THE MINISTRY of WOMEN
IN THE NEW TESTAMENT

"In this timely and much-needed study, Lee offers a balanced, scholarly, and accessible foray into New Testament and early church understandings and presentations of ministerial roles for women. Her holistic approach makes sense of both these often-difficult writings and their treatment in developing Christian traditions. Her powerful conclusion leaves no doubt about proper contextualization and paths forward in our continual interpretation of Scripture and tradition for the vocational calls of all people. As the apostle Paul says, 'No longer Jew or Greek, . . . slave or free, . . . male and female; for all of you are one in Christ Jesus. And if you belong to Christ, then you are Abraham's offspring, heirs according to the promise' (Gal. 3:28–29 NRSV)."

—**Sherri Brown**, Creighton University

"Scholar Dorothy Lee strongly urges the church to go beyond the biblical texts usually cited as obstacles to the full acceptance of women in the ministry and leadership of the church. Instead, she urges the church to turn to the deeper currents of Jesus's own example and to the New Testament vision of a church in which all women and men are recognized as equal sharers in the mission of the Risen Christ for the renewal of the world. Her study engages key New Testament texts and motifs and traces their evolving interpretations across time and cultures."

—**Donald Senior, CP**, Catholic Theological Union, Chicago

"Lee offers a fresh review of the relevant New Testament texts related to women and ministry. She looks at women not only in the Gospels and in Paul's letters but also in important passages in Acts, the Catholic Epistles, and Revelation, and she includes reflections on early Christian tradition and systematic theology. Newcomers to this conversation will find this book a great place to begin. Others will benefit from her discussions of the latest scholarship. Lee makes a well-rounded and compelling case for women in ministry."

—**Nijay K. Gupta**, Northern Seminary

"Lee is a biblical theologian, and this is evident in her outstanding study of women's ministry in the New Testament. Her biblical analysis is thorough as she carefully examines key texts. Her discussion of the 'household codes' helps readers to understand this particular genre, how it developed, and its purpose within a society where the gospel was preached in the face of hostility and persecution. She also moves beyond the biblical texts to other writings in the early church to examine how the canonical texts were received and interpreted in later centuries. Lee then moves into the theology of interpretation and reveals the deliberate suppression of women's leadership. I wholeheartedly recommend this book to all who seek to expand their knowledge of the Scriptures, the tradition, and theological thinking. Bravo, Dorothy."

—**Mary Coloe**, Australian Catholic University

"In her deeply researched yet accessible new book, Lee provides a much-needed antidote to the misperception that women in early communities of Christ followers were not community and church leaders. She aptly demonstrates from a variety of evidence and perspectives that the ministry of women flourished during the early Christian era."

—**Ally Kateusz**, Wijngaards Institute of Catholic Research,
Rickmansworth, London

"Lee brings together a knowledge of the scriptural and theological sources and a sensitive engagement with the many facets of the debate in this accessible and persuasive volume. She takes her readers through the varying voices of the New Testament as well as the lesser-known early church evidence for women's participation in the work of the gospel, and she tackles these questions with confidence from a theological and social perspective. This book will surely encourage respectful discussion among all who look to Scripture and tradition as they wrestle with contemporary challenges."

—**Judith M. Lieu**, University of Cambridge (emerita)

"Lee's study of the Christian traditions surrounding the ministry of women makes a major contribution to an important debate. This crucial discussion is too often marred by shrill dogmatism from both sides. Her analysis leads her to affirm convincingly that 'baptism is the primary symbol that draws women and men into a relationship with Christ that transcends all human barriers. . . . All Christians have the capacity to communicate Christ to others and to share his life in multiple forms of ministry.'"

—**Francis J. Moloney, SDB**, Catholic Theological College,
University of Divinity, Melbourne, Australia

THE MINISTRY OF WOMEN IN THE NEW TESTAMENT

Reclaiming the Biblical Vision for Church Leadership

DOROTHY A. LEE

Baker Academic

a division of Baker Publishing Group
Grand Rapids, Michigan

Published by Baker Academic
a division of Baker Publishing Group
PO Box 6287, Grand Rapids, MI 49516–6287
www.bakeracademic.com

Printed in the United States of America

Library of Congress Cataloging-in-Publication Data
Names: Lee, Dorothy A., author.
Title: The ministry of women in the New Testament : reclaiming the biblical vision for church leadership / Dorothy A. Lee.
Description: Grand Rapids, Michigan : Baker Academic, a division of Baker Publishing Group, [2021] | Includes bibliographical references and index.
Identifiers: LCCN 2020033259 | ISBN 9781540963086 (paperback) | ISBN 9781540964113 (casebound)
Subjects: LCSH: Women in Christianity—History—Early church, ca. 30-600. | Christian leadership—History—To 1500. | Women in church work—History—To 1500.
Classification: LCC BR195.W6 L44 2021 | DDC 270.1082—dc23
LC record available at https://lccn.loc.gov/2020033259

Baker Publishing Group publications use paper produced from sustainable forestry practices and post-consumer waste whenever possible.

22   23   24   25   26   27   28   8   7   6   5   4   3   2

To three outstanding leaders in the church:

Bishop Barbara Darling (d. 2015)
Archbishop Kay Goldsworthy, AO
Dr. Muriel Porter, OAM

Contents

Preface

THIS BOOK arose from a conversation with a group of women in a church that does not offer women any significant leadership roles. They asked for a study that would explore the New Testament texts and update recent research on women and the Bible. This monograph is the result. I myself am blessed enough to be part of a wider community that does encourage women's leadership, but I am also aware of forces that would move us back and reinstate a paternalistic ordering of our life together.

At its core the issue is one of interpretation: especially of the Bible but also, to a lesser extent, of Christian tradition. The biblical basis some claim for disqualifying women is a handful of texts, and in asserting this claim, these interpreters blithely ignore the weight of New Testament theology and the basic principles of the gospel. They insist on one meaning to the Bible, crystal clear but allowing for no different or opposing view. This kind of imperialism is against the very spirit of the gospel. There is diversity within the biblical text, and it must always be understood within its context, just as we need to be aware of our own. This is not an unfortunate reality we have to deal with but an opportunity to see how the incarnation embeds itself in the ordinary realities of our lives in Christ. Our own cultural framework can open new doors of meaning for us from these ancient texts. It is (part of) the meaning of Scripture as inspired by the Holy Spirit: the capacity to speak anew through the One who inspired and inspires.

I am not of course claiming that this book is the result of divine inspiration, but I am acutely aware of the many human inspirers. To my colleagues in the Trinity College Theological School, Melbourne, I owe my gratitude, especially the biblical scholars among them: Bob Derrenbacker, Rachelle Gilmour, Fergus King, and Christopher Porter. To Francis J. Moloney I owe a special debt for his endless encouragement of me, especially on this project. Also thanks are due to Brendan Byrne and Mary Coloe for regular lunches and regular inspiration. I am grateful to the Dalton McCaughey Library for its help, especially during a time of lockdown. And I am thankful for the graciousness and gentle encouragement of Bryan Dyer at Baker Academic and for the helpfulness and patience of Jennifer Hale.

To my wider family I owe far more than I can say: my sister and her family, my daughters and their partners, and my three grandchildren (Jemima, Theodore, and Harriet), who bring me a delightful mix of chaos and joy.

Lastly to my friend Muriel Porter, who patiently edited the volume and kept me upright, coherent, and grammatical, I am deeply thankful. To her and to two other eminent leaders in my church, Barbara Darling (now with God) and Kay Goldsworthy, the first female bishops consecrated in this country, this book is warmly and gratefully dedicated.

Easter 2020
Trinity College
University of Divinity
Australia

Abbreviations

General

//	parallel to	fl.	*floruit*, flourished
ca.	*circa*, approximately	i.e.	*id est*, that is
cf.	*confer*, compare	par.	parallel
d.	died	pl.	plural
e.g.	*exempli gratia*, for example		

Bible Versions

ASV	American Standard Version	NIV	New International Version
CEB	Common English Bible	NJB	New Jerusalem Bible
ESV	English Standard Version	NRSV	New Revised Standard Version
KJV	King James Version	REB	Revised English Bible
LXX	Septuagint	RSV	Revised Standard Version

Old Testament

Gen.	Genesis	1 Kings	1 Kings
Exod.	Exodus	2 Kings	2 Kings
Lev.	Leviticus	1 Chron.	1 Chronicles
Num.	Numbers	2 Chron.	2 Chronicles
Deut.	Deuteronomy	Ezra	Ezra
Josh.	Joshua	Neh.	Nehemiah
Judg.	Judges	Esther	Esther
Ruth	Ruth	Job	Job
1 Sam.	1 Samuel	Ps(s).	Psalm(s)
2 Sam.	2 Samuel	Prov.	Proverbs

Eccles.	Ecclesiastes	Obad.	Obadiah
Song	Song of Songs	Jon.	Jonah
Isa.	Isaiah	Mic.	Micah
Jer.	Jeremiah	Nah.	Nahum
Lam.	Lamentations	Hab.	Habakkuk
Ezek.	Ezekiel	Zeph.	Zephaniah
Dan.	Daniel	Hag.	Haggai
Hosea	Hosea	Zech.	Zechariah
Joel	Joel	Mal.	Malachi
Amos	Amos		

Old Testament Apocrypha

| 1 Esd. | 1 Esdras | Sir. | Sirach (Ecclesiasticus) |
| 2 Macc. | 2 Maccabees | | |

New Testament

Matt.	Matthew	1 Tim.	1 Timothy
Mark	Mark	2 Tim.	2 Timothy
Luke	Luke	Titus	Titus
John	John	Philem.	Philemon
Acts	Acts	Heb.	Hebrews
Rom.	Romans	James	James
1 Cor.	1 Corinthians	1 Pet.	1 Peter
2 Cor.	2 Corinthians	2 Pet.	2 Peter
Gal.	Galatians	1 John	1 John
Eph.	Ephesians	2 John	2 John
Phil.	Philippians	3 John	3 John
Col.	Colossians	Jude	Jude
1 Thess.	1 Thessalonians	Rev.	Revelation
2 Thess.	2 Thessalonians		

Introduction

THE WORDS OF MARY MAGDALENE to the other disciples in the Gospel of John—"I have seen the Lord" (*heōraka ton kyrion*, John 20:18)—set the scene for this study of women and ministry in the New Testament. Mary's words are her response to the appearance of the Risen Lord, who leads her from grief and loss to joy and hope. She is the first to meet Jesus after the resurrection and the first to be given the core message of Christian faith: that the Lord is risen and has triumphed over sin, evil, and death. She becomes, as the later church declared, the "apostle of the apostles" (Latin: *apostola apostolorum*). Yet her role and her ministry have not often been followed in the life of the church, despite the New Testament witness to a broader and more encompassing community and despite evidence from the early church of her leadership.

It may seem anachronistic to write a book on women in the New Testament. After all, surely the work has been done, the arguments canvassed, and the battle in good part won.[1] It would be nice to think such is the case, but unfortunately it is not. A number of publications and media sites have resurrected anew the traditional arguments against egalitarianism in home and church, while proclaiming themselves to be in favor of women's equality with men, and have promulgated it to a new generation of Christians.[2] These arguments have influenced particularly young men who are seeking positions of leadership for themselves while firmly excluding their female peers and calling for obedience from their wives. The old antiwomen arguments have reemerged in contemporary guise with forceful rhetoric and authority.

1. See, e.g., Stagg and Stagg, *Women in the World of Jesus*; France, *Women in the Church's Ministry*; Hewitt and Hiatt, *Women Priests*; Moltmann-Wendel, *Women around Jesus*; Schüssler Fiorenza, *In Memory of Her*; and Tetlow, *Women and Ministry*.

2. E.g., Köstenberger and Köstenberger, *God's Design for Man and Woman*. Against this, cf. Giles, *What the Bible Actually Teaches on Women*, especially 1–4.

1

On the basis of fresh readings of the New Testament material, women and men from the evangelical tradition are now arguing for egalitarian principles in church and home, where women and men have equal access to authority.[3] Roman Catholic women are questioning their church's denial of women's ordination.[4] The new research has come from different traditions across the church. The evidence has highlighted the role of ministry in leadership in the early centuries of the church's life and demonstrates the significant place women held within and beyond the ministry of Jesus. This research needs to be drawn together, especially in the light of the more recent backlash against women's ministry and women's equality. New insights run counter also to the claim that women's ordination and leadership was excluded in an unbroken line throughout the church's history.

Current Setting

In the Anglican/Episcopal church, for example, a woman was ordained priest for the first time in 1944—an ordination she exercised only briefly before protest prevented her from continuing—and she was not reinstated till 1971.[5] Since then, many other women have been ordained, including at senior levels.[6] Some women have already retired, and some have died, having carried out a faithful ministry, sometimes against fierce opposition.[7] A similar picture can also be drawn of many other denominations, particularly within Protestantism.[8]

Many laywomen, moreover, hold significant positions of leadership on parish and other church bodies. They chair committees; they preach; they evangelize; they are spiritual directors; they plan worship; they are church planters; they run church schools, colleges, and agencies; and they are involved in various forms of chaplaincy. In addition, women also continue to carry out their traditional duties in the church, ministering in service and care, a ministry often hidden and unacknowledged yet essential for the well-being of the church.

3. One such example is CBE International (Christians for Biblical Equality), which promotes equality between women and men on the basis of its interpretation of Scripture: "The Bible, properly interpreted, teaches the fundamental equality of men and women of all ethnic groups, all economic classes, and all age groups." https://www.cbeinternational.org/content/cbes-mission.

4. See, e.g., Wijngaards Institute for Catholic Research, https://www.wijngaardsinstitute.com.

5. The Rev. Dr. Florence Tim Oi was ordained in a situation of crisis in Hong Kong for the church; see The Li Tim-Oi Foundation, https://www.ltof.org.uk.

6. The Rt. Rev. Barbara Harris was consecrated bishop in the Episcopal Church in the USA in 1989.

7. See, e.g., Porter, *Women in the Church*; Porter, *Women in Purple*.

8. For a time line of women's ordination (that includes Unitarian and Jewish communities), see "Women as Clergy."

For all that, there are still places across the church where women are not permitted to be ordained, to preach, or to serve in a leading capacity. It is easy for those living in more open parts of the church to be complacent, but the battle to value and promote women's leadership is by no means won. Even in contexts that ordain women and permit female lay leadership, the numbers are still low for women as leaders, bishops, priests and pastors, chairs of committees, and even members of committees. This unbalance persists, even though women tend to outnumber men as members and adherents of the church.

Of greater concern is evidence of a reactionary movement in recent years against women's authority in Christian communities. Mark Driscoll, for example, the controversial and deeply conservative evangelist, has said that women cannot be ordained because "they are more gullible and easier to deceive than men."[9] Others are more guarded in their statements about women's nature but still react against the movement for women's ordination.[10] There are also examples of denominations that have stopped the practice of ordaining women. While a number of denominations across the world ordain women and recognize their leadership, others, such as the Roman Catholic Church and the Eastern Orthodox churches, do not permit women to be ordained and have no significant place for lay female leadership and authority. Unlike their more progressive equivalents, Protestant churches on the conservative end of the spectrum likewise withhold leadership from women, usually in the home as well as the church.

Another significant element in this discussion is the small number of women from indigenous communities and ethnic minorities in leadership roles, even in contexts that ordain women. Some of this may reflect diverse cultural values. But much of it is due to an implicit racism within white communities and the difficulties indigenous women and women of color find in attempting to break through racial and cultural barriers. The issue of women's ministry challenges not only male dominance but equally white dominance. Racism and misogyny are potent coworkers in this equation and make marginalization more extreme and painful for women of color than for white women.[11]

Opposing Views on Women

The situation is by no means unique. Many Christian churches reflect the same spectrum of female participation in ministry, sometimes within one

---

9. Quoted in Burk, "Mark Driscoll on Women in Ministry."
10. See, e.g., Milton, "Can Women Be Pastors?"
11. Studies in postcolonial theology offer challenges along these lines; see, e.g., Runesson, *Exegesis in the Making*, especially 17–50.

denomination and at other times across denominations.[12] It can go from full participation at the one end, which tends to represent the more progressive side, to almost entire exclusion from leadership at the other. This is the case particularly among Fundamentalists, who take a strict and conventional view of authority, either of passages from Scripture or of church teaching and tradition.

None of this is necessarily linked to the specific shape and form of theology or liturgy. The divide is not the familiar one between "evangelical" and "catholic"—between those who see the Bible as the sole authority and those who see tradition as having an additional (though dependent) authority—but rather between those who support women's participation in the full ministry of the church and those who restrict or oppose it. There is, in some circles, an implicit assumption that support for women's leadership is the sign of a contemporary "liberal" Christianity that has wandered far from its biblical and traditional roots and has been captivated by the values of the world. The fear is that by "giving in" on this issue, a string will be pulled that holds everything together, and the Bible and the church's deeply held values will unravel.

Most people who support women's leadership would emphatically deny such a charge. On one side of the church, there is a vigorous argument that the Bible itself needs to be read anew in each age and culture and that we cannot assume that the readings of previous ages are the only ways to interpret it. There is no single, fixed interpretation of biblical passages that cannot, under the dynamic presence and guidance of the Spirit, be questioned and reinterpreted. Such revisioning is already happening for some of the more controversial passages of the Bible about women's place in the church.[13] On the other side, the argument is that tradition itself is unfolding, developing, and growing as the Spirit leads the church into "all truth" (John 16:13). There is also considerable evidence that tradition itself, at least in the early days, was not monolithic or univocal but demonstrated a relatively broad diversity. Assumptions about what actually took place in the past, in both the early New Testament communities and the early church, can be and are being challenged as new data is uncovered.

None of this is necessarily to downgrade the authority of the Bible or the theological importance of the early ecumenical creeds and councils of the church. These form the riverbanks for Christian faith and practice. But they do not rule out questions raised by new contexts and new situations. On the contrary, these questions should be embraced by the church, which should

---

12. Lavinia Byrne takes an ecumenical approach to exploring women's spirituality across denominational and other divides, finding a commonality of authority and wisdom even amid the differences; see *Women before God*.

13. See, e.g., Evans, "For the Sake of the Gospel."

be confident in its own faith and spirituality. The church is not static; it is not, strictly speaking, primarily an institution at all but an organic body of faithful, God-serving people, stretching across time and space. Belief in the Spirit's ongoing presence in interpreting Scripture for new circumstances is part and parcel of Christian belief.[14]

Ancient Culture

Integral to our understanding of the Bible is awareness not only of our own context but also of the context of the ancient society out of which the early church and the New Testament writings arose. The problem is that we know very little about women's lives, and the little we know comes from men. The Greco-Roman and Jewish worlds were patriarchal and had a clear bias toward maleness. Rule and authority were widely considered to be primarily male prerogatives, and men were seen as endowed with the necessary qualities and virtues—such as initiative, reason, and courage—to equip them for their roles. Women, by contrast, were generally regarded as more fitted for domestic duties and were seen to have the requisite conventional virtues, particularly those of "modesty, loyalty and industry," in relation both to the family and to their engagement with the wider community.[15]

The point should not be overstated. The gender binary in the ancient world did not result in a clear division between the public and private spheres, since women were also involved in public life and had a sense of civic duty, including in relation to their domestic work. Ancient dwellings had public and private areas to which both women and men had access, with the family trade or business conducted usually from the home. The ancient Mediterranean world was governed by values of honor and shame, which affected women as well as men, with women, like men, able to deal in the currency of honor. Yet perhaps the overriding aspect of the value system was that personal identity was always set within the context of family relationships and the wider kinship group. In this world there was no notion of individualism or personal autonomy, for men certainly but even more so for women.

The cultural realities of life in the ancient world were made up of considerable diversity and tension that amounted in many places to contradiction.[16]

---

14. Many of these areas are beyond the scope of this book, including the church's response to revelations about clergy sexual abuse, the church's cover-up, the ongoing relevance of compulsory celibacy for priesthood, and the question of marriage and sexual orientation.

15. Hylen, *Thecla*, 23. See also Belleville, *Women Leaders and the Church*, 73–96.

16. See especially, Hylen, *Thecla*, 7–42.

While most women were powerless to resist patriarchal constraints and were subject, as a consequence, to subservience, suppression, and abuse, a few elite women were able to negotiate the complexities of the cultural norms to make important contributions to public life. In the Greco-Roman world, there were women who displayed initiative and held authority, women who were active in business, and women who exercised political power, directly or indirectly.[17] Women's literacy was not high and was much less than men's, and such education as women gained was through homeschooling.[18] But a minority of women were educated[19] who were either of elite status or slaves and freedwomen whose role was to teach children.[20]

Ancient literature, on the other hand, features female characters of courage and resourcefulness. For example, in Sophocles's play *The Antigone* (ca. 441 BCE) the hero of the story, Antigone (daughter of Oedipus), decides to bury her rebel brother against the king's explicit order. As a consequence he orders Antigone to be buried alive in a cave, where she then hangs herself. Antigone's strength of character lies in her courageous defiance of the king and her strong commitment to the moral duties of family and kinship over power, for which she is prepared to give her life. In the Athenian culture of the fifth century BCE, when Sophocles was writing and where women were particularly secluded and confined to the domestic sphere, these and similar portraits of Greek tragedy tell a rather different story from the misogynistic context of ancient Greece.

Formidable female deities, too, while not challenging patriarchal power, exercised a major influence on women and men's lives. One of the most popular cults in Rome was the cult of the Bona Dea (literally, "Good Goddess"), whose festival was celebrated by women only, at the homes of leading citizens as well as in private homes, during December. The Vestal Virgins, who were responsible for protecting the Roman state, kept the sacred fire burning, which symbolized the "hearth" of Rome. The Bona Dea was protector of Rome and also of her adherents. She was responsible for fertility and healing and was a powerful deity, part earth mother and part state guardian, whose unknown name and origins, along with her compassion and protective power, increased her prestige among worshipers.[21]

Women who were active in the public sphere were in a considerable minority, but they contributed alongside the more dominating class divisions. Within

17. See, e.g., Cohick, *Women in the World*, 225–56.
18. Westfall, *Paul and Gender*, 238–40.
19. E.g., Barnes, *Reading 1 Corinthians*, 37–64.
20. On the shape of women's daily lives in Greco-Roman culture and early Judaism, see Cohick, *Women in the World*, 19–32. See also Keener, *Acts*, 1:605–38.
21. Cohick, *Women in the World*, 167–73.

the fabric of social life, gender was only one of several factors regulating women's lives: "Legal categories of free, freed, and slave, but also relative wealth and pursuit of honor play major roles in determining the choices available for women."[22] The existence of such women reveals that ancient norms were complex, even while most women lived mainly under strict male control.

Judaism was similarly complex. As a religion it was patriarchal in its understanding of authority and leadership. At the same time, other cultural norms operated within its contours. In addition to the strong female figures of faith, heroism, and courage in the Old Testament, some Jewish women were synagogue leaders and exercised considerable influence on their religious peers, including men.[23] Such contradictions also made possible the developments we find in the New Testament around female authority. Jesus himself had an extraordinary way of relating to women, neither belittling nor patronizing them,[24] but his attitudes owe something not only to his radically inclusive vision of the reign of God (Greek: *basileia*) but also, in part, to his own cultural environment. Both the Old Testament and the Jewish practice of the day presented him with compelling women who, in their own contexts, were able to make active and impressive contributions to religious and civic life, contributions that were accepted and in some (though rare) contexts extolled.

Not that women in the ancient world were all on the same level, nationally or socially. Greek women had less power than Roman women, and elite women had significantly more power and freedom than women of lower classes, being able to initiate divorce and, to a certain extent, inherit property. Jewish women had less power, in one sense, but in another were given a greater degree of dignity and respect in their own culture, as attested in the biblical world.[25] And the culture itself made it possible for traditional roles to be negotiated. In this respect, it is impossible to separate the New Testament writings from the complexity of their heritage and wider context. The remarkable openness to women's ministry in these texts arises in part from the women of the Jewish and Greco-Roman worlds, even though primarily it comes from the example of Jesus's own ministry. His teaching and practice, as recorded in the Gospels and carried through into other New Testament writings, led the early church to sanction female gifts and leadership. It also explains something of the diversity of the New Testament texts, including those that retain something of the patriarchal hue of their environment.

22. Cohick, *Women in the World*, 22.
23. See Bernadette Brooten, who argues that there is evidence in Judaism of women as heads of the synagogue, leaders, elders, and even priests (*Women Leaders in the Ancient Synagogue*, 5–99).
24. Sayers, "Human-Not-Quite-Human," 121–22.
25. See, e.g., Tetlow, *Women and Ministry*, 5–29.

A Word on Interpretation

As we have come to realize more acutely over the past few decades, interpreting a text of any kind is a complex process. It is not simply a matter of reading the text and drawing out a meaning on which everyone will then agree. Church history tells us that such has never been the case. Part of this study on women is about presenting ways of interpreting the New Testament text in all its diversity, ways other than those we have always held.

There is considerable dispute in literary and biblical circles about where meaning in texts resides. Is it to be found in discerning the intention of the author, as is traditionally thought? In this view, authorial intention is to be discerned by scholars using all the tools of the historical-critical method, including word studies and an awareness of the historical context out of which the text arose.[26] The author's intention becomes the basis for discerning the authentic sense of the biblical text. He or she determines the meaning, and it is up to us as readers to accept or reject it.

More radically, some have proposed that meaning resides not with the author's intention but rather in the mind of the reader, who draws meaning and significance from the text. In this view, the reader gains the ascendancy in discovering meaning from within her or his own context; authority shifts now from the author to the reader. This view has given rise to the idea of multiple interpretations within the text—a view that, when pushed to its limits, means that it is almost impossible to argue for any one interpretation over another. It represents a potential collapse into subjectivity, where there is little or no control over the reader's interpretation.

The third option is that meaning resides primarily in the text as an objective reality, quite apart from its author or its reader. Of course a text has by necessity both an author and a reader, but the meaning to be communicated between the two is located within the contours and materiality of the text. This answer to the quest for textual meaning is particularly helpful in biblical studies, where there is no direct access to the biblical author. This view came from literary critics in the early twentieth century (part of the New Criticism) who argued that the text, whether or not the author is still alive, is all that we have to go on. They disliked the vague notion of authorial intention since, they believed, it might not always have been articulated successfully. Authors' intentions are not always clear in their writings, even to themselves. In this view, we find a shift in where authority lies: not in the author, to whose

---

26. For an excellent summary of this hermeneutical development, including the problem of translation, see Frank, "Do We Translate," 653–67.

intentions we have no direct access, and not in the creative imagination of the reader, but in the actual text itself.[27]

Nonetheless the reader still has a role to play in interpreting a text, even if the text itself remains central. New settings can uncover fresh insights that past generations may not have seen, just as aspects of the text they perceived may seem puzzling or irrelevant to us today. Paul Ricoeur speaks of the biblical text having a "surplus of meaning" that goes beyond its original context and can speak afresh to succeeding ages.[28] The text always has something "more" to reveal to new readers in new generations as it is read with dedication, intelligence, and imagination. That "surplus of meaning" is particularly discernible within the symbols and symbolic structures of the text, which are themselves grounded in theological truth and which lend themselves to variegated (though not endless) understandings.[29] In this sense, the text—though capable of more than one meaning—retains its objectivity and cannot mean whatever the reader wants. From this perspective, the text itself has both an authority and an intentionality that can be discerned by readers from within their own cultural setting. The text may also point in a fresh direction, creating a trajectory for future interpretations. The horizon of the text and the horizon of the reader need to meet for biblical meaning to emerge.[30]

For our purposes, this balanced view enables women, in particular, to read and reread the biblical texts from their own perspective ("horizon") to discern meanings for today. The text does not lose its objectivity, nor is it stripped of its implied author—particularly in the mind of the reader[31]—but rather it interacts with new contexts that enable it to speak in unimagined ways. Women have the capacity to illuminate the text in ways unforeseen by past, male-centered generations, grasping that "surplus of meaning" that, in theological terms, indicates the continuous, inspiring work of the Holy Spirit. The divine work uncovers meanings that speak as vividly to the present as to the past and transforms readers in renewed and life-giving ways. This kind of interpretation also requires more than one angle from which to view the text. Fresh readings are needed in the Christian community's interpretation of the Bible and are a fruitful means of rediscovering the gospel anew for contemporary readers.

27. See the collection of essays in Breu, *Biblical Exegesis*.
28. Ricoeur, *Interpretation Theory*, 55. Against this, cf. Kevin J. Vanhoozer, who argues for the objectivity of the author's intention (*Is There a Meaning in This Text?*, 106–11, 201–80).
29. Lee, *Flesh and Glory*, 4–7, 9–14.
30. For more on this model, see Thiselton, *Two Horizons*, 10–23.
31. Heinen, "Exegesis without Authorial Intention?," 7–23.

Focus of This Study

This study explores two points of focus for arguments against women's leadership. On the one hand, some claims are based on Scripture: that the Bible itself does not endorse women's leadership, except in relation to other women and children. Women, in this interpretation, are not permitted to be ordained, except in subservient roles. In any case, the argument emphasizes women's subjection and wifely submission. Headship in this model belongs exclusively to men, who are instructed to exercise it in love and not in a spirit of dominion or domination. This concept of power belonging exclusively to men is based on interpretations of several New Testament texts that appear to assert male headship within the family, and this becomes, in turn, the model for the church.

On the other hand, some claims arise from tradition: that church teaching has never endorsed women's ministry at the level of ordination and that priesthood necessitates maleness since the priest stands in the place of Christ. These two arguments form the basis for the more "catholic" opposition to women's ordination in, for example, the Roman Catholic and Orthodox traditions, including some forms of Anglicanism. In theory at any rate, the arguments need not of themselves rule out women's lay leadership or their participation in the diaconate, but if religious rule is built essentially on priestly power, women are thereby ruled out of decision-making, including women in religious life. It should be noted, however, that the Roman Catholic Church does not support the submission of wives to husbands. The marriage liturgy no longer asks the bride to obey the bridegroom, and one previous papal statement has spoken of wife and husband as sharing equal authority and responsibility within marriage.[32]

The purpose of this study is to revisit the arguments against women's full participation in ministry and leadership within the church. It does so from a biblical and theological point of view. Arguments from social justice are not of primary import in this debate, though they have their place. The real issues are theological and christological, concerning the nature of God and the significance of Christian identity in relation to Christ. It is not primarily a question of rights, therefore, and still less of individual rights to be ordained. No one can lay claim to such a right, though perhaps the church has the "right" to be served by those best fitted for service, regardless of gender. Even here, however, the language of rights is secondary to that of theological identity. What is at stake is the character of the church itself in its adherence to Christ, and its core vocation to be shaped in his likeness and to proclaim his saving presence in word and deed.

32. See Leonard, *Beloved Daughters*, especially 52–56.

This study argues from a New Testament perspective that women should have full access to the church's ministry, whether in lay or ordained ministries, and that this access needs to depend not on gender but rather on a sense of vocation and on the church's discernment of calling. All Christian women, like all Christian men, have one and the same fundamental vocation: to be disciples of Jesus Christ, a gift and a calling given in baptism. Thereafter, the particular form their ministry takes should not be restricted because they are women, just as it is not so restricted for men. Both focal points of disagreement, whether coming from the Bible or from the tradition, will be considered in the following discussion.

It is true that the language of ordination, along with its rites and rituals, arises only indirectly from the New Testament, as the evidence of formal structures of leadership is unclear in the early days and most likely differed from what transpired in the following centuries.[33] Thus any discussion of ordination is somewhat anachronistic, while as we will see, biblical teaching and early church practice are not so easy to distinguish. The historical development of ministry as threefold, while it can be glimpsed from the New Testament Epistles, arises in more developed form in the second and third centuries. Nevertheless, we will discover the traces of women's participation in this early period, mainly within but also beyond the pages of the New Testament.

Revelations of domestic abuse within Christian marriage are linked at some level to traditional teachings on women's place and lack of power within the church. These core issues around marriage and ministry represent a clarion call to the worldwide church to rethink theologically its position on women's roles and ministry. The question here is whether there is evidence of misogyny in much current church teaching that claims to be "complementarian."[34] The term is misleading, as advocates for women's full participation in ministry and leadership sometimes argue precisely on the grounds that women's perspective is unique and is needed to complement that of men, though in an egalitarian way. Whether a hidden misogyny drives some of this debate is worth considering at this point, a misogyny that results in exclusively male access to power and that feeds the uncertainties raised for men by the women's movement.[35]

---

33. Wijngaards, *Women in Holy Orders?*, 10–12.

34. For an extended challenge to this view on a biblical basis, see Giles, *What the Bible Actually Teaches on Women*.

35. It is worth remembering that the nineteenth-century movement for female equality, out of which the contemporary women's movement was born, was inaugurated by Christian women who were following gospel principles in seeking an equal status for women in the church. For more on this, see Porter, "Christian Origins of Feminism," 208–24.

The following chapters move, more or less, in canonical rather than chrono-logical order, with some historical and literary variation. Part 1, which com-prises the bulk of this study, deals with the New Testament itself: In the first chapter, I examine the first two Gospels to be written (Matthew and Mark). In the next two, we turn to Luke the Evangelist's two-volume work (Luke and Acts). Then the Gospel of John is explored for its narrative presentation of women as disciples of Jesus who were engaged in ministry, along with the other writings that are somewhat loosely attached to the Fourth Evangelist (the Johannine Epistles and the book of Revelation). The following chapter focuses mainly on the Pauline Letters: Paul's experience of working alongside women and the core principles of his theology, along with more difficult passages that seem to support women's silence and submission. Brief attention will be given to other New Testament writings that contribute to the subject matter (1 Peter, Hebrews, James). A number of these Pauline and other texts include the "household codes," with implications for marriage as well as ministry.[36]

Part 2 moves beyond the New Testament, beginning with a brief survey of the historical tradition in the early centuries of the church, especially in the light of more recent studies. Here claims to unanimity of practice are seen as anachronistic, reflecting a post-Constantinian setting that has forgotten the diversity of the early church's experience. This material is important, not only because it challenges the notion of an all-male priesthood and episcopate in an unbroken line but also because it reflects on New Testament practice and experience. Part 2 also explores theological issues, such as the significance of the incarnation for women, particularly in relation to the person of Christ in his divinity and humanity, the meaning of the virginal conception, and the symbolic role of icons. The significance of baptism for women is also included, pointing to a new, transformed understanding of Christian community.

The recognition of women's equality and mutuality with men in the proc-lamation of the gospel, as this study will argue, is a key challenge for today's church, along with the need to create structures protecting the weak and vulnerable. This recognition includes the overcoming of racial and cultural (and any other human-made) barriers that restrict women from the struggle to achieve universal equality. Women's full dignity and authority as children of God and disciples of Christ, whatever their race or culture, need to be included in new ways in order to fulfill the New Testament call to a transformed world, where "there is no longer Jew or Greek, there is no longer slave or free, there is no longer male and female; for all of you are one in Christ Jesus" (Gal. 3:28).

---

36. Examples of these New Testament instructions for the running of Christian households can be found at Eph. 5:2'–6:9; Col. 3:18–4:1; 1 Pet. 2:13–3:7. The epistle whose authorship is possibly female is Hebrews.

PART 1

WOMEN'S MINISTRY IN THE NEW TESTAMENT

Chapter One

Gospels of Mark and Matthew

WOMEN'S MINISTRY is a notable feature of Mark and Matthew, and their depictions of women, though not identical, are similar to each other. Women are followers of Jesus and are committed to his message, and their following of Jesus and service to him are exemplary. It is true that they are less prominent in these Gospels than men and that no specific call narratives for women are included. Yet what is remarkable is how, without denigrating or idealizing women, Matthew and Mark emerge from the limitations of their environment to give women's discipleship and ministry a significant place.[1]

The two Gospels belong closely together, since Matthew used Mark throughout as a primary source.[2] In one sense, both are writing biographies of Jesus, but they are doing so in the ancient rather than the modern sense.[3] They are concerned not to paint a neutral picture of Jesus as outsiders but rather to draw out the inner meaning of the events of Jesus's life and death and to bring others to faith and to deeper faith. Their intent is, in other words, "evangelical" in the strict sense of the word. Mark's Gospel is explicit about this intention and commences with the words "The beginning of the *good news* ["gospel," *euangelion*] of Jesus Christ,[4] Son of God"[5] (1:1). In the ancient world the word *euangelion* was used to denote a military victory,

---

1. On the ancient context of women, see Cohick, *Women in the World*.
2. See M. Bird, *Gospel of the Lord*, 160–62.
3. Burridge, *What Are the Gospels?*, 105–232.
4. See especially M. Bird, *Gospel of the Lord*, 5–12.
5. The words "son of God" may well be original, though missing in a few manuscripts; see Moloney, *Gospel of Mark*, 28–32.

which demonstrated divine favor—including a reward for the bringer of the news—or the emperor's accession, which brought hope for stability and peace. In the Greek translation of the Old Testament, it refers to God's reign and restoration of Israel, which is celebrated particularly in Isaiah. Whatever its context, the word *euangelion* carries with it a sense of joy and gladness, which for Israel is firmly located in God's sovereign rule.

The structure of the two Gospels is similar, with many of the incidents in Matthew following Mark.[6] There are also differences, indicating that Matthew, like Mark, is a skillful narrator and theologian in his own right. Matthew is considerably longer than Mark, and the author has added to Mark's account the birth narratives (Matt. 1:1–2:23), large blocks of teaching material throughout, and the appearances of the Risen Christ (28:1–20). These give emphasis to the picture of Jesus as teacher and Lord, confirming him, with the miracle stories, as Messiah and Son of God, authentic in word and deed.

Language of Discipleship

Those who gather around Jesus belong in any of three overlapping categories: followers of Jesus (from *akolouthein*, "to follow"), disciples (*mathētai*, "learners, students"), and the Twelve (*hoi dōdeka*). The term "disciples" is not used in Mark till 2:15 (where Jesus eats with tax collectors and sinners) nor in Matthew till 5:1 (at the beginning of the Sermon on the Mount). Before then, the main image is that of "following," as in the call of the four fishermen who leave everything behind to follow Jesus (Mark 1:16–20 // Matt. 4:18–22).[7]

In Mark, there remains a wider group of followers throughout that includes other males and also females, such as blind Bartimaeus and the Galilean women (Mark 10:52; 15:40–41).[8] Whether they formally belong among "the disciples" is not explicit, though it is sometimes implied. Such disciples/followers make up a committed group of Jesus's students and traveling companions—in addition to the Twelve—who function as a missional movement, with the Markan Jesus as their teacher and leader.

6. The authors of the two Gospels are never named within the text. Later tradition in the second century associates them with the apostle Matthew and John Mark, companion of Paul. Not all scholars accept these later traditions, especially since the Gospels originally circulated anonymously. See Davies and Allison, *Gospel according to Saint Matthew*, 1:7–58; Marcus, *Mark 1–8*, 17–24.

7. The mark "//" means the parallel or parallels found in other Gospels; the same is true for "par.," which means the parallel in one other Gospel.

8. These include the cleansed demoniac who is instructed to remain (Mark 5:18–20), prefiguring the post-Easter community; see Marcus, *Mark 1–8*, 353–54.

In Matthew, the phrase "his twelve disciples" can give the impression that disciples and the Twelve are one and the same (Matt. 10:1–2). This group seems to constitute the church, given their eschatological role in "judging the twelve tribes of Israel" (19:28).[9] Yet Matthew also indicates a larger grouping, such as those whom Jesus identifies as members of his family (12:49–50; 27:57). Imagery of discipleship is used also of the Galilean women (27:55–56). Thus, while "disciples" often refers to the apostles, others share the same characteristics:[10] relationship with Jesus, involvement in his ministry, and commitment to his mission.[11]

Given the imprecise limits around who belongs, it is easiest to use the term "disciples" in its broadest sense to include not only the Twelve but also the women and other men who follow Jesus. There are no clear lines of demarcation when it comes to those who identify with his ministry. When the Markan disciples try to prevent an exorcist from working in Jesus's name, Jesus allows the work to continue, since "no one who will perform a mighty deed in my name will be able quickly to defame me" (Mark 9:38–40). In the Gospels we find little clarity about where the boundaries lie, yet we find a clear understanding of what it means to be committed to Jesus.[12]

Women Disciples in Jesus's Ministry

The Galilean women who are devoted to Jesus show remarkable faith. The first of these in both Gospels is Peter's unnamed mother-in-law (Mark 1:29–31 // Matt. 8:14–15), whom Jesus heals of a deadly fever. She is so fully recovered by his healing touch that she at once rises from her bed and begins "to serve" or "minister" (*diakonein*) "to him" (Mark) / "to them" (Matthew). This might seem a male-oriented narrative: the woman no sooner rises from her sickbed than she is obliged to wait on demanding guests. It is more likely that this detail illustrates the totality of her cure; she does not need time to recuperate but rises from her bed full of energy and purpose. Moreover, the same verb is used for the ministry of the angels to Jesus in the temptation (Mark 1:13 // Matt. 4:11), and Jesus uses it to speak of his own ministry, including his death: "The Son of Man came not to be served/ministered to but to serve/minister" (*diakonein*, Mark 10:45

9. J. Brown, *Disciples in Narrative Perspective*, 39–43.
10. Carter, *Matthew*, 215–27.
11. France, *Gospel of Mark*, 94–95.
12. On the social status of the women around Jesus, see Corley, "Slaves, Servants and Prostitutes," 191–221.

// Matt. 20:28).[13] The woman's actions capture the true, self-giving nature of Christian ministry.[14]

Jesus's attitude toward women and power challenges the structures of his world, revealing a compassion and authority that are, for Mark, distinctively divine.[15] Girls and women find no revulsion from him but encounter his readiness to heal and save. The double narrative of the woman with a hemorrhage and the daughter of Jairus (Mark 5:21–43 // Matt. 9:18–26), where the one story is sandwiched within the other, is perhaps the best example of this openness toward females and their needs. A desperate woman, suffering from a disability that renders her physically weak, intervenes between Jairus's desperate appeal at his daughter's illness (Mark) / death (Matthew) and Jesus's response to it. The woman has an incurable medical condition that renders her ceremonially "unclean" (Lev. 15:25–30).[16]

The hemorrhaging woman is anxious not to draw attention to herself, yet she shows courage and faith in touching Jesus's cloak for healing (Mark 5:29). Mark adds a poignant note about how she became poor through costly attempts to find a cure (5:26). In both versions—though Matthew's is shorter—Jesus draws the woman forth and commends the strength of her faith publicly:[17] "Daughter, your faith has saved you; go in peace and be healed of your disease" (Mark 5:34); "Be confident, daughter; your faith has saved you" (Matt. 9:22). Restoring her to wholeness, Jesus claims kinship with her and confirms the power of her faith.

In Mark's version, the intrusion of the woman and the delay it causes means that, in the interim, the girl dies (Mark 5:35). Jesus enters the house to find full-blown mourning in progress, and he is met with derision about his capacity to waken the girl. The Markan Jesus raises her by touch and speech; he speaks in Aramaic, emphasizing the intimacy, and shows compassion in his command that she be fed (5:41–43).[18]

In Matthew's abridged version, the girl has just died when the "leader of the synagogue" approaches Jesus. With many of the details omitted, it seems at first a diminishment, a tale stripped of its drama. Yet Matthew

---

13. John N. Collins has argued that *diakonia* in the ancient world does not mean menial service but has the sense of a spokesperson, an agent, or one attending on another who is a superior person (*Diakonia*, 118–36). Yet the Gospels associate Jesus's ministry with humble service, which does not contradict his status as divine envoy; see Breed, "*Diakonia*," 349–68.

14. See Mitchell, *Beyond Fear and Silence*, 63–64.

15. For more on Mark's Christology, see Lee, "Christological Identity and Authority," 1–20.

16. The point about uncleanness should not be overstated; for a Jewish perspective, see Levine, "Discharging Responsibility," 70–87.

17. Cotter, "Mark's Hero," 59–60.

18. Cotter, "Mark's Hero," 76–78.

focuses more sharply on faith by paring back the details.[19] Thus we see more vividly the faith of the synagogue leader—who believes Jesus can raise his daughter from the dead (9:18)—and the faith of the hemorrhaging woman. In the case of the latter, the healing is tied not to her touch of Jesus's cloak, as in Mark, but to his words of kinship and affirmation; only at that point is she cured (9:22).

So while both females are the victims of grave misfortune beyond human power, Jesus has the capacity to heal them, indifferent to ritual or to social or gender considerations. Together the interwoven stories illustrate his capacity to reinstate the dignity of women and girls, while offering healing: "On the same day, when everything seemed hopeless, each is delivered into a new life. . . . One has the bold faith that dares to touch; the other is absolutely passive and unable to do anything for herself but receives Jesus's life-giving touch."[20]

There is another story of Jesus's encounter with a woman that seems to contradict this portrait of openness toward women. The narrative of the woman whose daughter is demon possessed and who begs for healing for her child seems like the opposite (Mark 7:24–31 // Matt. 15:21–28). This time it is a gentile woman, and Jesus is in the gentile region of Syrophoenicia.[21] At first, the Markan Jesus appears to repel the woman: "Let first the children be satisfied, for it is not good to take the children's bread and toss it to the dogs" (Mark 7:27). In Matthew's slightly longer and harsher version, Jesus at first ignores the woman before announcing that his ministry is only for Israel; he then adds similar words to what we find in Mark: "It is not good to take the children's bread and toss it to the dogs" (Matt. 15:26). If anything, the offense of Jesus at first ignoring the woman's situation, then comparing it to that of a dog begging for food at the table (dogs being unclean animals in Judaism), is intensified in Matthew, where she is identified as a Canaanite, representative of the ancient enemies of Israel.[22]

The narrative has occasioned controversy among modern interpreters. For some, it is a teaching lesson for Jesus himself, leading him from gender and racial prejudice to a ministry of openness and inclusion.[23] Such a reading, however, risks missing the literary form. Jesus's words about dogs and children are not

19. On Matthew's editing of the miracle stories, see Held, "Matthew as Interpreter of the Miracle Stories," 165–211.

20. Boring, *Mark*, 158.

21. Syrophoenicia was a region where, in economic terms, the wealthy gentile inhabitants drew on the labor of the Jewish peasantry in Galilee for their food, giving a political dimension to this encounter. She represents a people who have exploited the poor Jews of the region for food.

22. Davies and Allison, *Gospel according to Saint Matthew*, 2:547.

23. E.g., Ringe, "Gentile Woman's Story"; also Thurston, "Mark," 555.

a literal description but a parable,[24] with typical characteristics: a fictional and realistic narrative, centering on a metaphor that takes on symbolic meaning.[25] The parable narrates an imaginary but realistic scenario of dogs scavenging food from the table while the family eats, where the children have priority of access. The parabolic reading is confirmed in the woman's response. Far from taking umbrage, the woman takes the parable further and, in a sense, completes it. Keeping to the spirit of things, she adds a typical element: the dogs are fed the leftovers. Jesus concedes the point and grants the woman's request. In responding as she does, the woman accedes to the priority of Israel in God's salvation.[26]

The parable thus elicits the woman's faith,[27] acting ironically to connect the two characters. The female outsider displays an exemplary faith in contrast to the insiders, Jesus's disciples, who have so often failed to grasp his parables (Mark 4:10).[28] Here the parable validates the gospel's ability to cross boundaries and open locked doors. In Matthew, the woman uses the language of the community of faith to address Jesus—"Lord, son of David, have mercy on me!" (Matt. 15:22)—so that by the end, Jesus is deeply moved by her faith: "O woman, great is your faith!" (15:28). She plays an educative role in how readers are to approach him, with the same openness and trust: "This woman . . . not only becomes for us gentiles the forerunner of our faith, but her reply to Jesus teaches us how to speak."[29]

The wider narrative context in both Gospels is that of bread and eating (Mark 6:6b–8:21 // Matt. 14:1–16:12), with the two feeding stories—one in Jewish, the other in gentile territory—and the banquet for Herod's birthday.[30] The Syrophoenician/Canaanite story functions as a metaphor for the inclusion of the gentiles. It presents a vision of the grace of God, revealed in Jesus, crossing boundaries to those on the outside. The encounter with Jesus outlines the shape of the church's ministry. In the end, for Mark, Matthew, and their communities, Jesus's engagement with this gentile woman plays a decisive role in dissolving the boundary between Jew and gentile, demonstrating the true nature of discipleship and the inclusive character of Christian community.[31]

24. So Iverson, *Gentiles in the Gospel of Mark*, 52–54; Rhoads, "Jesus and the Syrophoenician Woman in Mark," 355–57.

25. Zimmermann, *Puzzling the Parables of Jesus*, 137–50.

26. Keener, *Gospel of Matthew*, 415–18.

27. Marcus, *Mark 1–8*, 468–71.

28. See Lee, "Faith of the Canaanite Woman," 12–29; Lee, "Clean and Unclean."

29. Hauerwas, *Matthew*, 144.

30. For a reading of this story that pays attention to its literary setting, see Moloney, *Gospel of Mark*, 144–48.

31. Scholars disagree on whether Matthew stands outside Judaism (Jewish-Christian) or within it (Christian-Jewish); Carter, *Matthew*, 66–91, takes the former, majority view, while David C. Sim, *Gospel of Matthew*, 109–64, takes the latter view.

The last story of a woman in Jesus's ministry in Mark is the widow who, despite her poverty, gives to the temple treasury from her means of subsistence (Mark 12:41–44).[32] The woman functions as a contrast to the scribes who love ostentation and seek honor (12:38–40), as well as to the rich who contribute from their largesse; her gift is interpreted by Jesus as of infinitely greater value.[33] She is a model of the truly devout person of faith who, in comparison to the rich man, shows the generous disposition of authentic discipleship (10:17–31). The widow displays her total love of God with heart, soul, mind, and strength (see 12:28–34),[34] revealing the values of God's reign. The story points to women characters "who exemplify the demands of followership, from bold faith in Jesus's life-giving power to self-giving in parallel to, or in recognition of, his self-denying death."[35]

Mary and the Matriarchs

The mother of Jesus appears in the first two Gospels, although, as Mark contains no birth story, Mary is not present in the early parts of his Gospel. Her one appearance in Jesus's ministry in Mark, apart from a solitary mention (Mark 6:3 // Matt. 13:55), is ambiguous. In the context of the dispute over the demons, where the Markan Jesus is accused of working under satanic power, his family tries to restrain him, perhaps in an effort to protect the family honor (Mark 3:21, 31). Jesus turns instead to his disciples as his true family: "Whoever does the will of God, that one is my brother and sister and mother" (3:35). In Matthew's version, where Jesus says much the same, there is no mention of the family's attempt to restrain Jesus (Matt. 12:46–50); the gathered disciples have priority over the family in relationship with Jesus. But in Mark, there is a sense of his mother and family not comprehending his mission: "The members of his blood family are unable to understand the urgency that drives Jesus in his task of proclaiming the kingdom. . . . They are 'outside' the kingdom preached by Jesus."[36]

What makes a difference in Matthew is the birth narrative. Admittedly Joseph plays a more prominent role than does Mary: the annunciation comes to him (in a dream), and he makes the decision to marry her (Matt. 1:24)—despite his initial reservations—then later to flee from Bethlehem to Egypt (2:13–15)

32. On gifts to the temple treasury, see A. Collins, *Mark*, 587–89.
33. France, *Gospel of Matthew*, 491–93.
34. A. Collins, *Mark*, 590.
35. Malbon, "Poor Widow in Mark," 123.
36. Moloney, *Gospel of Mark*, 82.

and finally to settle in Galilee (2:19–23). Joseph acts as a truly righteous person, in the tradition of his ancestor Joseph: he is just and merciful, portrayed as an entirely appropriate adopted father who cares for the vulnerable mother and child. It may seem a male-oriented picture, but nursing mothers stand in need of support in the demanding task of nurturing infants, a support that does not negate any strength of character.

Yet Mary's role is not passive and certainly not negligible in Matthew's birth story. The four unexpected women in the patrilineal genealogy point forward to her (Matt. 1:1–17): Tamar, who organizes offspring for herself through her father-in-law, Judah, alerting him to his responsibilities (Gen. 38; Matt. 1:3);[37] Rahab, a Canaanite prostitute of Jericho who protects the Israelite spies and is spared the destruction along with her family (Josh. 2; 6:22–25; Matt. 1:5);[38] Ruth, a gentile woman of faith and fortitude, who leaves her home behind to embrace Israel and whose mother-in-law arranges her marriage to Boaz (Ruth 1–3; Matt. 1:5);[39] and the "wife of Uriah," Bathsheba, whose sexual abuse by David leads to their second son, Solomon, becoming David's successor (2 Sam. 11:1–12:25; 1 Kings 1–2; Matt. 1:6).[40]

Each matriarch stands both within and without the ordinary line of descent: by ethnic identity, the means by which she becomes pregnant, or unconventional behavior. What they share is a "common dynamic" in which each threatens the status quo and each is, in turn, under threat herself.[41] Any irregularities in their path to motherhood do not make them sinners.[42] On the contrary, each is a hero in the story of Israel, placed in the line of descent from Abraham and David, conspicuous among the other biblical women (some of them better known) who remain invisible. Mary stands in their tradition because of the unusual nature of her pregnancy, but her faith and courage are implied in the story. If anything, she exceeds them because, in her miraculous pregnancy, she becomes the mother of the Messiah. The matriarchs are her foremothers in faith and courage, and she follows in their footsteps, linking hands with them across the generations. When the wise men arrive, it is Mary and her infant son whom they joyfully see, which leads to their worship of him; with her son she occupies center stage in this tableau (Matt. 2:11).[43] Together these women represent a female nar-

---

37. On Tamar in Gen. 38, see Clements, *Mothers*, 40–67.
38. Clements, *Mothers*, 68–95.
39. Clements, *Mothers*, 97–118.
40. Clements, *Mothers*, 121–44.
41. Gaventa, *Mary*, 107–10.
42. Moloney, *Living Voice of the Gospel*, 132–34.
43. Clements, *Mothers*, 194–230.

rative line running through Matthew's Gospel in Jesus's ministry,[44] a line focused on those on the margins and on shaping an inclusive community that welcomes them.[45]

Another matriarch who features in Matthew's story is Rachel, wife of Jacob and mother of Joseph and Benjamin (Gen. 29–35; Matt. 2:17–18). This reference forms part of the five Old Testament quotations throughout Matthew's birth narrative, tying the story of Jesus to the story of Israel. This particular quotation goes back to the exile and the time of Jeremiah, who prophesied the desolation of God's people (Jer. 31:15), but it reaches further back to the narrative of Jacob, his wives, and his children, at the beginnings of Israel as a nation. Rachel is the foremother of the Southern Kingdom, Judah, and Jeremiah depicts her weeping as her descendants are led into exile, where "she personifies the voice of sorrow."[46] Matthew connects this to the massacre of the baby boys in Bethlehem, as Jesus replays and relives ("recapitulates") the story of Israel, achieving that covenant righteousness so often absent.[47] Rachel is the grieving "mother in Israel" (Jer. 31:15), her tears representing those of the Bethlehem mothers and also her descendants, whose deaths foreshadow that of Jesus himself.[48]

More extraordinary still is that at the end of a list of male begettings God bypasses the male line altogether and effects the incarnation—the presence of Emmanuel, "God with us" (Matt. 1:22–23)—through the female line alone (1:16). As a virgin, Mary is the guarantor of Jesus's humanity; he is not half-human and half-divine but wholly human in and through her femaleness, as well as wholly divine. The genealogy is significant for Jesus's adopted father and for the traditions of Abraham and David, which shape Jesus's identity throughout the Gospel—but his humanity is dependent solely on his mother.[49] Though a man, he is conceived, nurtured, and born only of a woman. That gives the Matthean (and Lukan) Jesus a profound connection with women that other men do not possess.[50] The virginal conception is a key theological point in understanding not only the incarnation but also Jesus's relationship to women.[51]

44. Elaine Mary Wainwright sees Matthew's inclusive vision marred by the way women are silenced (*Towards a Feminist Critical Reading*, 325–29).

45. Lee, *Friendly Guide to Matthew's Gospel*, 13–15.

46. Kennedy, "Jeremiah," 445.

47. Boring, "Gospel of Matthew," 146–47.

48. O'Connor, "Jeremiah," 276.

49. On the virginity of Mary in Matthew and Luke, see B. Byrne, *Lifting the Burden*, 26–27.

50. For more on this theme, see chap. 9, "Women and the Virgin Mary."

51. See Clements, *Mothers*, 166–68.

Female Characters as Antiheroes

Not all women behave in exemplary ways in Mark and Matthew. Both Gospels narrate the story of John the Baptist's death, a tale of political injustice at the highest levels (Mark 6:17–29 // Matt. 14:3–12), prefiguring the passion of Jesus. The chief culprit is Herod Antipas, who despite the respect that, according to Mark (6:20), he has for John and his teaching, imprisons the Baptist for criticizing his marriage to his sister-in-law, Herodias. In the context of a banquet to celebrate Herod's birthday with the powerful figures of Galilean society, Herodias's daughter—who is his stepdaughter and niece—dances before the company. It is so unusual for a royal princess to dance at an all-male banquet that this part of the story is sometimes seen as legendary.[52]

Yet the scene illustrates an immoderation that is characteristic of Herod Antipas: the lavish banquet held in his own honor with the leading citizens and the rash promise to his stepdaughter following the dance (Mark 6:23 // Matt. 14:7). Mark and Matthew portray Herod as a ruler of extravagance and folly, as full of self-importance, as childishly willful and morally bankrupt in his marriage to his sister-in-law and in his desire to protect his honor, saving face at all costs.

What role do the two female characters play in this drama? Herodias manipulates her husband into executing the Baptist in revenge for John's rebuke of her marriage. Mark is explicit in portraying Herodias's desire to have John dead, though she has been powerless up till now to achieve it (6:19). Lacking the fear of popular opinion that has stayed her husband's hand, she seizes the opportunity to manipulate him. Mark's Gospel presents her as an example of power that cannot brook criticism from those deemed inferiors, and thus the Gospel exposes the hypocrisy of power and that of the elite, male or female.

The daughter, never named in the story, is described as a "girl" (*korasion*, 6:22, 28), which is the same word used of Jairus's twelve-year-old daughter (5:41), who is also called a "child" (5:39–41).[53] Perhaps the narrative presents the daughter as the victim of parental abuse, both in the dance and in her mother's terrible demand. From this perspective, Herod and Herodias are guilty not only of judicial murder but also of using their daughter to gain what they want: first with the dance and then with its reward. On the other hand, the girl is on the verge of being old enough for marriage in the ancient context. She shows herself willing and, on her own initiative, adds reference to the "platter," demanding that the execution take place "at once."

52. The story of the dance is absent from Luke (3:18–20; 9:7–9) and from Josephus (*Jewish Antiquities* 18.116–19). On the historicity, see Davies and Allison, *Gospel according to Saint Matthew*, 2:464–66.

53. On the age at which a girl could be engaged, see Bovon, *Luke 1*, 49.

Though young, she mirrors the designs of her mother in playing on the moral feebleness of her stepfather. These figures contrast with the Syrophoenician/ Canaanite woman, who displays a deep protective care of her daughter,[54] as does Jairus with his daughter.[55] "Women can be villains as well as heroes" in these two Gospels.[56] The story illustrates that women are not idealized but that, like men, they are capable of misusing power to justify immoral conduct.

Women in the Passion

Herodias's behavior highlights the exemplary conduct of the women disciples. The passion stories of Mark and Matthew are bounded on either side by the fidelity of women. The anointing at Bethany, which commences the passion narrative,[57] displays the insight of an unnamed women who prophetically anoints Jesus's head, revealing her awareness and proclamation of his destiny and identity (Mark 14:3–9 // Matt. 26:6–13). In both cases, the story is sandwiched within the contrasting tale of Judas's betrayal of Jesus to the authorities (Mark 14:1–2, 10–11 // Matt. 26:1–5, 14–16). This act of ministry by a woman has hardly been acknowledged in the history of interpretation, confused with the Lukan story of the sinful woman (Luke 7:36–50) and sidelined in favor of men's ministry—though for none of their actions does Jesus utter such portentous words as he does concerning this woman.

The key word here is "good news" or "gospel" (*euangelion*). First and foremost it is Jesus who proclaims the good news of God's reign (Mark 1:14–15; Matt. 4:23; 9:35; 11:5), since he also embodies it (Mark 1:1). Thereafter, the apostolic community proclaims it as part of its identity and mission given by Jesus (Mark 8:35; 10:29; 13:10 par.). The same word, "good news," used in the story of the anointing, interprets the woman's action as a prophetic, evangelical sign: "Wherever the gospel is proclaimed, what she has done will be told in remembrance of her" (Mark 14:9 // Matt. 26:13).[58] The woman's anointing is integral to the proclamation of the gospel and the articulation of its meaning. No other action by a disciple is given quite this significance in the Gospels. To comprehend, honor, and proclaim the death of Jesus as divine King lies at the heart of ministry and is exemplified by the woman's intelligent and insightful action. That is how the passion narrative begins.

54. Marcus, *Mark 1–8*, 402–3.
55. See Betsworth, *Reign of God Is Such as These*, 101–14.
56. Malbon, *In the Company of Jesus*, 66.
57. The anointing stories in the other Gospels are different and may not reflect the same incident.
58. Boring, *Mark*, 384–85; B. Byrne, *Lifting the Burden*, 202–3.

Following the death of Jesus, both Mark and Matthew relate for the first time the presence of a group of women who have been with Jesus on the journey from Galilee (Mark 15:40–41 // Matt. 27:55–56). Who are these women? We know little of their background. Three of the most prominent are named in Mark: Mary Magdalene, Mary the mother of James the Less and Joseph, and Salome. Matthew agrees with Mark but omits the reference to "many other" Galilean women and the description of James and refers to the third woman simply as "the mother of the sons of Zebedee." It may well be that her name is Salome. If so, it is an important description for Matthew, since in his account the same woman, mother of the apostles James and John, has requested the seats of honor for her sons in Jesus's kingdom (Matt. 20:20–21). In Mark it is the two disciples themselves who make the request, suggesting that Matthew has added the reference to their mother. In Matthew Jesus responds to her sons rather than to her, implying that they have put her up to it—although it indicates her own lack of understanding, as well as that of her sons. There is a small parable here. The sons disappear at Jesus's arrest along with the other male disciples and are not present at the cross (Matt. 26:56b). Their mother, by contrast, remains courageously with Jesus in his suffering and death. Her understanding has changed since her first appearance. She has now grasped the message of the cross that James and John have as yet failed to understand:[59] "Her presence serves as a foil for her sons' cowardly absence."[60]

Salome does not appear elsewhere in the Gospels. Against her identification as the wife of Zebedee, it could be argued that Mark makes no reference to her family in naming her, which is unusual for females, who are generally defined by the males of their family. But this could also indicate a prominence that transcends family ties. Salome is also mentioned in later writings beyond the New Testament as a disciple and the sister of Mary mother of Jesus (see John 19:25), as well as the midwife at the birth of Jesus.[61]

This passage (Mark 15:40–41 // Matt. 27:55–56) is also the first mention of Mary Magdalene in Mark and Matthew, and her name appears at the head of the list, as it does in most cases in the Gospels. It is now recognized that Mary is not a prostitute in any of the Gospels and that her main association is in relation to the cross and resurrection. She is most likely an early disciple of Jesus, as she is numbered among the Galilean women before Jesus's journey to Jerusalem, among whom she is eminent. This view of Mary's significance brings her into the foreground, where previously the tradition (particularly in the West) has misunderstood her as a penitent sinner—and the worst kind of

---

59. Moltmann-Wendel, *Women around Jesus*, 119–27.
60. Davies and Allison, *Gospel according to Saint Matthew*, 3:638.
61. See Traverso, "Art and the Gospels."

female sinner at that.[62] But Mark and Matthew depict Mary as a woman of exemplary faith and strength of character. She is indeed capable of bearing the role assigned to her as witness to the cross and burial and as proclaimer of the resurrection. Her role and character place her among Jesus's most prominent disciples and as a leader in the early community.[63]

The second woman listed, also named Mary (Mark 15:40 // Matt. 27:56), is identified by her motherhood of two (presumably) known disciples, James the Less and Joses (= Joseph). Two other characters named "James" appear in Mark and Matthew: James the son of Alphaeus, one of the Twelve (Mark 3:18 // Matt. 10:3), and James the brother of Jesus (Mark 6:3 // Matt. 13:55). It is possible that this Mary is an unknown disciple of Jesus identified by her sons, known to the early community but unknown to us. But her name and that of her sons are so common in the Gospels that, from our point of view, they fail to isolate her from other women of the same name.

Another possibility is that she is the mother of Jesus. Two of the names fit Jesus's siblings, particularly James, who became a disciple of Jesus and the leader of the Jewish-Christian community in Jerusalem (Gal. 1:19; 2:9–12); he is also associated with the Letter of James. James and Joses/Joseph are listed first among the four brothers of Jesus (Mark 6:3 // Matt. 13:55).[64] There is certainly a Gospel tradition that the mother of Jesus is present at the cross, and it may be that John's Gospel, knowing the Synoptic tradition, clarifies that this Mary is the mother of Jesus (John 19:25–27). On the other hand, it is unlikely that Mark and Matthew would not make explicit her relationship to Jesus.[65]

Some have argued that the first two evangelists are embarrassed by these Galilean women and leave it till the last minute to mention them.[66] But we need to note the tendency in biblical narrative to mention an important detail not at the beginning of the story, where we might expect it, but later, when it is needed.[67] This view is supported by the striking way the women are described. Only at this point does their behavior part company with that of their fellow disciples; they act here as "God's bearers of hope."[68] Admittedly, they are standing "from afar" and not at the foot of the cross. But they are closer than their male colleagues, who are nowhere in sight, and we do not know

---

62. On Mary Magdalene in the Gospels, see chaps. 2–4 on Luke-Acts and John. See Haskins, *Mary Magdalene*; Ristine, *Mary Magdalene*.

63. On the women followers, see Ricci, *Mary Magdalene and Many Others*, 171–77.

64. Jesus also has sisters as well as brothers (*adelphai*, Mark 6:3 // Matt. 13:56).

65. Davies and Allison, *Gospel according to Saint Matthew*, 3:637–38.

66. See, e.g., Dewey, "Women in the Gospel of Mark," 28.

67. Alter, *Art of Biblical Narrative*, 66.

68. Luz, *Matthew 21–28*, 575.

whether the authorities would allow the friends and relatives of a crucified man to approach and to remain in the place of execution.[69]

The women are described in two ways. First of all, Mark tells us, "When [Jesus] was in Galilee, they used to follow him" (Mark 15:41). Matthew's version of this makes it clear that they have followed him to Jerusalem: "Who were following Jesus from Galilee" (Matt. 27:55). In other words, these three women are disciples of Jesus, because "following" is the main image of discipleship, as we have already seen. Mark also mentions the "many other women going up with him to Jerusalem." This is an extraordinary picture: rarely, if ever, do we picture the journey to Jerusalem as including a large group of women. Hollywood reinforces the imagery, as we view Jesus marching ahead, followed (literally) by twelve men. Yet the Gospels depict many women, not just a handful, who have left homes, families, and occupations to accompany Jesus. The iconography of twelve-men-plus-Jesus needs to be challenged to portray Jesus's disciples in accord with the Gospels.

The contrast with the Twelve is equally significant. For Mark, the Twelve are given a dual role: "to be with" Jesus and "so that he might send them out to proclaim" (Mark 3:14b). Whereas they succeed in mission (6:7, 30), they fail dismally to be his companions following the Last Supper and desert him at his arrest (14:50). This desertion coheres with their lack of understanding on the road to Jerusalem as Jesus foretells his suffering and death (8:31–33; 9:31–35, 38; 10:28, 32–45). Mark's Gospel presents, in other words, "a widening chasm not just between Jesus' faithfulness and the disciples' faltering ways, but also between their own calling and their inability to fulfill it."[70]

At the beginning of Jesus's ministry, the first four to be called by Jesus—Peter and Andrew, James and John—respond by following him at once (*akolouthein*, Mark 1:18, 20 // Matt. 4:20, 22). In the passion story, the same four who have failed to follow Jesus to the cross are replaced by the three who do not fail. The women's discipleship emerges confidently into the foreground,[71] in striking contrast to the men's discipleship, which has, for the time being, fallen into the shadows.

Second, both Gospels describe the women as "ministering" to Jesus (*diakonein*): "who . . . used to . . . minister to him" (Mark), "ministering to him" (Matthew). This is the same verb we have found elsewhere to describe the core work of Christian ministry. It is the same ministry that defines the work of Jesus, including not only his teaching and healing but also his journey to the cross. It sums up what it means for Jesus to live and die as Savior, and

---

69. Luz, *Matthew 21–28*, 572–73.
70. Henderson, *Christology and Discipleship*, 248.
71. Keener, *Gospel of Matthew*, 689–90.

it articulates the form and practice of the ministry bequeathed to his community of disciples.[72]

The same ministry will continue into the resurrection story (Mark 16:1–8 // Matt. 28:1–20). The women disciples replacing the Twelve are the privileged ones who become witnesses to the resurrection and its profound message of hope. We would expect this message to be given directly to the Twelve, who should be there. But their absence paradoxically makes it possible for the women to take over their role and become, in effect, Jesus's apostles. The dual role of being Jesus's companions and apostles is embraced by the Galilean women disciples. As a consequence, women become the primary witnesses of the resurrection, with astonishing implications for their ministry both then and now.

The Ending of Mark and Matthew

At this point, the narratives of Mark and Matthew part company. Mark's narrative is terse, and the ending at 16:8 is difficult to interpret. In the second century two endings were added to Mark that reflect a different style and either may have come from another, lost Gospel or may represent a summary of the other Gospels. The longer ending relates the story of an appearance of Jesus to Mary Magdalene, who faithfully reports it to the grieving disciples and is not believed (16:9–11). Only when Jesus appears to two other disciples do the rest believe (16:12–13). Jesus's subsequent appearance is to the Eleven, who are chided for their rejection of the testimony of "those who saw him raised" (16:14). This reference can signify only Mary Magdalene and the other women disciples, whose testimony is vindicated. In this account, the primary witness of the resurrection is Mary Magdalene, whose testimony is rejected by the apostles, by implication on gender grounds, reinforcing her prominence.[73]

Mark's Gospel as we now have it narrates no story of Jesus appearing to anyone, although it indicates such an event in the near future in Galilee (16:7). The women disciples, having heard the message from the angel and having been given the command to proclaim it to Peter and the other disciples—"go, tell"—run from the tomb, trembling and overwhelmed, and say "nothing to anyone, for they were afraid" (16:8). Here the Gospel seems to have concluded,[74]

---

72. Matthew is the only evangelist to speak explicitly of the church (16:18; 18:17); see Kingsbury, *Matthew*, 157–60.

73. For more on the longer ending, see Moloney, *Resurrection of the Messiah*, 18–25.

74. For the view that Mark refrains from committing the final episode to writing because of its political danger to a community suffering persecution in Rome, see Billings, "End of Mark's Gospel," 42–54.

and the ending has provoked considerable debate. Is there a lost ending?[75] If not, why would Mark end his Gospel so abruptly? If he did, how are we to read the women disciples' flight from the tomb and their silence?

On the one hand, some argue that the women disciples fail at this point in the narrative, with Mark turning, as it were, to face the reader with the challenging question, How will you respond to the message of the resurrection? In this view, both men and women are failures who, without the strength of Christ's risen presence, are disobedient and in disarray.[76] Though they all fail, God does not fail—and God's triumph is definitive above and beyond human failure.

There is, on the other hand, a counterargument that the women disciples have not failed at this point. Rather, they are overcome by the fear that is natural at an epiphany. The stone moved away from the tomb and the presence of an angel are the very last things these women are expecting as they reach the tomb (Mark 16:3); they have come to anoint Jesus's body and mourn him (16:1). In this view, the women are terrified also by the message that Jesus is risen. Their flight and silence are a temporary reaction to the astonishing news that renders them overwhelmed and tongue-tied. It is literally an ineffable event, an event that cannot be spoken of, at least initially.

This second interpretation is not an attempt to demonstrate the superiority of the women over the men for ideological reasons. The eleven disciples are terrified of being arrested along with Jesus, as Peter's denial and his subsequent grief make plain (Mark 14:66–72). The women disciples are less vulnerable to arrest. Moreover, their fear at the tomb, which is not described by Mark, does not seem to be caused by any danger from the authorities. It is more likely that their response is the comprehensible human reaction when coming face-to-face with a divine epiphany, which is a common biblical motif.[77] This reading makes more sense of the Markan narrative as a whole, while also leaving open the possibility of a lost ending that tells of the women's proclamation.

Matthew's account has unusual features and difficulties of interpretation that are very different from those in Mark. Only two women disciples go to the tomb—Mary Magdalene and the "other Mary"—but nothing is said of their intention to anoint Jesus's body (Matt. 28:1). They come to "see" the tomb and, presumably, to mourn. Here Matthew gives weight to the anointing that has already occurred (26:6–13), where the unnamed woman has poured expensive oil over Jesus's head, acknowledging his royal and

---

75. For this view, see France, *Gospel of Mark*, 670–74.
76. See, e.g., Hooker, *Gospel according to St Mark*, 382–87; Boring, *Mark*, 448–49; and Moloney, *Gospel of Mark*, 22–23, 348–54.
77. Lightfoot, *Gospel Message of St Mark*, 80–97; also A. Collins, *Mark*, 799–800.

messianic status, which Matthew has established from the beginning (1:1–17). Strangely enough, the "mother of the sons of Zebedee," despite her courage in following Jesus to the cross, is not included in the resurrection narrative. Why Matthew omits this woman is unclear. Perhaps he sees her role fulfilled in her readiness to share Jesus's cup of suffering (20:22–23), or perhaps his account is not meant to be exclusive: other disciples may be present whom he does not mention.

Matthew implies that the women witness the pushing back of the stone by the angel, who is so dazzling and terrifying a figure that the guards at the tomb faint in shock (28:2–4). This coheres with the Markan ending, where other human beings are overwhelmed at the presence of the angel. When the angel invites the women to witness the emptiness of the tomb and gives them the commission to proclaim the message, they immediately obey it: they go and they tell "with fear and great joy" (28:5–7). Any ambiguity for the implied reader is hereby explicitly resolved. Matthew, the first interpreter of Mark, interprets the women's response as that of holy fear and joy, making it clear that they obey the angel's (and Jesus's) message.

Is Matthew's version of the story a correction of Mark or a clarification? Much will depend on how we interpret Mark 16:8. If it is disobedience, then Matthew is rectifying Mark's account, showing emphatically that they do not in fact disobey the angelic command.[78] This view would seem to be bolstered by the existence of the longer ending (Mark 16:9–20), indicating the early community's unease with the unsettling ending of this Gospel. If, however, the Markan women are awestruck and silenced but not disobedient, Matthew is clarifying an ambiguity that he, and others, have recognized.

What follows the women's departure in Matthew is unexpected: on the way they meet Jesus, who confirms the good news and their commission (28:8–10). From a narrative point of view, there is no need for this appearance. The women disciples already believe, are already filled with Easter joy. His appearance is an act of grace, a gift not needed but one that is welcomed with faith, emphasizing the importance of the women's commission. They are the first to meet the Risen Lord, to fall at his feet in worship, and to be given the commission to proclaim the resurrection.[79]

There is no gender competition among disciples in Matthew's Gospel; nonetheless the scene where the men require the women's testimony "reflects the gospel's power to transcend gender restrictions."[80] Jesus meets the Eleven

---

78. So Moloney, *Resurrection of the Messiah*, 44–48.
79. See Friedrichsen, "Commissioning of Women Disciples," 270–78.
80. Keener, *Gospel of Matthew*, 702.

on the mountain in Galilee and gives them the commission to proclaim the gospel, with the assurance of his abiding presence (28:16–20). The problem is one of interpretation: the epiphany of the risen Jesus on the mountain is invariably emphasized at the expense of the epiphany at the tomb. Yet both commissions are integral to the Matthean narrative, and both play their part in the good news of Jesus risen from the dead. In one sense, the Eleven are the primary witnesses to the resurrection, as their experience takes place on a mountain, the place of revelation.[81] In another sense, the primary witness belongs to the two who meet the triumphant life of heaven in the place of death and are the first to see, believe, worship, and bear witness.[82] Their message is believed. Both groups represent the church in its proclamation of the resurrection.

The unexpected presence of women where we might expect men takes us back to the genealogy. As we have seen, we encounter there four women in a male-only genealogy who prefigure the unique role Mary will play in giving birth to the Messiah (Matt. 1:1–17). The women of the genealogy are Old Testament prototypes of the women disciples at the tomb, who bear witness to the resurrection of the Messiah.

CHART OF GALILEAN WOMEN IN PASSION AND RESURRECTION NARRATIVES OF MARK AND MATTHEW

NAME	RELATIONSHIPS	TEXT	IDENTIFICATION	NOTES
Mary	Mother of Jesus	Mark 3:31–32 // Matt. 12:46; Mark 6:3; Matt. 1:16, 18–25; 2:11, 13–14, 19–21	Unlikely to be mother of James and Joses/Joseph	
Mary		Mark 15:40 // Matt. 27:56; Mark 16:1–8 // Matt. 28:1–10	"The Magdalene"	
Mary	Mother of James the Less and Joses/Joseph	Mark 15:40 // Matt. 27:56; Mark 15:47 // Matt. 27:61; Mark 16:1–8 // Matt. 28:1–10		From Judea, if wife of Clopas/Cleopas
Salome		Mark 15:40; 16:1–8	Mother of James and John, wife of Zebedee?	
	Mother of sons of Zebedee	Matt. 20:20; 27:56	Salome?	Does not come to tomb in Matthew
Other women		Mark 15:40 // Matt. 27:55		Larger group

81. Mountains are important throughout Matthew: see Donaldson, *Jesus on the Mountain,* 30–50, 82–83.
82. Bauckham, *Gospel Women,* 277–79.

There is one other point to be made for both Gospels. The women disciples are the witnesses in Mark and Matthew not only of the resurrection in general but also of its materiality.[83] It is the *emptiness* of the tomb to which they bear witness. Any denial of the physical nature of the resurrection is a denial of the women's testimony, which is particularly striking in a context where the witness of women was given little or no credence. The idea that the empty tomb can be bypassed in favor of a spiritualized appearance tradition is to deny not only the materiality in which Christian faith is grounded but also its dependence on the faithful testimony of Jesus's female disciples, whose witness is vindicated in the Gospels. The women join with the angelic messengers to bear witness to the resurrection and its mysterious materiality in the empty tomb.[84]

Presence and Absence

A further factor, often ignored, is that women are present in many scenes—such as crowd scenes—where they are not explicitly mentioned. In reading these two Gospels, we need to take into account women's hidden presence. Unless it is clear they are absent, such as in the Sanhedrin, the male-only Jewish council, we should assume that women are present in many scenes alongside men. Women form their own group among the disciples, but that does not mean they are not present in more general scenes. In this task, as in any study of the ancient world, "we must exercise more imagination to repopulate the ancient landscape with women . . . because women were everywhere, present publicly at all social levels."[85]

Yet it is hard to deny women's absence from several scenes in the Gospels. There is no story in Mark or Matthew of a woman being called. No woman is present at the transfiguration, despite its centrality in both Gospels (Mark 9:2–9 // Matt. 17:1–8).[86] At the Last Supper, Mark and Matthew refer only to the Twelve as Jesus eats the Passover meal (Mark 14:17 // Matt. 26:20). Although it is possible that women, and other men, were present,[87] the first two Gospels do not mention anyone else—perhaps because the Twelve have a symbolic role, connecting Israel to the church through the new Passover.

---

83. In some circles women could not be witnesses, although there is no prohibition in the Torah. In some circumstances, women could swear oaths, and their religious testimony—e.g., as prophets—could be taken seriously. See Maccini, *Her Testimony Is True*, 63–97.

84. For more on the bodily resurrection, see R. Williams, *Resurrection*, 91–112.

85. Cohick, *Women in the World*, 321.

86. Lee, *Transfiguration*, 130–31.

87. See Maguire, "Bible, Liturgy Concur." The article contains the painting *Last Supper* by Bohdan Piasecki, which includes the presence of women and children.

As we have seen, a notable feature of Mark's Gospel—though present in softer form in Matthew—is that the Twelve often fail to understand Jesus's ministry. This feature stands alongside the privileged position they hold throughout his ministry. Peter, James, and John are present at the raising of Jairus's daughter in Mark (Mark 5:37) and the transfiguration. Their hardness of heart (Mark) or weakness of faith (Matthew) is particularly apparent in the passion narrative, as we have seen, where they betray, deny, or desert Jesus (Mark 14:50 // Matt. 26:56b). This failure of ministry is compensated by those who do understand and who serve Jesus to the end, and they consist largely of women. So, while absent from some scenes, women are faithfully present in others, reflecting Jesus's inclusive ministry.

Leadership in a New Key

In outlining his understanding of leadership, Jesus speaks of a new way of being in the community of disciples (Mark 10:42–45; Matt. 20:25–28). This pattern is seen above all in Jesus's crucifixion, which is the ultimate act of renunciation of power, exposing him to an irretrievable loss of honor in the culture of his day.[88] While this death is exemplary for Christians, it is more fundamentally a saving event by which sins are forgiven and death is overcome, where the structures of the world are dismantled by the advent of God's eschatological reign.

The disciples are not to uphold patriarchal domination, as in the Roman-Hellenistic world, but rather to embrace a countercultural model of leadership.[89] Jesus endorses "the topsy-turvy nature of *true* greatness, which is experienced by those who have given up all claims to conventional power and instead have turned themselves into servants of their fellow human beings."[90] Yet Christians have often ignored the challenge and proceeded to set up similar structures of domination within the family and the church. Loving service and servanthood are the traditional prerogatives of women in their domestic environment. If women are models of leadership in Jesus's teaching, how can they subsequently be excluded?

Conclusion

When we take Mark and Matthew together, we are left with a profound impression of the strength and resilience of women's discipleship. Women

---

88. Lee, *Gospels Speak*, 18–20.
89. Giles, *What the Bible Actually Teaches on Women*, 82–83, 90–93.
90. Marcus, *Mark 8–16*, 755.

are not mentioned as frequently as men, and their role is less visible than the Twelve.[91] Yet in many ways, their ministry exceeds that of the apostles, and their role goes far beyond their cultural context. This portrait of women reflects the ministry of Jesus and his extraordinary openness to women as disciples. It also reflects, as we will see in a later chapter, the experience of the earliest church, where women were given unprecedented access to leadership in the early community.[92] To Mary Magdalene and the other Galilean women, with their fearless following of Jesus and their witness to him in the earliest communities,[93] we owe a debt of gratitude as we see women's leadership expand today. As ministers to Jesus, modeling the ministry he himself embraced, and as witnesses to his death, burial, and resurrection, the women are given a role in Mark and Matthew well beyond cultural stereotypes, a role that enables their daughters-in-faith today to stand alongside male leaders in the Christian community.

Yet the role forged by the earliest communities was all-too-soon eroded, eventually limiting women to a discipleship of invisibility and a ministry that confined itself to traditional and nonthreatening female roles. Eventually, only the successors to the Twelve were to be seen as authoritative, not the women disciples who in so many ways surpassed them and who gained for other women a ministry that the church is still struggling to embrace. This picture of women's exemplary discipleship will be confirmed as we turn to the writings of Luke.

---

91. On the Twelve, see Giles, *What the Bible Actually Teaches on Women*, 87–89.
92. See below, chap. 5.
93. Bauckham, *Gospel Women*, 295–304.

Chapter Two

Writings of Luke

Gospel

TAKEN TOGETHER, the Gospel of Luke and the Acts of the Apostles present us with something of a conundrum in regard to women—unusual given that the same author, Luke, wrote both texts.[1] In particular the Gospel itself seems to accord women a high status, with significantly more female characters than any of the other Gospels. This feature includes Luke's tendency to pair stories of women and men, such as the healing of the crippled woman and the healing of the man with dropsy (13:10–17; 14:1–6). Acts contains fewer female characters than Luke's Gospel, and not many women have explicit leadership roles. There are no women among the reconstituted Twelve (1:15–26) or the seven chosen for a diaconal role (6:1–6), and the two main characters are Peter and Paul.[2]

This conundrum has given rise to a variety of conclusions. Some have argued that Luke is a champion of women, preeminent among the New Testament writers, and an early feminist—not only on account of the number of women in the Gospel but also because of the significant roles they play.[3]

1. The New Testament speaks of "Luke the beloved physician" (Col. 4:14; 2 Tim. 4:11; Philem. 24), a companion of John Mark and Paul. But "Luke" was a common name, and there is no evidence of any specialized medical knowledge on his part. See Fitzmyer, *Gospel according to Luke*, 1:35–53.
2. For a brief outline of the differences, see Seim, *Double Message*, 3–4.
3. See, e.g., Kopas, "Jesus and Women," 192–202; also Leonard Swidler on the Gospels in general, including Luke (*Biblical Affirmations of Women*, 161–290).

Other, more negative studies see Luke as including additional female characters in the Gospel for the purpose of relegating them to traditional roles: "To restrict the participation of women to the bounds of discreet behavior."[4] Thus, in one view, Luke is the great supporter of women's ministry, while in the other, Luke subordinates women's role[5] both in the ministry of Jesus and in the early Christian community.[6] Still another view argues that Luke's message is both positive and negative for women, a "double message" that reflects ambiguity: one in which women's discipleship is commended but their leadership restricted.[7] This controversy will form part of our discussion on Luke and Acts in this and the following chapter.

New Testament Connections

The Gospel of Luke has a dual association within the New Testament writings. In the first place, it is closely allied to the Gospels of Mark and Matthew, the three together forming the Synoptic Gospels. It was perhaps written in the 80s or 90s, around the same time as Matthew. There is general agreement that, like Matthew, Luke used Mark as a major source in the writing of his Gospel (see Luke 1:1). Where there is disagreement is on the question of whether Luke (along with Matthew) used a second, hypothetical source called Q, a Gospel collection of mainly Jesus's sayings from which both evangelists have drawn, though in different ways. This is the preferred view of most scholars, as it explains the common words of Jesus that Matthew and Luke share, though often in different locations.[8]

The main alternative to this theory is that Luke's Gospel represents a creative reworking of both Mark and Matthew, where the evangelist had access to Matthew as well as Mark.[9] In this case, there is no need to postulate a Q source, and Luke would represent a second rewriting of Mark via Matthew. This may seem an attractive alternative at first, as it dispenses with the need for Q, but it is hard to see why Luke has made some of the changes he has to Matthew's Gospel, especially to the carefully crafted collections of Jesus's sayings. In the end, the Q theory, along with Mark,

4. D'Angelo, "Women in Luke-Acts," 461.

5. Jane Schaberg begins her commentary on the Gospel with a warning: this is "an extremely dangerous text, perhaps the most dangerous in the Bible" (Schaberg and Ringe, "Gospel of Luke," 493).

6. For an outline of the conflict, see Karris, "Women and Discipleship in Luke," 2–5.

7. Seim, *Double Message*, 249–56.

8. See, e.g., Kloppenburg, *Q, The Earliest Gospel*, 1–40.

9. One of the main contenders is Mark Goodacre; see, e.g., *Case against Q*.

makes the most sense of Luke's Gospel and offers the best solution to date of the synoptic problem.[10]

Second, the Gospel of Luke, with its focus on Jesus's ministry, is closely tied to its second volume, the Acts of the Apostles, which narrates the story of the early church, beginning with Pentecost (Acts 2:1–13) and concluding with Paul's arrival in Rome (28:11–31). The texts are separated in the canonical ordering of the New Testament, but Luke specifically refers to his "first book" at the beginning of Acts: "In my first book, I mentioned all the things which Jesus began to do and teach" (1:1). The two volumes are fused together by the story of the ascension, which concludes the Gospel and opens the Acts of the Apostles (Luke 24:50–53; Acts 1:2–11), though there are differences between the two accounts. More generally, there are striking similarities between the way events are narrated in Luke and in Acts, and the style of writing is common to both.[11] It is clear that the texts are intended to be read together as two parts of one overarching narrative.

As in the other two Synoptic Gospels, women belong under the umbrella of "disciples" in Luke. In Luke's Gospel there is the same sense of ambiguity around the language of discipleship, as well as overlap, so that no strict boundary line is drawn between who is in and who is out. In fact, the ministry of the Lukan Jesus has a much better reception among the outsiders than the insiders. If anything, Luke makes the point clear by explicitly including women as followers of Jesus early in the Gospel (Luke 8:2–3).

Women as Prophets

The significant role played by women in the Gospel of Luke is immediately apparent in the birth narratives. Within these stories, several women are depicted as prophets: Mary, Elizabeth, and Anna. Not only are they prophets, but they also play a decisive role in the understanding of revelation and the significance of the birth of Jesus. Through them in particular Luke introduces his message of salvation, and he demonstrates its acceptance in the women's active response.

Eminent among these is Mary, who is depicted as a young woman of remarkable faith and courage, contrasting with the priest Zechariah—in an early example of Lukan pairing—whose response to the annunciation by

10. A further possibility, if we want to dispense with Q, is that Matthew has made use of both Mark and Luke, rather than Luke making use of Mark and Matthew; see Garrow, "Streeter's 'Other' Synoptic Solution," 207–26.

11. On the similarities, see, e.g., Stephens, *Gospel of Luke*, 19–54.

Gabriel is deemed inadequate and lacking in faith (Luke 1:20): "Because he asks in unbelief, the sign becomes a punishment."[12] Mary is one of the few biblical characters who are particularly favored by God, a favor she finds troubling rather than comforting (1:28–30).[13] Her questioning of the angel is not interpreted as disobedience, and her final response is a powerful statement of exemplary faith and strength of heart. There is nothing timid or passive in her yes to God: Mary "unreservedly embraces the purpose of God, without regard to its cost to her personally."[14]

In the following visitation scene, where the two mothers meet (1:39–45), the elder woman with the higher status—on account of her age, lineage, and marriage to a Judean priest—gives way before the young woman from Galilee, because of the greater status of Mary's conception.[15] Elizabeth recognizes Mary's belief in the word of God, with all the heartache it will mean for her (2:35), and the presence of the Holy Spirit enables Mary to proclaim the Magnificat: the song of praise that sets out the revolutionary dynamic of Luke's Gospel (1:46–55). Without a hint of jealousy Elizabeth is full of wonder at the role her young relative has been given and awe at the depth of Mary's faith. She, too, stands under the influence of the Spirit, while her response to Mary's visit echoes the words of Gabriel in the previous scene.[16]

Elizabeth's prophetic role in this scene is paralleled by that of the prophet Anna, who greets Jesus in the temple at his presentation. Paired with Simeon, likewise an elderly prophetic figure (2:25–35), the aged Anna has many years of faith and dedication to God in the temple behind her; she is the ideal widow, dedicating herself entirely to the worship of God through prayer and fasting.[17] This spiritual depth enables her to recognize at a glance the significance of the child as she enters the scene of Simeon's prophecy. Her reaction to the infant is a rendering of thanks to God, which is the appropriate response to God's saving action in Jesus.[18]

Not only does Anna render thanks to God, in keeping with her whole life, but she also proclaims the message to others. Following on from Simeon's words, Anna recognizes in this child the "redemption" (lutrōsin, 2:38) of Israel

---

12. Bovon, *Luke 1*, 32.
13. Reid, *Choosing the Better Part?*, 66–67.
14. J. Green, *Gospel of Luke*, 92.
15. Just, *Luke 1:1–9:50*, 63.
16. Gaventa, *Mary*, 143–45.
17. On the role of widows in the New Testament church, see Thurston, "Widows," 745.
18. Luke uses different verbs to refer to the response of praise in his Gospel: "bless," "glorify," and "praise" (1:64; 2:13, 20, 28; 4:15; 13:13; 17:15; 18:43; 19:37; 23:47). With Anna, the word employed is unusual and occurs only here in the New Testament (*anthōmologeito*); it means something like "give thanks in return."

and proclaims it to all who, like her, are living in expectation of the divine intervention on behalf of the people of God. Although Anna is given no direct speech at this point, unlike Simeon,[19] she takes on the wider and more public task of proclaiming the child's birth. Redemption will necessitate also Jesus's death and resurrection, so Anna's words are prophetic. She is an impressive figure here: "The dignity of old age, a deep passion for God, and prophetic inspiration stand behind and give credibility to her witness to Jesus."[20]

To return to the central figure of Mary, two further points emerge about her in Luke's birth narrative. In the first place, she is, in effect, the first Christian in Luke's narrative, the first to believe in, and respond wholeheartedly to, God's calling (1:26–38).[21] Second, the story is generally associated with the biblical form of annunciation stories around the birth of a child,[22] and more immediately, it is compared with the annunciation to Zechariah (1:5–20).[23] At least five elements of this literary form are present in the annunciations to Zechariah and to Mary: the appearance of an angel (Gabriel, 1:11, 26); the proclamation of God's word (to Zechariah, that Elizabeth will bear a son; to Mary, that she will become the mother of the Messiah; 1:13, 31); the overcoming of a barrier (Elizabeth's barrenness and Mary's virginity, 1:7, 34); and a sign endorsing the message (for Zechariah—ironically—his muteness; for Mary, Elizabeth's pregnancy; 1:20, 36).[24] To these we might add a further element: the response of the person addressed by God (Zechariah's initial disobedience and later obedience; Mary's willing consent; 1:18–20, 38).

At the same time, the annunciation to Mary acts as a prophetic call or commissioning narrative:[25] "She wraps herself in the mantle of a prophet, one inspired by God to proclaim the hidden things God is accomplishing among the people."[26] Isaiah's call narrative, for example, has a number of distinctive elements: a divine *confrontation*, which is the epiphany of God in the temple (Isa. 6:1–2); an introductory *word*, which is the proclamation of the divine holiness (6:3); an objection apparent in the prophet's statement of

19. This aspect can be used to argue that Luke tends to silence women—although Anna is not silenced, even if her words are narrated in indirect speech. According to Reid, however, for Luke "the voices of woman prophets are never heard" (*Choosing the Better Part?*, 93). This must surely except the voices of Mary and Elizabeth.

20. Nolland, *Luke 1–9:20*, 125.

21. Fitzmyer, *Gospel according to Luke*, 1:341.

22. See, e.g., the angelic annunciations to Hagar about the birth of her son, Ishmael (Gen. 16:7–14), and to Manoah's wife about the birth of her son, Samson (Judg. 13:3–5).

23. See Bovon, *Luke 1*, 47–48.

24. L. Johnson, *Gospel of Luke*, 38–39.

25. As argued by E. Johnson, *Truly Our Sister*, 247–51.

26. Gaventa, *Mary*, 133.

inadequacy (6:5); a *reassurance* given by one of the seraphim with the glowing coal from the altar (6:6–7); and a *commission with an assent* to follow (in some call narratives this element includes a *sign*), evident in the question of who will go and the prophet's response: "Here am I; send me!" (6:8).[27] In this sense, the shape of the annunciation story to Mary overlaps with the call narrative, which Luke "deftly combines" with it.[28]

The *divine confrontation* is the appearance of the angel Gabriel (Luke 1:26–27). The introductory *word* is the angel's greeting of her (1:28). Mary's sense of *inadequacy* is captured in her incomprehension at both the greeting and its explanation (1:29, 34). The *reassurance* comes from the angel, intending to calm her fear (1:30) by explaining the agency of the Holy Spirit, who will make the impossible possible (1:35–37). Finally, her *assent* to the *commission* is a strong statement uttered with confidence and resilience: "Behold, the servant [*doulē*; literally, "slave"] of the Lord! May it become for me according to your word [*genoito moi kata to rhēma sou*]!" (1:38). And the *sign* offered is that of Elizabeth's miraculous pregnancy (1:36–37). The assent is reiterated at the end of the following scene—which confirms the depth and insight of Mary's faith (1:42–45)—where Mary, under the sway of the overshadowing Spirit,[29] proclaims joyfully the salvation that has come to Israel's poor (1:46–55).

To round off the picture of Mary in Luke's Gospel, we need to note that her response fulfills the words of Jesus on two further occasions, once when Jesus describes his true family as those who "hear the word of God and do it" (8:21) and once when he tells an enthusiastic woman in the crowd extolling Mary's physical motherhood: "Blessed rather are those who hear the word of God and guard it" (11:27–28). This is precisely what Mary does in Luke.[30] Her strength of faith in the unimaginable word of God, her intrepid acceptance of her vocation, her prophetic voice, and her close association with the Spirit mean that her presence with the apostles at Pentecost is both comprehensible and even necessary; she belongs among Jesus's family in both a literal and a metaphorical sense.

Women as Suppliants

Women from Galilee are recipients of Jesus's ministry in the Gospel of Luke, including the women we have encountered in the other two Synoptics. Thus

---

27. See Guyette, "Genre of the Call Narrative," 54–58.
28. E. Johnson, *Truly Our Sister*, 248.
29. E. Johnson, *Truly Our Sister*, 251–54.
30. Fitzmyer, *Gospel according to Luke*, 2:927.

Simon's mother-in-law is healed of a "high fever" (Luke 4:38–39), as she is in Mark and Matthew, yet strangely, in Luke, this is the first mention of a disciple and apostle who is not yet a follower of Jesus, not until the miraculous catch of fish in the next chapter, when Simon Peter leaves everything to follow Jesus (5:11). Jesus simply enters his house as if his intention is not primarily to see Simon at all but rather to heal his wife's mother (his wife being the second, though hidden, woman in the story).

Luke underlines the totality of the woman's cure at the mere sound of Jesus's word, emphasizing the divine power to "rebuke" the illness rather than the healing tenderness of touch, as in Mark and Matthew (Luke 4:39). Luke's concern is to demonstrate Jesus's authority over the ills, human and demonic, that afflict human life: "Demon possession, sickness, sin, and death are all manifestations of creation's bondage in its fallenness."[31] The story thus has the features more of an exorcism than of a simple healing story. "Rebuke" is precisely what Jesus does in the previous story of the demon-possessed man (4:35) and in the following verses when the demons try to speak (4:41), as if here, with the woman, he is silencing the raging voice of the fever. Her readiness to respond with service has its own dignity and significance, illustrating not only the power Jesus has over all forms of evil but also the power that he freely restores to her.

One of the additional stories Luke brings to the Gospel is that of the widow of Nain (7:11–17),[32] which pairs with the previous story of the centurion (7:1–10). Both are about death: the much-loved slave who is dying and the son who has just died and is on the way to burial. Jesus is motivated by compassion for the woman; as a widow she has lost not only her only and beloved son but also her sole means of support (widows were among the poorest and most socially vulnerable). We could translate Jesus's response more vividly as "his heart went out to her" *(esplangchnisthē*, 7:13), a response that is reinforced by his immediate words to the woman: "Do not go on weeping." Luke tells us that in raising her son to life, Jesus "gave him to his mother" (7:15). Here again Jesus shows deep concern for the particular vulnerabilities of an unsupported woman in a male-oriented world.

The story of the sinful woman is another Lukan addition, though there are loose parallels elsewhere. The woman who weeps over Jesus's feet and anoints them with perfumed oil, drying them with her unbound hair, is a conspicuous example of Jesus's core mission in Luke. The Gospel portrays a woman who

---

31. Just, *Luke 1:1–9:50*, 201.
32. Note the parallels with the widow of Sarepta, whose son Elijah raises from the dead (1 Kings 17:17–24; Luke 4:25–26); see L. Johnson, *Gospel of Luke*, 116–20.

experiences forgiveness of sins and who moves from the literal margins into the middle of the banquet scene, becoming unwittingly the center of attention because of Jesus's response to her actions (7:36–50).[33] The story is similar but not identical to the stories of anointing in the other Synoptic Gospels. Unlike in Mark and Matthew, however, the Lukan woman is explicitly described as a sinner who anoints Jesus's feet in the context of his Galilean ministry. In the other Synoptic accounts the woman anoints Jesus's head and is never identified as a sinner; her prophetic act occurs at the beginning of the passion narrative (Mark 14:3–9 // Matt. 26:6–13). Many commentators assume that both versions go back to a single event,[34] but it is also possible that they describe more than one event in the ministry of Jesus.[35]

Later Christian tradition has tended to harmonize the two events, with preference for Luke's picture of the penitent sinner.[36] Mark and Matthew are then read in the light of Luke. This reading does an injustice to the first two Gospels, whose own story of a prophetic anointing by an unnamed woman, who clearly qualifies as a disciple of Jesus and a prophet, is overlooked. But it also does disservice to Luke's version. The woman is not explicitly called a prostitute in the narrative, though it may be implied,[37] but the real interest is not in the precise nature of her sin but in her identity as one among the "sinners"—those who, for various reasons, stand outside the moral and ritual law and thus outside the covenant community of Israel. Throughout Luke's Gospel the sinners are the ones who, again and again, are drawn to Jesus and his acceptance of them, while the authorities are increasingly alienated from him.

Nothing expresses this revolutionary dynamic more than the three "lost" parables later in Luke's Gospel (15:1–32). In the parable of the lost son, the climax of the three, it is not clear at the end whether the elder brother, the righteous son who contrasts with the profligate younger son, will enter the banquet at his father's invitation (15:25–32). The sinners and outsiders symbolized in the younger son, in other words, show an insight entirely lacking in the religious insiders, of whom the elder son is the representative in the parable (15:1–2).

---

33. On women's presence at meals in the Greco-Roman and Jewish worlds, see Corley, *Private Women*, 24–79.

34. See, e.g., Fitzmyer, *Gospel according to Luke*, 1:684–86; Bovon, *Luke 1*, 291–93. For the differences between the Gospel accounts, see Vinson, *Luke*, 228.

35. L. Johnson argues that Luke's story is very different from the other Gospels, and he thinks the resemblances are superficial (*Gospel of Luke*, 128–29).

36. Schaberg and Ringe, "Gospel of Luke," 504–5.

37. Her presence at the (probably all-male) banquet gives an indication of her profession, as does her touching of Jesus (Corley, *Private Women*, 124–25).

The woman thus represents a group of alienated people whom Jesus welcomes with unreserved hospitality.[38] In this context her tears imply gratitude as much as, if not more than, penitence. Toward the end of the story, in indirect and direct speech, Jesus describes her sins as already forgiven: to paraphrase, "Your sins have been and are forgiven [*apheōntai*]" (7:47–48). It is unclear from this declaration exactly when the woman's sins are forgiven, and this issue has been one of major dissension in this story. Although it may occur at the banquet itself, thus suggesting the tears are those of penitence, it is more likely that she has already experienced forgiveness and intrudes into the inner circle at the banquet to express her profound sense of gratitude.[39] In either case, forgiveness implies acceptance, welcome, belonging: "The woman's actions are simultaneously indications of and reasons for her forgiveness."[40] The one who is Son of God and Savior in this Gospel draws the woman, and others like her, into the center of covenant friendship and community, into the very heart of God.

There is more to this story than forgiveness. The unnamed woman without status or any sense of belonging contrasts strikingly with the named Simon, the "righteous" insider and religious leader. The Lukan Jesus (never a comfortable dinner guest!) points out how meager Simon's hospitality is in the ungenerous face he displays to Jesus and his blatant disapproval of Jesus's reception of the woman's touch. The woman, by contrast, shows the hospitality and generosity lacking in Simon's welcome: she "washes" Jesus's feet, she kisses him, and she anoints him with oil (7:44–46), all the things Simon has failed to do as host. In effect, the woman takes over the role of host, ministering to Jesus out of a deep-seated awareness of salvation. Her hospitality and ministry arise out of self-knowledge and recognition of Jesus's identity as Savior, knowledge that Simon lacks in both respects.

Luke then follows Mark in telling the double narrative of Jairus's daughter and the woman with a hemorrhage (8:40–56), one story sandwiched within the other,[41] but he does so in his own way. The narrative portrays two females in desperate plights, the first a girl approaching womanhood—twelve years old—who, as her parents' only and beloved daughter, is dying (8:41–42). The second person is a woman who is most likely menopausal, at the other end

---

38. Cf. Schaberg and Ringe, who argue that "by erasing the female prophet," Luke has robbed the story of its power ("Gospel of Luke," 505). This conclusion underestimates the power of the Lukan story.

39. See B. Byrne, *Hospitality of God*, 87–89.

40. Bovon, *Luke 1*, 297.

41. On the parallels and dramatic effects of the intercalation, see J. Green, *Gospel of Luke*, 343–44.

of her reproductive life and afflicted by a menstrual complaint that renders her unclean. Twelve years she has suffered from this debilitating ailment, which has also reduced her to poverty (8:43–44).[42] The two stories clash; Jesus's healing of the woman means delay in the healing of Jairus's terminally ill daughter. He even stops to interrogate the woman because he knows the power has been drawn secretly from him. He thus brings her into the public sphere to narrate her story, including her healing (8:47), and he rehabilitates her not only physically but also socially. Claiming the intimacy of kinship with her—"daughter"—he bestows on her the blessing of peace (8:48).

The episode then returns to the first story with the news of the girl's death—the tragic consequences of the delay. Jesus is neither surprised nor dismayed by the news. Once again indifferent to the ritual laws of purity, he enters her room with her parents and three of the apostles, grasps her by the hand, and with a commanding word betokening his power—not only over serious illness and social isolation but also over death itself—he raises her to life (8:54–55). Thus the two females, the woman and the girl, are serendipitously connected through their physical contact with Jesus, despite differences in age, status, and wealth, becoming joint recipients of the divine power over disability, social alienation, and death.

The story of the disabled woman forms another Lukan pair with the man suffering from dropsy: both of them are healed by Jesus on the Sabbath, resulting in controversy with the authorities (13:10–17; 14:1–6). The woman is suffering from something very like osteoporosis, a thinning of the bones, which results in back pain, the inability to stand upright (and therefore carry out many everyday tasks), and the potential for falls and fractures. Eighteen years is a considerable time to suffer such debilitating symptoms. Jesus liberates the woman on his own initiative, using word and touch (13:12–13a); in characteristic Lukan style, she responds at once by glorifying God, indicating the perceptiveness of her faith (13:13b).

In defense of his action in healing the woman on the Sabbath, Jesus describes her in two ways: as a "daughter of Abraham" and as someone whom (literally) "Satan bound for, behold, eighteen years!" (13:16). Jesus expresses compassion at her suffering and its longevity, indignation at Satan's captivity, and consciousness of her dignity within the people of God. His liberation of her (cf. 4:18–19) in the terms of an exorcism attests to his acute awareness of women's suffering (which is often bypassed in male-oriented cultures in favor

---

42. Does "she spent all her livelihood on doctors" belong in the original text? It is lacking in the best manuscripts but seems a typical Lukan summary of Mark 5:26; Metzger, *Textual Commentary*, 121.

of men's suffering), an awareness that leads him into serious conflict with the authorities—the kind of conflict that will take him ultimately to the cross.

These stories of the contact of suppliant women, who are in need of forgiveness or healing, with Jesus demonstrate in part the power and compassion of Jesus's ministry, which is particularly geared toward those whose lives, for social, medical, or other reasons, are marginalized and impoverished. They demonstrate his capacity to see into the lives of women, regardless of the cost to himself, and his power to restore their dignity. At the same time these stories illustrate the faith of the women in their encounter with Jesus, a faith that is resilient in the face of adversity and disapproval, a faith to be emulated by the readers of the Gospel.

Women in Discipleship and Ministry

The story of the anointing makes an apposite introduction to Luke's recounting of the presence of women among Jesus's disciples (8:1–3). This is a passage of critical importance in the Gospel, and its significance is often overlooked. Luke has brought forward the reference to the women followers of Jesus, who are not cited till the passion narrative in the other two Synoptics (Mark 15:40–41 // Matt. 27:55–56). The context in Luke is Jesus proclaiming the good news of God's reign in word and deed in the earlier parts of his ministry in Galilee (Luke 8:1). The implication is that those accompanying Jesus are also participants in that proclamation. His companions fall into two parallel groups: the Twelve and the Galilean women. There is an inner group of men and an inner group of women who continue to follow Jesus and engage in ministry with him throughout his career.[43] And just as Peter is the leader of the men's group, so Mary Magdalene is the leader of the women's.[44] Not all suppliants in Luke's Gospel follow Jesus literally, but these Galilean women are not simply "recipients of Jesus' healing power . . . but have received Jesus' invitation to follow him and have responded, not only by following but by serving."[45] They are members of Jesus's family, fully incorporated into his circle of disciples.[46]

The women's engagement in ministry is emphasized at this point: they "ministered to them/him out of their resources" (Luke 8:3). A number of

43. Bauckham, *Gospel Women*, 110.
44. Ricci, *Mary Magdalene and Many Others*, 129. Others take a more negative view, arguing that Luke sees the women offering hidden support in return for their healing, confirming his repressive agenda; e.g., Reid, *Choosing the Better Part?*, 132–34.
45. Vinson, *Luke*, 243.
46. Vinson, *Luke*, 243–46; Bauckham, *Gospel Women*, 161–65.

manuscripts read "ministered to *them*," meaning that the women disciples ministered to Jesus and also the Twelve.[47] Other manuscripts have "him," indicating that the ministry is primarily directed to Jesus himself. While both readings can be justified on external evidence, and commentators tend to prefer "them,"[48] the latter makes some sense internally, as Luke sets the two groups on either side of Jesus and in relationship to him.[49] Of the major translations, only the KJV uses "ministered," whereas more modern translations use "provided for" (RSV, NRSV, ESV, NJB) or "helped to support" (NIV). The verb is *diakonein*, which is more usually translated as "serve" or "minister." Either our main translations dislike the notion of women ministering, or they make unduly narrow and stereotypical assumptions about the nature of that service. The word implies that women have responded in a radical way in Jesus's mission. In this respect, their attitude toward wealth is equivalent to that of the Twelve, who leave their possessions to follow Jesus. Here the holy women, in obedience to the Lukan command that disciples surrender their possessions (14:33),[50] use their wealth to fund Jesus's mission.[51]

The women's association with Jesus arises from their experiences of healing and exorcism at Jesus's hands, from bodily ailments or demon possession (8:2). The ancient world tended to associate the two in a way that may seem foreign to us, but evil spirits were often seen as the cause of physical disability. Today in the Western tradition we seek the cause of these ailments in medical rather than demonic terms. Even so, such power need not imply that the sick or disabled person is in any way to blame for her condition; rather she is a tragic victim of circumstance. The women's following of Jesus therefore arises out of a sense of physical and spiritual liberation to which they respond by joining his family of disciples.

Three of the women are named, accentuating their prominence: Mary Magdalene (a character common to all the Gospels), Joanna, and Susanna. They are drawn to Jesus by virtue of his healing power. Here Luke gives prominence to women's perceptiveness and insight in their following of Jesus and their ministry to him. It is a significant list. This is the only reference to Mary Magdalene outside the passion and resurrection narratives in the Gospels. Unfortunately, due to narrative proximity, and for no other reason, tradition

---

47. Schaberg and Ringe assume "them" and take this as a Lukan devaluing of women's ministry ("Gospel of Luke," 506).

48. See, e.g., Fitzmyer, *Gospel according to Luke*, 1:698.

49. Karris, "Women and Discipleship in Luke," 5–7.

50. For this theme in Luke's Gospel, see also 6:25; 8:14; 12:13–21, 33–34; 16:13–14, 19–31; 18:18–30; 21:1–4.

51. Bauckham, *Gospel Women*, 113–14.

in the West has associated her with the sinful woman of the previous story, assuming that the "seven demons" imply a sexually abandoned lifestyle rather than a medical illness. Yet nothing in the Gospels warrants this deduction, and it does much to reduce the impact of Mary's role as a Lukan key witness of and participant in Jesus's ministry.

A significant element in the description of Mary is her second name, "Magdalene." In the Gospels she is mostly described simply as "Mary, the Magdalene."[52] The name is generally taken to be a reference to her geographical place of origin, a village on the shores of the Sea of Galilee. The name derives from the Hebrew word *migdal*, which means "tower": a place overlooking the sea from which shoals of fish might be identified. According to Joan Taylor, however, there is no reference to "Magdala" as the name of a town in the literature of the period. It is more likely, she suggests, that "Magdalene" is a nickname given to Mary by Jesus, indicating something in her appearance or character as a "tower of strength."[53] Luke's unusual use of the phrase in this passage, "Mary, the one *called* [*kaloumenē*] Magdalene," does indeed suggest a nickname rather than a place name. Elsewhere Jesus gives nicknames to Simon ("Peter," Mark 3:16 // Matt. 10:2; 16:18) and to James and John ("Boanerges" or "Sons of Thunder," Mark 3:17). In Acts, the community gives Joseph the nickname "Barnabas" ("Son of Encouragement," Acts 4:36). If the same phenomenon is present here, the epithet underscores Mary's role as a leader in the circle around Jesus.

Joanna is a particularly intriguing figure, since marriage to Herod's steward Chuza places her in royal circles within the Herodian court[54]—with its pro-Roman culture, its flamboyant wealth, and its laxity toward Jewish religious practices. It also places her in connection with Herod Antipas, who beheaded John the Baptist (Luke 9:9) and whom the Lukan Jesus describes as "that fox" (13:32). She is very different from the other women around Jesus. Her presence says something of the diversity among Jesus's disciples, particularly in class terms. It may even represent a challenge to the Galilean peasants to have to mix with an associate of Herod and his court. As a member of the elite, Joanna is moving across otherwise impassable boundaries: "Such a person would experience a serious loss of status if found to be socializing with groups other than his own."[55] We can thus imagine how costly such a move might be: from a context where "those wearing expensive clothes and living on rich food are in royal palaces" (7:25) to the simplicity, roughness, and

---

52. Mark 15:40, 47; 16:1, [9]; Matt. 27:56; 28:1; Luke 24:10; John 19:25; 20:1, 18.
53. Taylor, "Missing Magdala," 205–23.
54. On Chuza, see Bauckham, *Gospel Women*, 150–61.
55. Rohrbaugh, "Pre-industrial City in Luke-Acts," 136.

relative poverty of Jesus's lifestyle, where "the Son of Man has nowhere to lay his head" (9:58). This is the lifestyle of Jesus's traveling companions, whom Joanna joins; it is a context in which her status and class count for nothing. Her joining of Jesus's disciples thus represents "a conversion to the poor."[56] She is mentioned again as being present at the empty tomb and becomes a witness of the resurrection (24:10).[57]

Nothing is known of Susanna, except that her name means "lily"; this is the only place she is mentioned in the New Testament. She is not named explicitly as being present at the empty tomb, her place in this list of women being taken by "Mary, the mother of James" (24:10). For all that, we should assume, on the basis of 8:2–3, that Susanna is present throughout Jesus's ministry, including at his passion, death, and resurrection, along with the other women disciples who, Luke tells us, follow Jesus to the end.

There is a further feature to this short but revealing passage. Luke speaks of "many other women" engaged in the same discipleship and ministry (8:3). As we saw in the previous chapter,[58] when we think of Jesus's journey to Jerusalem, we do not usually imagine "many women" to be among the group. Hollywood depicts only Jesus and the Twelve, and even the 2018 movie *Mary Magdalene* presents her as the only woman to accompany Jesus and the Twelve on their travels.[59] Readers of the Gospels are familiar with the Twelve, who leave behind family and occupation to follow Jesus. But here women have done the same, leaving behind other commitments to follow Jesus, even a married woman such as Joanna! We need to reimagine the journey of Jesus's ministry in terms that cohere with the Gospels themselves. It is not a singular group of twelve men and Jesus but a wider community that not only includes women but also singles them out. This is another example of Luke's pairings, where the twelve named apostles and the three named women, along with "many others," parallel each other in their wholehearted commitment to Jesus—which is apparent in their relinquishment of wealth and other human ties—and to his ministry.

Luke's story of Jesus sending out the seventy (or seventy-two) on mission is also significant in relation to women's ministry in the Gospel (10:1–12, 17–20). These disciples are to travel light and in pairs (10:1, 4), and they are to proclaim the reign of God and heal the sick (10:9), going ahead of Jesus and preparing the way for him (10:1). This is the first occasion on which a large group of disciples embarks on the mission of Jesus, and it follows a similar

---

56. Bauckham, *Gospel Women*, 150.
57. Bauckham identifies Joanna with the apostle Junia (*Gospel Women*, 165–202).
58. See above, chap. 1, "Women in the Passion."
59. See Davis, *Mary Magdalene*.

pattern to that of the Twelve in the previous chapter (9:1–6), except that this second mission is a preparation for Jesus's own (10:1). There is nothing in the narrative to indicate that those engaged in the mission are men only and that women are excluded.[60] On the contrary, this larger group of disciples is everywhere in sight in Luke's Gospel throughout Jesus's ministry, and it unquestionably includes women as well as men.[61] Most importantly, awareness of this factor challenges the assumption that, unless women are mentioned explicitly, they are absent. Women play a key role in the ministry of Jesus, and they (Mary Magdalene, Joanna, Susanna, and "many others") are likely to be active participants in this mission, given their substantial place among Jesus's closest followers.

Women as Models

A number of women appear in Luke's Gospel as models of discipleship and ministry. Perhaps the best-known example is during Jesus's visit to Martha and Mary in Bethany (10:38–42), where Martha hospitably invites Jesus into the home she shares with her sister, Mary (10:38). Martha then "serves" Jesus, engaging in that *diakonia* that lies at the heart of Christian discipleship and ministry.[62] Mary, sitting at Jesus's feet and listening to his "word," provokes criticism from Martha, who is discontented with Mary's choice and wants Jesus to intercede on her behalf.

This is a brief story, though not without its difficulties and ambiguities. Some regard the story as hostile to women and full of contradictions, seeing Luke as dividing the sisters against each other and preferring the quiet and passive Mary to the strong-minded and articulate Martha.[63] There are, however, two interrelated textual problems in the early manuscripts that make a difference to the way we interpret the story. The NRSV translation represents one version of the manuscript evidence, the shorter version, where Jesus informs the irritated Martha that only one thing is needful—namely, the choice that Mary has made: "But the Lord answered her, 'Martha, Martha, you are worried and distracted by many things; *there is need of only one thing*. Mary has chosen the better part, which will not be taken away from her.'" In this version, Martha and Mary are separated by their choices, where the one has

60. Collinson, "Women Disciples," 572.
61. Vinson, *Luke*, 319–20.
62. On the link with *diakonia*, especially as it is associated with Martha, see Ernst, *Martha from the Margins*, 177–223.
63. E.g., Reid, *Choosing the Better Part?*, 144–62; Schaberg and Ringe, "Gospel of Luke," 507–8.

chosen wisely and the other has chosen unwisely; only the one choice is valid, and Mary possesses it. Martha's choice to serve is here discounted.

By contrast, the NIV represents the other manuscript tradition, which opts for the longer version as the more original: "'Martha, Martha,' the Lord answered, 'you are worried and upset about many things, *but few things are needed—or indeed only one*. Mary has chosen what is better [literally, "the good part"], and it will not be taken away from her.'" Here the interpretation shifts so that it is clearer that Jesus is speaking of food and its preparation: only a few dishes are needed, and indeed one dish is probably sufficient. It is more apparent now that the choice lies not between service and listening to the word but rather between laboring with elaborate forms of hospitality and paying heed to Jesus's teaching. There is a further alternative manuscript reading at Luke 10:39 that places both women initially at Jesus's feet and is reflected in neither the NRSV nor the NIV: "And she had a sister called Mary *who also was seated* at the Lord's feet and listening to his word." In this reading, Martha leaves her position at Jesus's feet in order to prepare an extravagant meal and resents what she is now missing.[64]

In both cases, the longer reading makes more sense of the narrative and its context, though Luke 10:41 is not an easy sentence in any version.[65] Luke does not elsewhere downplay ministry, whether performed by males or females. The real issue is Martha's anxiety, which is caused by taking on burdensome cultural responsibilities for hospitality that make her understandably resentful and place her at a disadvantage to her sister. In the end, it is not Martha's service that is chided but rather the fact that she is "*distracted* [*periespato*] by much serving" (10:40), suggesting that something is amiss in the expectations she has taken on: "The fundamental antithesis is not between hearing and serving, but between hearing and agitated toil."[66] Yet Jesus's response to Martha is sympathetic rather than judgmental, as is indicated by the repetition of her name.[67] In the end the text summons Martha, in effect, to join (rejoin) her sister, leaving aside social anxieties and keeping the food preparation to a minimum, in keeping with Jesus's teaching on food and anxiety (12:22–31).

By contrast, Mary's place at Jesus's feet is far from passive. This is the primary pose of discipleship: actively learning from Jesus, the Teacher. It is

64. On the manuscript evidence in favor of the longer ending, see Wasserman, "Bringing Sisters Back Together," 439–61.

65. See Lee, "Martha and Mary," 197–220. Note my change of opinion in favor of the longer version.

66. Seim, "Gospel of Luke," 746–47.

67. Marshall, *Gospel of Luke*, 452.

a pose that is more usually the preserve of men and that also provides them with training for their own future teaching.[68] Her role in Luke's Gospel is one of unqualified faith and love. She sits at Jesus's feet, a place of honor and insight in this Gospel (5:8; 7:38; 8:35, 41; 17:16; cf. Acts 22:3), a role not normally assigned to women; she has "joined the road of discipleship."[69] Her place at Jesus's feet represents for the evangelist the openhearted, self-giving love of the true disciple who wants to learn and to share that learning through teaching.

In this sense, Mary is a model of true discipleship, while her sister, though a sincere disciple, is an example of how service can go awry if it moves away from simplicity of life through cultural demands and loses its focus on the word of Jesus. Mary is an example of an authentic disciple who knows where the center lies. Martha, too, is a disciple who shows exemplary faith in Jesus in her welcome of him, yet she needs to rediscover the same center and to live without anxiety for provisions. This is a simple message, both for men and for women, yet it has greater implications for women. No longer confined to the domestic sphere, women here are liberated from responding endlessly to burdensome demands that prevent them from caring for their own spiritual needs. Jesus does not make such demands nor restrict women to their traditional role. Luke's use of women to make this lesson sends a signal to all disciples, placing women on an equal plane with men so that men, too, can learn from women's exemplary discipleship.

Other female characters in less dramatic ways appear as models of discipleship. First, Jesus uses two comparisons between his own generation and those of the past in Israel: the queen of the South and the people of Nineveh will condemn the present generation for its response because they responded well to the lesser figures of Solomon and Jonah, respectively (Luke 11:31–32). Second, the widow puts two small coins in the temple treasury out of her subsistence, while others give of their surplus (21:1–4). In these two examples, women are portrayed as models of wisdom, insight, and self-giving generosity. Two female figures in parables also function as models: the woman seeking her lost coin, who serves as a paradigm of the divine seeking of the lost (15:8–10), and the widow with the unjust judge, who demonstrates the gospel values of persistence in prayer and divine justice (18:1–8).[70]

---

68. Keener, *Acts*, 1:600–601.

69. J. Green, *Gospel of Luke*, 435.

70. Luke has few negative portrayals of women in his Gospel: Herod Antipas, rather than his wife, is blamed for the murder of John the Baptist (3:19–20; 9:7–8); Lot's wife is an eschatological warning (17:32); and a serving girl accuses Peter of being an associate of Jesus (22:56–57).

Women at the Cross and Empty Tomb

Later in Luke's Gospel we meet the Galilean women at the cross and empty tomb. They stand at a distance near the cross, along with those who are designated by the vague phrase "all those known to him" (*pantes hoi gnōstoi autō*), which is probably a reference to Jesus's disciples in general.[71] The women are described as "co-following" (*synakolouthousai*) Jesus from Galilee (Luke 23:49), and their identity as disciples who have traveled with Jesus from Galilee is underscored, as they prepare spices and myrrh for his burial, becoming the main witnesses of his death, burial, and resurrection: "For Luke, the women are uniquely faithful to Jesus, and function as the eyewitness link between these critical events."[72] They are devout women, devout not only to Jesus but also to the law of Moses; rather than going straight to the tomb, they wait and obey the fourth commandment: "On the sabbath they rested, according to the commandment" (23:55–56).

Being witnesses to Jesus's death and burial places the "myrrh-bearing women" in a uniquely privileged position when it comes to the tomb. They are the first to reach it on Easter morning. On their arrival they hear the message of the resurrection from two dazzling angels who instruct them to "remember" Jesus's words (24:4–6a). The idea of "remembering," for Luke, is a key component of faith, present in the immediate faith-response of the women disciples; in previous uses it refers to words or deeds said or done by God, who is utterly trustworthy (1:54, 72; 22:61; 23:42).[73] The women disciples demonstrate their trustworthiness and ongoing fidelity to Jesus in the encounter at the tomb by responding with faith and faithfulness to the angels' message and with spiritually attuned memories. Their remembering leads them to action: they return to tell the good news to the other disciples in a spirit of faith and joy (24:6b–8). They are not believed by the Eleven and the other disciples—with the apparent exception of Peter (24:12)—for whom their story of the resurrection represents but "idle words" (24:11).

Luke again names three of the women—Mary Magdalene, Joanna, and Mary the mother of James—two of them from the list at 8:2–3, with Mary the mother of James replacing Susanna in those who are named. Indeed, the number of named female disciples across Luke's Gospel adds up to seven, a number that may be intentional, paralleling that of the number twelve.[74]

---

71. J. Green, *Gospel of Luke*, 828. Luke has omitted the Markan reference to the disciples' flight (Mark 14:50); only Peter follows "at a distance" (Luke 22:54).

72. L. Johnson, *Gospel of Luke*, 385.

73. Just, *Luke 9:51–24:53*, 967–68.

74. These are Mary the mother of Jesus, Mary Magdalene, Joanna, Susanna, Martha and Mary of Bethany, and Mary the mother of James; so Vinson, *Luke*, 242.

Seven is a common symbol and a divine number in biblical narrative, generally signifying completeness or abundance. And once again, as at 8:3, "other women" are also present who have journeyed with Jesus not only to Jerusalem but also to his passion. For this reason, the women disciples play a major role as witnesses of Jesus's crucifixion, death, burial, and resurrection.

Grieving is another aspect of Luke's passion story. On either side of the crucifixion are people who are weeping over Jesus's fate, and they include women (23:27–30, 48). Jesus indeed addresses them as "daughters of Jerusalem" (23:28). The message is a grim, prophetic "oracle of judgment" that calls on Jerusalem to turn to Jesus in order to prevent the coming judgment (a reference to the destruction of the temple and the fall of the city in 66–70 CE).[75] Luke's reference to them as "the people" (*ho laos*, 23:27) usually denotes the ordinary folk who are supportive of Jesus; here those mourning will be the victims of violence.[76] It would seem that, in Luke's view, the Jerusalem women do not approve of Jesus's death and see the crucifixion as a tragic event, indicating their sympathy with Jesus. Yet he in turn indicates his sympathy for them in the coming suffering of the next generation, particularly of the most vulnerable: women and children.

Luke does not explicitly recount a tale of Jesus appearing to a woman disciple, although they are the first to receive the news of Jesus's resurrection and the first to proclaim it to the other disciples. But in the Emmaus story (24:13–35) the second, unnamed disciple who accompanies Cleopas may be a woman—possibly the same Mary mentioned in John's Gospel as the "wife/mother of Clopas" (John 19:25). It would be consistent with Luke's habit elsewhere in the Gospel of pairing women and men. On the other hand, the two travelers speak as if they identify with the unbelieving men rather than the believing women in the episode at the tomb, making it less likely that the companion of Cleopas is female (Luke 24:22–23).[77] The reference to "some of us" going to the tomb further identifies the two with the male disciples, and specifically Peter (24:22–28). The women disciples who have gone to the tomb do not need such an appearance, as they have already come to Easter faith (24:8). What is clear from this story is that the two are heading in the wrong direction and that the appearance of Jesus on the road and at their meal reorients them to Jerusalem, where they return in faith (24:33).[78]

75. J. Green, *Gospel of Luke*, 815–17.
76. L. Johnson, *Gospel of Luke*, 374–75.
77. B. Byrne, *Hospitality of God*, 205.
78. The icon by Sr. Marie-Paul Farran, OSB, portrays the second disciple as female; see Jones, "Unnamed Emmaus Disciple."

There seems to be an exception to the men's unbelief. Yet the story of Peter is a confusing one. He goes to the tomb and finds it empty and leaves feeling "amazed," although there is a textual problem with this verse (24:12).[79] When the two Emmaus disciples return, it is to hear that the rest of the disciples now believe in the resurrection on the basis of Jesus's appearance to Peter, which is not narrated at this point (24:34). It would seem that it takes a male disciple to verify the women's testimony from the empty tomb and the angels; without masculine authority to confirm the news, the women are simply not believed. Nevertheless, the women's testimony has priority, however shaky it may appear to patriarchal eyes. There is an extraordinary "audacity" in their proclaiming of the Living One, an audacity to which Peter alone responds; here we observe "the verve of Peter in the tracks of Mary Magdalene and her companions."[80]

It is surprising that, despite the list of witnesses to the resurrection who have testified thus far (including the holy women, the two companions in the Emmaus story, and the apostle Peter, 24:34), and despite also the risen Jesus's greeting of peace (24:36),[81] the gathered disciples respond with panic and terror at his appearance.[82] They need to be convinced in palpable ways that he is not a ghost (*pneuma*, "spirit," 24:37–40) before they can allow themselves to rejoice. This reaction might suggest that only the apostles, along with Cleopas and his fellow traveler, are present for Jesus's appearance.

Yet the narrative relates that Jesus's self-revelation is made to "the Eleven *and their companions* [literally, "those with them"]" (24:33). Who are these companions? Most likely they are "the whole company of Jesus' followers who have thus far remained in Jerusalem."[83] This company includes the Galilean women. They, too, are therefore appointed to be witnesses of Jesus's resurrection—as they already have been witnesses at the cross, burial, and empty tomb—and of his message of forgiveness to all the nations (24:46–48). They, too, are among those instructed to wait in Jerusalem for the coming of the Spirit, who will empower them for their mission and ministry (24:49). More than that: the women disciples, too, will witness his ascension, worshiping him and returning to the temple in Jerusalem to express their joy and gratitude (24:52).

In images of the ascension in various forms of pictorial art, the figure of Mary the mother of Jesus is usually depicted,[84] particularly in Eastern icons.

79. See Marshall, *Gospel of Luke*, 888–89.

80. Bovon, *Luke 2*, 360.

81. Despite the doubts about the second half of this verse, it is likely to be original; see Nolland, *Luke 18:35–24:53*, 1210.

82. Bovon, *Luke 2*, 390.

83. J. Green, *Gospel of Luke*, 853.

84. Fernandes, "Analyzing Art."

Not only is she present in the iconography; she is at the center of the disciples, her hands raised in prayer.[85] This coheres with the description of her presence among the gathered disciples in prayer before Pentecost (Acts 1:14). More importantly, in these traditions of the ascension Mary, in company with the apostles, signifies the church, and therefore her presence is theologically necessary. From our perspective, this aspect underlines the presence of women—even if they are represented in icons by only the one woman—at Jesus's appearance and ascension in the Gospel of Luke.

CHART OF GALILEAN WOMEN DISCIPLES IN LUKE

NAME	RELATIONSHIPS	TEXT	IDENTIFICATION	NOTES
Mary	Mother of Jesus	Luke 1:26–56; 2:1–52; 8:19–21; 11:27–28 (8:3; 23:49, 55–56); Acts 1:14		Main character in infancy narratives (apart from Jesus); her obedience confirmed in Jesus's ministry; present at Pentecost
Mary		Luke 8:2 (23:49, 55–56); 24:10 (Acts 1:14)	"The one called Magdalene"	Most likely a nickname given by Jesus: "strong tower"
Joanna	Wife of Chuza, Herod's steward	Luke 8:3 (23:49, 55–56); 24:10 (Acts 1:14)	From elite class; healed by Jesus; financial supports	Not mentioned in other Gospels
Susanna		Luke 8:3 (23:49, 55–56; 24:10); (Acts 1:14)		Only here in Luke
Mary	Mother of James	Luke (8:3; 23:49, 55–56); 24:10 (Acts 1:14)	Mother of James the Less and Joses/Joseph (Mark and Matthew); "the other Mary" (Matt. 28)	Husband = probably Clopas/Cleopas; may be Judean rather than Galilean (displacement of Susanna)
Other women		Luke 8:3 (23:49, 55–56); 24:10 (Acts 1:14)		Probably with other disciples when risen Jesus appears; present at ascension in Luke-Acts, and possibly also Pentecost

A final comment on Luke's Gospel is to note Jesus's teaching on leadership as servanthood, which is also present in the Gospels of Mark and Matthew. In Luke's case, however, this teaching occurs at the Last Supper, at the heart of the church's life, in the context of the Eucharist and the impending passion

85. David, "Going Up? Icons of the Ascension."

of Jesus, with which it is closely associated (22:24–27). The disciples are squabbling for power, and over against them Jesus sets his own teaching and his own pattern of leadership. Despite the world's notions of greatness and power—using the metaphor of the table, where the one who dines is greater in status and honor than the one who serves—Jesus places himself alongside the servant, the woman, the inferior: "I am in the midst of you as the one serving" (22:27). This challenge to the disciples reflects Luke's theme throughout the narrative of the overturning nature of the gospel: the "Great Reversal."[86] The message, particularly in its solemn setting, emphasizes the transformed ordering of the church's life, a direct challenge to paternalistic power, which demeans, diminishes, and excludes women (among others). The cross is the ultimate symbol of power overturned and of the new order inaugurated in Jesus's death and resurrection. There is an irony in forbidding women the gift of servant leadership in the church despite Jesus's teaching. More importantly, such passages challenge the patriarchal nature and use of authority.

Conclusion

Luke's Gospel presents a panoply of women who are connected to Jesus at profound levels, including at times of crisis in their own lives. Women act as prophets and as models of discipleship. They are suppliants who respond in faith and self-giving to Jesus's healing power, and they are acknowledged as his disciples from the beginning of the journey to Jerusalem. The first Christian in the Gospel is Mary, the mother of Jesus, who shows an extraordinary level of faith and courage in assenting willingly to what God asks of her. Other women follow suit, a number of them named explicitly—names we do not encounter elsewhere, such as Joanna and Susanna. Women are not included among the Twelve, but a female grouping around Jesus has considerable prominence in the Gospel narrative. No woman receives a resurrection appearance, yet women show themselves swifter to believe on lesser evidence. We turn now to Acts to complete the picture and to draw conclusions, where we can, about Luke's overall depiction of women in his two-volume work.

---

86. Just, *Luke 9:51–24:53*, 844–46.

Chapter Three

Writings of Luke

Acts of the Apostles

NO PICTURE OF LUKE can be completed without attending to his second-volume work, the so-called Acts of the Apostles. Women are significantly less prominent in Acts than they are in the Gospel in terms of number and visibility. Gender pairing is also less frequent, though it is not entirely absent.[1] The main characters in Acts are Peter and Paul, Peter being the leading apostle through whom the gospel is first proclaimed at Pentecost, who experiences persecution from the authorities in Jerusalem, and who brings the first gentiles into the church. By contrast, the story of Paul—who is only called an apostle in one context (14:4, 6, 14), Luke generally restricting the title to the Twelve—constitutes the second major section of Acts, with his collusion in Stephen's martyrdom, his conversion, his missional journeys, and his final visit to Rome in captivity. As with the Gospel, a key question here is whether Luke ultimately gives any place to women's leadership in the community or whether he reflects a later context where patriarchal control is being reestablished and projected back onto the past in the story of the earliest church. The question is raised more sharply for Acts than for the Gospel, but it also reflects on the Gospel and its presentation of women. This chapter will explore the women of Acts and then draw some conclusions about the women in both Lukan writings.

---

1. Omitting married couples, examples are Tabitha and Aeneas (Acts 9:32–43) and Damaris and Dionysius (17:32–34).

Women's Presence

Though less visible, women are present in the Acts of the Apostles. Their stories are interlaced with the missional work of Peter and Paul. Their presence needs to be recognized, though it is further minimized in Luke's writing style by androcentric (male-centered) language, in which the women's presence is somewhat concealed. This factor presents a challenge for later readers, who, without comprehending how such language operates in its cultural context, tend to make women disappear even further from the narrative. When the whole church in Acts gathers together to pray or make decisions, women, too, are present among them. At other important junctures of the church's life, such as the Council of Jerusalem (15:1–21), we should again assume the presence of female believers. Women as well as men are among the converts to Christian faith, and no distinction is made between them in terms of their depth of faith (17:4, 12, 34). We need a new imagination to reread some of these scenes.

Luke is explicit in Acts that women are present at Pentecost with the Twelve (1:14; they are now reconstituted with the addition of Matthias, 1:13–26). We should especially note the reference to Mary the mother of Jesus, who having been present (by necessity!) in the birth narratives of the Gospel is also present at the "birth" of the church and belongs within the fledgling Christian community.[2] With her is a group of women: the same Galilean women, including Mary Magdalene, Joanna, Susanna, and Mary the mother of James, who have formed an integral part of Jesus's ministry, death, burial, and resurrection. With the holy women are also Jesus's brothers, or, more likely, "brothers and sisters,"[3] among whom is James, the Lord's brother.[4] Later iconography tends to exclude the group of women and the relatives of Jesus, with the exception of the mother of Jesus, who, as we have seen, is present and sometimes seated in the central teacher's chair.[5]

Oddly enough, it would seem that the Galilean group of women are not present after all for the subsequent resurrection appearances and the ascension, at least as the narrative of those events are retold in Acts 1:1–11. Luke is a little vague about who is present and for what. Reading Luke 24:36–53

---

2. Fitzmyer, *Acts of the Apostles*, 215–16.

3. The Greek word *adelphoi* can mean "brothers" in an exclusive sense, referring only to male siblings (e.g., Luke 20:29), or it can be inclusive, meaning "brothers and sisters" (Luke 21:16). Less frequently, the feminine form, *adelphai* (sisters), is added (Luke 14:26).

4. James is mentioned three times in Acts: 12:17; 15:13; 21:18. For more on his place in the New Testament, see, e.g., Painter, *Just James*.

5. "Pentecost Icon as an Icon of the Church."

gives the impression that all the gathered disciples are with Jesus when he appears, which includes the women and also other men outside the eleven apostles (Cleopas and his companion, for example). Yet in Acts, Luke specifically refers to the "apostles," with whom the risen Jesus meets to give instructions for a period of forty days (Acts 1:2), and following the ascension, the two angels appear to address them as males (literally, "Galilean men," 1:11).[6] Admittedly, Luke wishes to focus on the reconstituted Twelve, who play a role across Luke-Acts as the bridge between Jesus's ministry on earth and the ministry of the early church. By Acts 1:14, however, it becomes clear that others, including women disciples, will be involved in the dramatic events about to unfold. The Twelve are part of a wider community that includes women and members of Jesus's own family.

The male-centered language, however, may function in a rather different way. As elsewhere in Acts, it is possible that Luke uses "men" (*andres*) in an inclusive sense, even though more usually in Greek it contrasts with "women" (*gynaikes*); the plural form *anthrōpoi* is the more common expression for human beings. If so, this is a further example of androcentric writing, where women are in attendance but not explicitly mentioned.[7] Later in Acts, there is a reference to two Athenian converts, one male and one female, who are referred to in the same way: "Some *andres* having joined him believed, including Dionysius the Areopagite and a woman named Damaris" (17:34). Here the context makes it plain that *andres* should be translated "people" rather than "men" and that Luke can use the term in a more general fashion. Is it possible that, for Luke, others are present with the Risen Christ for those forty days, including the holy women, and also hear his teaching? Or is this a further example of the discrepancies between the two ascension stories? The likely solution is that Luke's vision is more narrowly focused in the Acts story and is not particularly concerned about other disciples who may or may not be present at the scene.

Women as Prophets

For all this, women do play a number of roles in Acts that, though not as numerous or prominent, cohere with the Gospel of Luke. For example, women are depicted as prophets in Acts. Being present at Pentecost with Mary the

6. Reid adds the absence of the Galilean women as a further example of Luke's exclusion of women throughout his two-volume work (*Choosing the Better Part?*, 42–43).

7. See Blomberg, "Today's New International Version." For the opposing view, cf. Marlowe, "Confusion of Semantics."

mother of Jesus, the Galilean women fulfill the prophecy from Joel that Peter quotes in his Pentecost sermon:

> In the last days it will be, God declares,
> that I will pour out my Spirit upon all flesh,
>   and your sons and your daughters shall prophesy. (Acts 2:16–21;
>   Joel 2:28–32)

At Pentecost, the Spirit is given not only without measure but also without regard for gender. These prophets are described from Joel as "slaves" (Acts 2:18), implying that the Spirit is already overturning the present world order for class divisions as well as gender.[8] Daughters as well as sons, whatever their social status, will receive the same, equalizing gift of prophecy from the Spirit. The mother of Jesus, Mary Magdalene, and the other Galilean women present at Pentecost are the first women to receive the gift of the Spirit, which ensures their shared vocation with men in the church's mission. The role of prophet, held by male or female, "illustrates the heart of Luke's programmatic message, which includes Spirit empowerment for both genders."[9]

We saw in the last chapter that the annunciation to Mary of Nazareth functions also as her commissioning narrative, using a pattern that derives from the Old Testament. Acts contains a similar narrative in the account of Saul's conversion. It follows the same pattern as the commissioning of Isaiah and of Mary (and also of Peter at Luke 5:1–11). The *divine confrontation* is blinding light on the road to Damascus (Acts 9:3). There is an introductory *word*, demanding Saul to explain why he is persecuting Jesus (9:4–5). Saul feels *inadequate* and is overwhelmed by the experience of being blinded for three days (9:8). *Reassurance* is given: Saul is visited by a reluctant Ananias at God's instruction (9:17). Finally, there is a *commission* and *assent*, with a *sign:* Saul, after being baptized, regains his sight and begins to proclaim the good news of Jesus (9:18–20). It is significant that Paul's commissioning is preceded by that of Mary, emphasizing the priority of her prophetic role and her mission to bear the Son of God.

The role of Mary and other women as prophets is a countercultural message in the ancient world, where "no woman was perceived as equal to a man in terms of her worth to the state."[10] The ancient pagan world had female-oriented religious rites and cults, such as the religion of Demeter, the cult of Isis, and the Vestal Virgins in Rome, in which women served as religious

---

8. Jennings, *Acts*, 34–35.
9. Keener, *Acts*, 1:603.
10. Sawyer, *Women and Religion*, 31.

devotees and prophetic and priestly figures. In most cases, however, these religions confirmed women's status quo within a patriarchal world.[11] The picture is more complicated and ambivalent within Judaism, where women might have significant religious power in some places but where the structure of the temple itself, in which women could go no further than the Court of the Women, kept them further from the center, the place of sacrifice, than it kept men.[12] Yet at Pentecost women are given a new level of access to spiritual life and are able to receive and donate the gifts of the Spirit without change to their female identity. In early Christianity, moreover, the role of the prophet was highly prized in Christian worship (Rom. 12:6–8; 1 Cor. 12:4–11; 14:1–5; also Eph. 4:11–13). Pentecost may lie behind us in today's church, but its full and radical implications for women's ministry still lie in the future.

Much later in Acts we learn of four sisters who are prophets, daughters of Philip the evangelist (as opposed to the apostle Philip): "To him there were four daughters, unmarried, prophesying" (Acts 21:9). These women, who "ride the wings of the Spirit,"[13] have no direct role in the narrative, which tells the story of Paul's decision to return to Jerusalem and his arrival, en route, at Caesarea. They are mentioned in an aside, as part of the identification of Philip, who is one of the Seven and a missionary (6:5; 8:5–7, 26–40). It is likely that these four unmarried women were well known in the church and highly regarded, and that Luke refers to them for that reason.[14] Certainly the church historian Eusebius, who was from Caesarea himself and who became bishop there in 314 CE, seems to include them among the "great luminaries" of the church in the Roman province of Asia.[15]

Women in Discipleship and Ministry

A number of other individual women in Acts are singled out by Luke for their discipleship and ministry. Some are suppliants, recipients of ministry. For example, Tabitha (with the Greek name Dorcas, both names meaning "gazelle") from Joppa fits both categories, as she is engaged in a practical and much-needed ministry among the poor (9:36–42) and is named explicitly a

---

11. Sawyer, *Women and Religion*, 59–72, 119–29.

12. Sawyer, *Women and Religion*, 73.

13. Jennings, *Acts*, 197.

14. C. K. Barrett sees no necessary connection between their unmarried status and their spiritual gifts, pointing out that Priscilla, though married, also has spiritual gifts, even if of a different kind (*Acts of the Apostles*, 994–95).

15. Bruce, *Book of the Acts*, 399–400. Eusebius, *Ecclesiastical History* 5.24.2–3 (Lake, 1:271–72, 287).

disciple. Luke employs the feminine form of the word "disciple," *mathētria*, which is not found elsewhere in the New Testament (9:36).[16] This description gives greater stress to her Christian identity and the form that her ministry takes, which parallels that of the Seven, a ministry focused on the needs of widows (6:1–6). Her ministry, too, is focused on widows, who were known in the ancient world for being poor because they lacked a male figure to provide for them financially. When Tabitha becomes ill and dies, Peter, summoned by the church there, approaches her deathbed, where the widows show him, in tears, the clothing she has made for them (9:39). God raises her from the dead, restoring her to life and to her ministry in caring for the needy, and the miracle results in many coming to faith (9:40–42). In this story, the gender aspect is explicit: a woman engaging in ministry on behalf of other women in need. Jennings points out that "Peter declares an unmistakable truth: women matter. This woman matters, and the work she does for widows matters. It matters so much that God will not allow death the last word. . . . Tabitha is an activist who lives again in resurrection power."[17]

Mary the mother of John Mark is another believing woman who has a church in her home, of which she is most likely both the host and the leader (12:12). That the house is commodious enough to hold the community and that she has at least one slave suggest Mary's comparative wealth. Like some of the Galilean women, she is another of the well-to-do women who support the cause of Christ (cf. Luke 8:3) and are heads of house churches: "Mary underscores what the story of Tabitha also reveals, the insistent presence and leadership of women in the early church."[18] It is here that the Christian community gathers during a period of intense persecution from Herod Agrippa I (grandson of Herod the Great),[19] who is acting to ingratiate himself with the religious authorities in Jerusalem and who will soon die as a consequence of his persecution.[20] At this time the apostle James is put to the sword (Acts 12:2), and Peter is thrown into prison and heavily guarded (12:3–4).

After his miraculous escape from prison through angelic intervention, Peter returns to the house church of Mary to find them deeply engrossed in prayer on his behalf, without realizing that the answer to their prayers is already standing and knocking at the gate. Note the small mention of the

---

16. The same noun is used of Mary Magdalene in the noncanonical Gospel of Peter 50 (Ehrman and Pleše, *Apocryphal Gospels*, 384).

17. Jennings, *Acts*, 100–101.

18. Aymer, "Acts of the Apostles," 542.

19. Herod Agrippa I is no different in this respect from Herod Antipas, his uncle, who in the Gospel is responsible for the death of John the Baptist and at least in part responsible for Jesus's death (Luke 9:9; 23:7–12).

20. On the hubris of Herod Agrippa I, see J. Green, "Acts," 750–51.

slave Rhoda, who is also a believer and who answers the door, sees Peter, and runs back to announce his arrival while leaving him standing outside. Rhoda is not believed (12:6–17)—a response to women that we have already encountered at the empty tomb.

Another prominent female disciple in Acts is Lydia of Thyatira (16:11–40), who is a leading businesswoman in Philippi and works in the dyeing of purple cloth, a luxury item. It is hard to be certain of Lydia's status; it may be that she is a freed slave who works at the production end of the business. On the other hand, she seems to be a woman of some means, which argues for a higher status, or at least a higher income.[21] Paul and Silas attend an intriguing event by the river: a gathering of women on the Sabbath to pray. Paul's normal custom in Acts is to go first to the Jewish community before approaching the gentile, pagan world. Here is a group of women gathered together for prayer, a group that probably includes, in addition to Jewish women, gentile sympathizers who are attracted to Judaism and participate in its worship without first becoming Jews. It is not an official synagogue, but it may be a prayerhouse used by the Jewish community for worship. Its proximity to the river makes it an appropriate site for Jewish ritual washings.[22] The reference coheres with other groups of devout women across Luke-Acts who are strongly committed to their faith and take seriously its obligations, including that of prayer. Lydia, who is a "worshiper of God," is probably a gentile, since her name is pagan. Under divine inspiration, she is deeply impressed with Paul's preaching—"The Lord opened up her heart" (16:14)—and the two missionaries stay in her home at her hospitable insistence, during which time she and her household are baptized (16:15).

In terms of hospitality in the ancient world, Lydia changes the status of Paul and Silas from outsiders and strangers to guests who belong.[23] Following the incident in the city, which leads to the imprisonment and release of Paul and Silas, Lydia again receives them into her home, this time in an act of courage in the face of irate citizens (16:40). The implication is that Lydia becomes the patron and leader of the Christians who begin to gather there;[24] certainly her hospitality and generosity mark her as a disciple.[25] Lydia's experience and that of her household work in the narrative as a gender pair with the experience

21. The description does not necessarily mean that Lydia is wealthy, but at least she is a woman of independence, including financial; see Holladay, *Acts*, 321.

22. There are, in any case, textual problems with the verse. It is unlikely to be a synagogue in a place with so small a Jewish population (Fitzmyer, *Acts of the Apostles*, 585).

23. Malina and Pilch, *Social Science Commentary*, 213–15.

24. On patronage, see Moxnes, "Patron-Client Relations," 242–50.

25. Holladay, *Acts*, 322.

of the jailer, another head of house who is also converted and baptized, along with his household (16:25–34). Note that Lydia, as the founding member of the church in Philippi, is the first European convert in Acts.[26]

The incident that leads to the imprisonment of Paul and Silas involves a second female character, very different from Lydia. This woman has no money of her own, no independence, and no control over her life.[27] She is a slave girl (*paidiskē*)[28] who is possessed by a "*pythōn* spirit" in pagan religion (a "spirit that enabled her to tell the future").[29] She divines their identity and cries out after them persistently, "These people are slaves of the Most High God, who are proclaiming to you the way of salvation!" (Acts 16:17). It is likely that, for Luke, this is an evil spirit who seeks power over the two by naming them. But it may also reflect the girl's own distress at her life of subjection to pagan powers; the fact that she follows Paul day after day suggests that she desperately craves something from them.[30] After days of this obsessive behavior, Paul, in exasperation, turns and exorcizes the spirit—the only exorcism in Acts—at once freeing the frenzied girl from her possession:[31] "The point was not to silence her voice but to release it from its networked captivity."[32] His impulse, however, is not particularly astute politically, as it infuriates the pagan owners, who having lost a lucrative source of income (16:19), now arrange to have him and his companion cast into jail. We can perhaps imagine the girl thereafter being taken up into Lydia's community.

Educated Women

Two women in Acts are educated, by implication and by context. The first is a woman named Damaris, who is converted to Christian faith by Paul during his visit to Athens (17:34). Her presence on the Areopagus in the group of people who enjoy intellectual debate suggests a certain level of education, which makes her something of an exception in Athens, where women were

---

26. J. Green, "Acts," 755.

27. Gaventa, *Acts of the Apostles*, 238.

28. *Paidiskē* is a feminine, diminutive form of "child" (*pais*) and signifies a female slave, but it is unclear whether this means she is literally a child or a grown woman of low status.

29. So the CEB translation, to which the NIV is similar. "Divination" is used in the NRSV and ESV and "soothsayer" in the NJB. *Pythōn* links the girl to the Delphic oracle, the Pythia, in Greek religion who is able to predict the future, though usually in highly veiled and ambiguous language. For Luke, the source of such power is demonic.

30. Jennings, *Acts*, 160–61.

31. On "alternate states of consciousness" in the ancient world—also a common feature throughout Acts—see Malina and Pilch, *Social Science Commentary*, 117–18, 185–87.

32. Jennings, *Acts*, 160–61.

generally confined to the domestic sphere. Nothing further is said of Damaris, apart from her association with others who come to Christian faith. In the context of the religious debate Paul has with the Athenians, the main point at issue is the resurrection of Jesus from the dead, which "challenges reality, reorients how we see earth and sky, water and dirt, land and animals, and even our own bodies."[33] It is this resurrection faith that Damaris embraces.

The most significant of the women—not just in Acts but also elsewhere in the New Testament—is Priscilla, who is a theologian in her own right along with her husband, Aquila. It is unusual that Aquila's name often appears following hers, not only in Acts but also in the Pauline corpus (see Rom. 16:3; 2 Tim. 4:19). Priscilla is clearly the more prominent and gifted of the couple. They share a common leather trade with Paul and become his fellow missioners (Acts 18:1–4),[34] accompanying him on some of his travels (18:18). They are also thrown out of Rome with other Jews on the edict of Emperor Claudius (18:2) sometime between 41 and 54 CE,[35] and their lives have clearly been turned upside down by the conflict in Rome.

In Ephesus, according to Acts, they meet Apollos, a brilliant young orator, preacher, and teacher from Alexandria who is well educated and comes from a city known for its intellectual culture. Yet, according to Acts, he is seriously ill-informed on matters of the faith. Luke is not very precise about these theological limitations, but since Apollos is described as "knowing only the baptism of John" (18:25), the narrative suggests that he needs further teaching on Jesus's resurrection and ascension.[36] Priscilla and her husband take him aside and teach him a better understanding, particularly of Christian baptism (18:24–28). It is ironic that Ephesus is the same location at which Timothy is ministering, where women are supposedly instructed to be silent and forbidden to teach (1 Tim. 2:11–12).

Women as Antiheroes

Acts refers just once to women persecuting Christians, specifically Paul and Barnabas (13:13–51). These are influential women within the community of Antioch in Pisidia (located in the Roman province of Asia Minor and distinct from Antioch in Syria). Paul's outspoken preaching in the synagogue has led to many converts among the Jewish people and roused the wider city to take an interest. Luke tells us that a number of hostile people from the synagogue,

33. Jennings, *Acts*, 178.
34. Keener, *Paul, Women, and Wives*, 514–17.
35. Suetonius, "Deified Claudius" 2.25.4 (Rolfe, 5:53).
36. Parsons, *Acts*, 263.

probably enraged at the success of the mission within their community, incite the influential women and men of the city—most likely pagans—with the result that Paul and Barnabas are forced to leave (13:50–51). There are also later repercussions (14:19), though these do not bring Paul's ministry there to an end (see 14:26–28).

One individual in particular stands out in opposition to the examples of devout and leading women within the Christian community: Sapphira, the wife of Ananias (5:1–11). She and her husband are early converts to Christianity, and both join in the sharing of possessions and surrender of wealth for the good of the poor and vulnerable—actions that, for Luke, are such a critical sign of authentic discipleship. The couple conspire together to deceive the fledgling community, offering a part of their subsistence as if it were the whole (5:1–2). They seek honor and status for their generous giving while at the same time surreptitiously holding back on their wealth; they are half-hearted and deceptive in their commitment to a community where generosity, wholehearted devotion, sincerity, and openness of heart are the hallmarks of discipleship. Is their real sin holding back property or lying to God? Perhaps it is something of both, but it certainly includes their "resistance to the new order where possessions will no longer divide and establish social hierarchies and where living by faith overcomes the worship of the other gods: money and possessions."[37]

This is a serious blemish in a fresh and enthusiastic young community, and the punishment of Ananias and Sapphira is severe: each falls down dead at Peter's feet when he confronts them with their deception. Peter does not actually kill them, but his words are powerful and have an extraordinary effect. It may be that the sin is more serious than the modern reader can conceive.[38] But it may also arise from the ancient practice of "pointing the bone," often associated with magic, which involves a figure of authority pronouncing a word of judgment that leads, literally, to a person's death. If so, the cause is as much psychological as physical, embedded in cultural assumptions and leading to collapse at the commanding words of censure.[39] Never again in Acts does such an incident occur, suggesting that the early church has learned something of the numinous authority its leaders possess by their very speech.[40] If so, Sapphira and Ananias's plot is an example of a sin that has unforeseen and tragic consequences. As readers we may disapprove of their scheming and

---

37. Jennings, *Acts*, 52–53.

38. For Gaventa, this is essentially a conflict between God and Satan, indicating the awesome power of God over evil, especially as it arises from within the community (*Acts of the Apostles*, 101–3).

39. King, "'Pointing the Bone,'" 12–34.

40. King, "'Pointing the Bone,'" 32–33.

deception, but it is hard not to feel dismay at its consequences. Nor is it clear from the text that this is an inappropriate response: "The deaths of Ananias and Sapphira are a tragedy within the life of the new community when the use of authority and the power that goes with it lead to death rather than to repentance and change."[41]

Women across Luke-Acts

This survey brings us back to the questions with which we began the previous chapter: Is Luke-Acts a dual work that enhances women's discipleship and ministry for the reader, or does it diminish women's participation in the circle around Jesus and the early church? Why does the Gospel contain so many additional female characters in comparison to the other Gospels, while the Acts of the Apostles has, relatively speaking, so few? Is Luke a protofeminist who extols women's participation or a traditionalist who thinks women should be kept firmly in their place? The answers generally given, as we have already seen, represent alternative views: either that Luke, though endorsing women's following of Jesus, does not believe that they should take on leadership roles in the church, as evident (apparently) from Acts, or that Luke's agenda in Acts reveals he has added women to the Gospel only in order to hammer home their subservience.[42] Both views, though in stark contrast at one level, have a good deal in common: they accept that women in Acts (or rather the lack of them) should determine how we interpret women in the Gospel, and both views affirm that women are given only passive and inferior roles in the Christian community.

CHART OF WOMEN BELIEVERS AND SYMPATHIZERS IN ACTS

NAME	RELATIONSHIPS	TEXT	IDENTIFICATION	NOTES
Certain women		1:14	Galilean women followers	Devoted to prayer in early community and present at Pentecost
Mary	Mother of Jesus	1:14		Devoted to prayer in early community and present at Pentecost
Daughters and slave women		2:17–18	Female prophets	Peter quoting from Joel 2:28–32 about last days fulfilled at Pentecost

41. King, "'Pointing the Bone,'" 33.

42. Note, however, the significant modification of these alternatives in Seim, *Double Message*, 249–60.

NAME	RELATIONSHIPS	TEXT	IDENTIFICATION	NOTES
Sapphira	Wife of Ananias	5:1–11		Withheld funds deceitfully; killed
Women believers		5:14	Jerusalem	Emphasizes that early community is mixed
Women baptized		8:12	Samaritan women	Result of Philip the evangelist's preaching
Women persecuted		9:2	Persecuted by Saul	Emphasizes Saul's fanaticism: even women arrested
Tabitha/ Dorcas		9:36–42	Disciple in Joppa	Cares for poor (widows); dies and is raised by Peter
Mary	Mother of John Mark	12:12–17		Peter escapes from prison; comes first to Mary's house, where she is leader of house church
Rhoda		12:12–17	Servant of Mary	Fails to let Peter in
Mother of Timothy		16:1	Believer	Does not appear but is responsible for Timothy's faith
Gathering of women		16:13	Jewish women in Philippi	Gathered for prayer, and Paul and companions join them
Lydia		16:14–15, 40	God-fearer in Philippi (from Thyatira)	Businesswoman (in purple cloth); converted and baptized and invites Paul and companions to stay with her; probably a woman of some means; they stay with her after release from prison; she is probably the leader of a house church
Leading women believers		17:4	Thessalonica	Conversion after hearing Paul in synagogue; Jewish women
Greek women believers		17:12	Berea	Diaspora Jewish women or God-fearers?
Damaris the Areopagite		17:32–34	Athens	Converted after Paul's preaching, along with Dionysius the Areopagite
Priscilla	Wife of Aquila	18:2–3, 18, 24–26	Corinth	Part of the believing couple who meet Paul and share his trade; travel with him to Ephesus and teach Apollos

NAME	RELATIONSHIPS	TEXT	IDENTIFICATION	NOTES
Wives and children		21:5	Believers	Meet Paul in Tyre and accompany him as he leaves
Daughters of Philip	Unmarried daughters of Philip the evangelist	21:8–9	Four prophets; Caesarea	Mentioned in passing; Paul and companions stay with them

Part of the problem lies in the title itself: "Acts of the Apostles" gives the impression that it narrates the whole story of the early church, centered on the twelve apostles.[43] In reality, Acts mentions very few of them, and James, the Lord's brother, despite his prominence as a leader in the church in Jerusalem (e.g., Gal. 2) receives only a handful of references (Acts 12:17; 15:13; 21:18). In any case, the characters in Acts, female as well as male, are "subsidiary to the larger story of divine activity."[44] There are a number of suggestions for a better and more accurate title for this text, such as "The Acts of the Holy Spirit," although no single theme is sufficient in itself to capture the theological focus of Acts.[45]

One theme that does consistently play across both Luke and Acts is that of the inclusive nature of the gospel: first as preached and taught by Jesus and as manifest in his death and resurrection, and second as proclaimed at Pentecost by the Spirit and throughout the subsequent mission stories. The universal nature of Jesus's ministry, which welcomes sinners, outsiders, women, and Samaritans, is palpable in Acts through the Holy Spirit in the capacity of the apostles and holy women to speak in other languages at Pentecost—to address people within the realities of their own culture and context (Acts 2:4). This universal intent extends to the inclusion of the gentiles in the divine mission through the Holy Spirit and through the presence of the Risen Christ "to the ends of the earth" (1:8). In this vision, women are included and confirmed in their discipleship and capacity for prophetic leadership.

Doubtless many today would love to see the ministry of a Phoebe or a Junia in Acts in action, alongside that of Peter and Paul, and more signs of the activity of the Galilean women disciples. Social and political activists may wish to see more evidence of a challenge to Hellenistic society and the Roman Empire: examples of programs to combat wider social poverty, to challenge oppressive structures, and to demonstrate the full participation

43. The manuscript originally had no title. Later scribes called it "Acts" to fit in with similar writings in the ancient world; "of the apostles" was added later still (Matthews, "Acts of the Apostles," 12).

44. Gaventa, *Acts of the Apostles*, 27.

45. For an outline, see Willimon, *Acts*, 8–11.

of slaves in the life of the early community. From this angle, something of the breadth and potential of the Third Gospel to transform human lives and human community at every level may seem somewhat narrowed in Acts, as if we are observing both the promise of the good news and its partial implementation in culture. "If the church could not immediately surmount ethnic and cultural barriers, we should not be surprised if the earliest communities developed egalitarian sensitivities only gradually and not everywhere at once."[46] In this regard, we need to be wary of assessing Luke against the standards of women's advancement in our own age and culture. Judged against the standards of his historical contemporaries, Luke's writings give women more attention and greater status than most.[47] The trajectory for the future direction of the church is already there in Luke's inclusive vision of the good news. Craig Keener wonders whether it is conceivable that "just as the Spirit eventually led most Jerusalem Christians beyond their ethnocentrism . . . , the promise of Pentecost in 2:17–18 suggests similar crossing of gender barriers in the future, an ideal that the earliest community about which Luke writes had not fully attained."[48]

Conclusion

We have seen something of the place and role that women have in Acts as disciples of Jesus and leaders in the early church. As we have noted, men are more prominent and numerous than women, reflecting the culture of the times, but that itself makes the presence of the women and the roles they play more remarkable. Women cooperate in the spreading of the gospel message in the stories from the early life of the church. Women's presence and power are still countercultural and reflect Jesus's extraordinary relationships with women, where their gifts and abilities are recognized and valued. It is noteworthy that in Acts women are not the possessions of their fathers and husbands: "What is important in Luke's ordering of things is where people are located in relationship to the gospel, not where they are located in the patriarchy."[49]

Not only does Luke present women engaged in ministry, but the text of Acts offers a trajectory for women's future leadership in the church. This is an essential aspect of biblical interpretation. It is not just a question of counting heads or listing positions across the gender divide. It is also essential to

46. Keener, *Acts*, 1:600.
47. Keener, *Acts*, 1:587–99; Gaventa, *Acts of the Apostles*, 43–44.
48. Keener, *Acts*, 1:603.
49. Gaventa, *Acts of the Apostles*, 44.

recognize the direction the text faces, drawing out implications that may not be fully realized or realizable within the cultural practicalities of the original context. Once again we confront an ambiguous story, not only or even primarily in the case of Acts but rather in subsequent generations, who did not always take the direction to which the text points. Instead, in some ways, parts of the church became increasingly captive not to the liberated and inclusive Lukan message of the gospel beyond cultural limitations but to the culture itself and its discomfort with women's leadership.

Chapter Four

John's Gospel

WOMEN have considerable prominence in the Gospel of John. While it contains fewer female characters than Luke, women are clearly significant and highly regarded in the Fourth Gospel[1]—though a few scholars disagree with this widespread estimation.[2] John's Gospel uses a similar pattern to Luke of pairing women and men—although, because of the long narratives, there are fewer examples: the mother of Jesus and the royal official (both at Cana), Nicodemus and the Samaritan woman, Mary of Bethany and Judas, the mother of Jesus and the beloved disciple, and Mary Magdalene and Thomas.[3] In some contexts women have roles not accorded them in the Synoptics (such as Martha at John 11:27), but in others women are absent, as in John 21.[4]

John's Gospel, the last of the canonical Gospels to be written (in the 90s), is rather different from the other Gospels in structure. For a number of years interpreters tended to assume that John was completely independent of the other three Gospels.[5] These days we are more aware of the interconnectedness

---

1. R. Brown, *Community of the Beloved Disciple*, 183–98; Schneiders, "Women in the Fourth Gospel," 35–45; Conway, *Men and Women in the Fourth Gospel*; and Beirne, *Women and Men in the Fourth Gospel*.

2. Adeline Fehribach sees women throughout the Gospel as "marginalized," while the Gospel has an "androcentric and patriarchal function" (*Women in the Life of the Bridegroom*, 169). For an overview of gender in John, see Conway, "Gender and the Fourth Gospel," 220–36.

3. See Beirne, *Women and Men in the Fourth Gospel*, especially 219–23.

4. Many consider John 21 an addition to the Gospel, possibly by the evangelist; see Moloney, *Gospel of John*, 545–46; Zumstein, *L'Évangile selon Saint Jean*, 2:289–302.

5. E.g., R. Brown, *Gospel according to John*, xli–li; D. Smith, *Johannine Christianity*, 145–72; Keener, *Gospel of John*, 1:40–51.

of the Gospels, and it is likely that John knew one or more of the Synoptic Gospels, even if he does not draw from them to the same extent as, for example, Matthew does from Mark. Luke, in particular, has a close relationship to John. Yet awareness of the points of similarity between the two traditions—the Synoptic and the Johannine—does not diminish the special way in which John narrates the story of Jesus and the particular theological perspective he brings to the New Testament, particularly in relation to women.

Women as Disciples

We encounter in this Gospel women whom, in the majority of cases, we have met already in one or another of the Gospels (Mary the mother of Jesus, Mary Magdalene, Mary the mother/wife of Clopas, Mary and Martha of Bethany) and, in another case, a woman who is unknown to the Synoptics (the Samaritan woman). While their discipleship is exemplary in John, women also struggle with faith, and their growth in believing, through misunderstanding, makes it possible for the reader to identify with them. This is also a feature of characters in general in this Gospel. For this reason, there is a greater stress on women as individuals in their encounters with Jesus, with only one context portraying women disciples as a group (19:25–27; cf. 20:2). The main characters of the Gospel with exemplary faith are John the Baptist, the beloved disciple, and the mother of Jesus.[6]

Only a few explicit female characters are portrayed negatively in John. We might include the female guard at the gate of the high priest's courtyard (18:16–17) who asks if Peter is one of Jesus's disciples, ensuring no allies of Jesus are given entry. The genders of those who question Peter on the two further occasions in the courtyard are not given (18:25–27). At the same time, we should assume, unless told otherwise, that women are present in crowd (*ho ochlos*) scenes, such as the "bread of life" narrative or the Tabernacles narrative; they move at first toward faith but later in the opposite direction (6:36; 8:37). In this case, women, like men, are capable of moving away from faith.

Like other Johannine characters, women mostly belong in much longer narratives in John than in the other Gospels. This is a distinctive feature of the Fourth Gospel, where the short, pithy stories and sayings of the Synoptic Gospels are replaced with fuller narratives and longer monologues by, or dialogues with, the Johannine Jesus.[7] This is a characteristic of John's liter-

6. Lee, "Witness in the Fourth Gospel," 1–17.
7. See Marianne Thompson, *John*, 2–8; Anderson, *Riddles of the Fourth Gospel*, 51–60.

ary style and displays his interest in the movement of single characters from unbelief to faith (and sometimes vice versa), which is a feature of male as well as female characters, including Pilate (18:28–19:16a).

An important question in John, as in the Synoptics, is the extent of the group called "the disciples" (*hoi mathētai*). The word is found throughout the Gospel, mainly of Jesus's disciples, although occasionally of disciples of John the Baptist (1:37; 3:25) and, in one context, disciples of Moses (9:28).[8] At no point does John's Gospel make it plain who exactly belongs among this group. In the first sequence of the Gospel, five gather around Jesus, two of whom have been disciples of the Baptist (1:35–51). In the final sequence of the Gospel, seven disciples meet the Risen Lord, among them Peter and the beloved disciple (21:2–3). In between the first and last chapters, several others are explicitly named: Thomas, Judas the betrayer, another Judas (14:22), and Joseph of Arimathea, though his discipleship is secret (19:38). The Twelve are mentioned in two contexts, are not enumerated, and are not explicitly named "apostles" (6:67; 20:24).[9]

Other language is also used to identify those who are attached to Jesus, and this category includes women. Sometimes it is the language of love, as in the case of the Bethany family (11:1–12:11) and the beloved disciple (13:23; 19:26; 20:2; 21:7), or it is that of believing, though the faith of believers may be partial or temporary (2:23–25; 8:31). Sometimes it is the presence of certain characters in their response to Jesus that indicates their faith and following: the Samaritan woman, for example, or the mother of Jesus along with her sister, Mary the wife/mother of Clopas, and Mary Magdalene at the cross. This also is the case with Nicodemus, who is not identified as a disciple but acts as one in burying Jesus (19:39).

A further group associated with Jesus is made up of his *adelphoi*, which can mean "brothers" or "brothers and sisters" (though translators tend to assume the former).[10] These have a somewhat uneasy relationship with Jesus and though attached to his ministry in some contexts (2:12), in others they demonstrate their lack of faith and their misunderstanding of the nature of his mission (7:5). Indeed Jesus dissociates himself from their presence and journeys separately to Jerusalem for the Feast of Tabernacles (7:10).[11]

---

8. For an outline of discipleship in relation to covenant, see Chennattu, *Johannine Discipleship as a Covenant Relationship*, 89–179.

9. For John's focus on personal discipleship rather than institutional structures, see R. Brown, *Community of the Beloved Disciple*, 83–88.

10. On the accuracy of inclusive translation, see Strauss, "Current Issues," 115–41.

11. On the *adelphoi* of Jesus in the Tabernacles narrative (7:1–3:59), see Wesley, *Son of Mary*, 212–55.

As for those who accompany Jesus at various points in his travels to and from Judea, the Gospel does not identify them. The impression in the Cana to Cana cycle (2:1–4:54) is that Jesus journeys with a small group of men—perhaps only the five mentioned in John 1:19–51—since they are shocked at Jesus speaking with a woman (4:27). Following the Samaritan conversion, there is the possibility of women participating in Jesus's ministry, especially if the gender barrier has been overcome. In the feeding story, it is unclear whether women are among the disciples, though their presence among the crowd can be inferred. Thomas appears among Jesus's disciples at 11:16, though he has not been included before. The same vagueness characterizes the second half of the Gospel, where those present at the Last Supper are never enumerated. If we work on the principle that females are included unless we are told otherwise, then women are present for this event.[12]

John has no interest in pinning down the exact names or numbers of those who accompany Jesus, particularly on his third visit to Jerusalem. What is significant, however, is that both Martha and Mary confess their faith in Jesus at the turning point of the narrative, just as it moves toward the final Passover meal, within days of his crucifixion. And on the other side, four women have remained with him to the end and are present at the foot of the cross. That these women, including Mary Magdalene and the mother of Jesus, are absent from Jesus's travels and Last Supper is hard to imagine. The most likely scenario is that women are incorporated into the community of gathered disciples for much of Jesus's ministry. This point coheres with the Synoptic tradition.

Mothering Faith

In order to grasp the significance of women in the Fourth Gospel, we need to begin with the central theological motif, that of the incarnation.[13] For the evangelist, the one who has dwelled with God from all eternity and through whom the universe is made (1:3) enters the material world, becomes "flesh" (*sarx*), and reveals the divine radiance of love and light (1:14). Here the "fundamental line of ontological difference" between Creator and creation "has been crossed and overcome in the Incarnation, yet also not obliterated."[14] Though Jesus is male, the divine Word does not identify only with men but with a humanity that includes male and female, and indeed embraces the

---

12. Lee, "Presence or Absence," 1–20.
13. See Schnelle, "Johannine Theology," 669–80.
14. Coakley, *God, Sexuality, and the Self*, 57.

whole of creation.[15] To become a child of God, for John, means to regain a lost identity through a new birth from the Spirit of God, who as we later learn, gives birth to believers, women and men, by faith in Jesus (1:13; 3:3–5).

Because the Gospel begins with creation and contains no birth narrative, we do not meet the mother of Jesus until his ministry. After the gathering of the first group of disciples (Andrew and Peter, Philip and Nathanael, and the unnamed disciple, 1:35–51), Jesus attends a wedding in company with them and with members of his family, including his mother and his *adelphoi* ("brothers and sisters," 2:1). The episode is a difficult one, and much ink has been spilled in discussing the problems of the narrative.[16] What is the meaning of Jesus's apparent rebuff of his mother, when she points out to him the lack of wine (2:3)—a major source of shame in a culture where hospitality is everything?[17] What does he mean by the words *ti emoi kai soi* ("what is it to me and to you"), and why does he address her as "woman" instead of "mother" (2:4a)? What is the "hour" that has "not yet come" (2:4b)?

We need to bear in mind two points here. First, it is not intended as a psychological or stereotypical narrative—depicting a son's difficult relationship with his mother[18]—but is a stylized and symbolic account, outlining the narrator's theological direction for the Gospel. This helps us interpret Jesus's response to his mother, which seems otherwise sharp and unconventional (2:4). Here the notions of "wedding," "stone jars," and "wine" each take on metaphorical meanings for John that are derived from the Old Testament and Jewish ritual practice. The wedding imagery points to the final banquet (Isa. 25:6–8; 55:1–2), and the water jars signify the cleansing practices of Judaism.[19] The miracle symbolizes, therefore, that the end time is now present in Jesus, who is "the good wine" kept till last (John 2:10). Far more than rescuing the family from social disaster, Jesus ignites the flame of God's final coming, God's ultimate rescue of human beings from darkness and death. And this salvation is couched within the framework, the mindset, the rituals and beliefs, of Judaism. In this sense salvation is indeed "of the Jews" (4:22).[20]

15. On the use of "flesh" to suggest also creation, see Lee, *Flesh and Glory*, 43–45.

16. For a succinct overview of the various interpretations, see Gaventa, *Mary*, 194–97.

17. On the social customs of weddings, see Keener, *Gospel of John*, 1:498–501.

18. Though mothers and sons formed close bonds in the ancient world; see Wesley, *Son of Mary*, 95–118.

19. See Keener, *Gospel of John*, 1:509–13.

20. John's Gospel does not view Judaism as superseded; for the Fourth Evangelist, the Old Testament and Judaism provide the symbolic matter for an authentic understanding of the Johannine Jesus. For more on this see Lee, "Significance of Moses in the Gospel of John," 52–66.

In this scenario the mother of Jesus plays a vital role. Though outspoken in bringing the issue to Jesus's attention (2:3), she is not discouraged by his reaction (2:4–5), which signals "from the start that divine power will not be prompted by occasions of human need such as arise from time to time."[21] There is perhaps an element of misunderstanding: she sees only a social problem that her son can rectify, while he perceives an event that will set in motion the whole train of his ministry. If his response represents a challenge to her understanding, it has the effect of not discouraging or puzzling her, so that "the sense of bafflement is only increased by the failure of Jesus' mother to share in it."[22] Her confidence is apparent in her turning to the servants: "Whatever he says to you, do!" (2:5). She grasps the centrality of trust in, and obedience to, the word of Jesus, which is the authentic response to be emulated by the disciples present. Although some have suggested that Jesus is distancing himself from his mother as kin,[23] it is also the case that her "maternal" role is extended beyond Jesus to the newly fledged disciples as she points them to the efficacy of Jesus's word: "She is the first person in the narrative to show . . . that the correct response to the presence of Jesus is trust in his word."[24] The mother of Jesus comes to believe at a deeper level in the life-giving capacities of her son.

The Cana story sets in motion Jesus's ministry together with the miraculous "signs" (*sēmeia*) and "works" (*erga*): "The story hints at events that lie ahead rather than prosaically announcing a program that mechanically unfolds."[25] It has a programmatic quality to it within the wider Johannine narrative. The signs throughout this Gospel have, as their purpose, not a demonstration of divine power but the revelation of Jesus's glory as it will be revealed on the cross.[26] Glory is a major theme of the Gospel, signifying the loving and life-giving radiance of God, once displayed at Sinai and in the temple and now definitively revealed in the incarnation.[27] The mother of Jesus plays an important role in bearing witness to that glory, a witness that leads the disciples to faith (2:11). The strength of her faith is the point more than Jesus's desire to distance himself from her. This same witness is evident at the end of the Cana cycle as Jesus challenges the royal official with an apparently discouraging statement, which likewise serves to bring out a remarkable faith

21. B. Byrne, *Life Abounding*, 54.
22. Lieu, "Mother of the Son," 66.
23. E.g., Marianne Thompson, *John*, 60–61, who also argues here that Jesus redefines the meaning of "kin" at the foot of the cross (19:25–27).
24. Moloney, *Gospel of John*, 68.
25. Gaventa, *Mary*, 198.
26. Frey, *Glory of the Crucified One*, 288–90.
27. On glory, see Bauckham, *Gospel of Glory*, 43–62.

(4:48–49). Jew and gentile, female and male, combine in the Cana to Cana cycle, at the beginning and end, to reveal the transforming effects of believing in the life-giving word of the one who is the Word.

Second, the wedding story at Cana needs to be interpreted in light of the passion, where the mother of Jesus again appears, for the second time in the Johannine tale. Throughout the Gospel Jesus refers to his "hour" (e.g., 12:23; 13:1), and each time it signifies the moment of his death and exaltation on the cross, where the glory of his identity as Son as well as the Father's love for him and for the world are fully disclosed.[28] The reference to his "hour" at the wedding is the first in a series of pointers to the passion, where the mother of Jesus will play a key role. Although the glory of Jesus is manifest in the incarnation and throughout his ministry, it reaches a revelatory climax on the cross. The wedding points to the cross through the presence of the mother of Jesus and the motif of glory.

Throughout the passion narrative, John presents a number of symbols that indicate salvation, revealing that Jesus gives life to believers through his death on the cross.[29] One of the key symbols is the moment when Jesus donates the beloved disciple to his mother and his mother to the beloved disciple (19:25–27). The scene has given rise to considerable controversy among Johannine interpreters. Even without the more inflated claims, it means more than a dying son's care for his aging mother;[30] Jesus, after all, has siblings who are perfectly capable of caring for their mother. In part it signifies Jesus's love for "his own" (13:1; 18:8–9). More importantly, it represents the founding of the Christian community[31] in the mutual, familial love of these two foundational disciples.

When we put the two stories together, the wedding and the cross, we see that the family imagery in the Cana story sets the scene for the full revelation of the fictive family of believers at the cross. At the wedding, Jesus is with his mother, his disciples, and his brothers and sisters, who accompany him to Capernaum (2:12). These same siblings later in Jesus's ministry demonstrate a lack of faith, despite their enthusiasm for his "signs" (7:5). This disjunction within the biological family leads to the creation of the fictive family at the foot of the cross—and includes the mother of Jesus in both. No longer is she defined by her motherhood to Jesus; now that motherhood is to be exercised within the family of believers. "Through his death and resurrection, Jesus

28. On the "hour" in relation to Johannine eschatology, see Zimmermann, "Eschatology and Time," 292–310.

29. Lieu speaks of the death and resurrection of the Johannine Jesus as an irresolvable paradox: "His birthing a dying, his dying a birth" ("Mother of the Son," 77).

30. Moloney, *Gospel of John*, 503–4.

31. Moloney, "Woman and Mother in the Fourth Gospel," 270–79. Against this reading, cf. Lieu, "Mother of the Son," 69–70.

gathers together the children of God who are brothers and sisters to each other and to him, and the claims of his family outweigh biological claims."[32]

The motherhood imagery, first introduced at Cana, is not lost. It coheres with the maternal Spirit, who gives birth to believers, and with the role of Jesus himself, from whose side blood and water flow in imagery connected to birth (19:34). The same nurturing, maternal love exists within the Christian community in its embrace of all who come to faith in Jesus (cf. 20:31). Maternal symbolism plays a role in the development of faith, therefore, within the Christian community.[33]

A further feature of the role of the mother of Jesus is the title "woman," which may be an allusion to creation, where Eve is "the mother of all living" (Gen. 3:20; cf. Sir. 40:1). If so, it reinforces the role of the mother of Jesus as mother within the fictive family.[34] Patristic writers regard Mary as an Eve figure, contrasting the disobedience of Eve with the obedience of Mary. Yet other women in John's Gospel are also referred to as "woman," notably the Samaritan woman (John 4:5–7) and Mary Magdalene (20:13, 15). Some in the early church also saw Mary Magdalene as a figure of Eve, particularly in her proclamation of the resurrection to the other disciples.[35]

Finding and Proclaiming

The Samaritan Woman

Not only do women play a nurturing role in John, but they also act in "apostolic" ways in two key texts.[36] We have already noted that the word "apostle" does not appear but that there is a good deal of "sending" language, in relation to both Jesus and his disciples ("apostle" means literally "one who is sent").[37] The first example of this ministry occurs in the Samaritan woman's encounter with Jesus (4:1–42). The wider narrative context is the Cana to Cana cycle (2:1–4:54), where the overall theme is entry into eternal life. In contrast to Nicodemus in the previous chapter, who has all the status the Samaritan woman

---

32. Marianne Thompson, *John*, 400.

33. For more on this, see Lee, *Flesh and Glory*, 150–59.

34. For a different view of the significance of this scene, cf. Gaventa, who argues that it represents the beginning of Jesus's ascension and his separation from those closest to him in his human life—i.e., his mother and the beloved disciple (*Mary*, 215–21). Lieu prefers to see an Eve parallel not in individual Johannine characters but in the parable of the woman in labor (16:21; "Mother of the Son," 71–75).

35. See, e.g., Gregory the Great in Elowsky, *John 11–21*, 354.

36. R. Brown, "Roles of Women in the Fourth Gospel," in *Community of the Beloved Disciple*, 187–92.

37. On the Johannine Christology of "sending," see Schnelle, "Johannine Theology," 681–86.

lacks and who is unable to move to faith at this point (3:1–10), she displays an openness to faith and begins slowly but surely, through misunderstanding, to grasp the significance of Jesus's identity and gift.

The narrative begins with the overturning of the roles of water giver and thirsty one. Initially the woman is the water giver and Jesus, after a long journey and in the midday heat, is thirsty and needs access to the well.[38] The woman objects, not on her own account but because she assumes that the Jewish Jesus will not want to drink from her (Samaritan) vessel,[39] since Samaritans are effectively regarded as unclean gentiles.[40] Unaffected by these distinctions, Jesus ignores issues of ritual cleanness and instead reveals himself as the true water giver, offering her "life-giving water" (4:10).[41]

At the end of the first scene, the woman has moved in her understanding and now sees Jesus as an authentic water giver, although she assumes mistakenly that this is a superior brand of water (4:15). In attempting to progress her understanding, therefore, Jesus turns the conversation to something more personal. He does so by revealing his knowledge of her marital status, not in a moralistic or judgmental spirit but in order to uncover her "thirst for life."[42] The woman has had five marriages through death or divorce (women could not initiate divorce in Judaism) and is now in an irregular relationship, possible with a married man ("the one you have is not *your* husband," 4:18).[43] This may illustrate her desperation: "She needs the protection and support of a husband, but has settled for what she can get."[44] Far from resenting this intrusion into her life, however, she embraces it with enthusiasm, recognizing Jesus as a prophet (4:19)—later, with some hyperbole, she will describe Jesus as someone who has told her "everything [she] ever did" (4:29). She at once raises the fundamental dividing issue between Jews and Samaritans: the proper place of worship (4:20).

In his response, Jesus leads the woman to a deeper comprehension of worship, with himself as the true sacred site, the temple where God's glory dwells (4:21–25; cf. 1:14; 2:21).[45] Faced with the patent disapproval of the returning

38. For more on this passage, see Lee, *Symbolic Narratives of the Fourth Gospel*, 64–97.

39. On the translation and textual problem here, see Lincoln, *Gospel according to Saint John*, 168, 172–73.

40. On Jews and Samaritans, see Keener, *Gospel of John*, 1:598–603.

41. This is Johannine ambiguity: the literal meaning is "flowing water," as opposed to the still water of the well, but Jesus means the water that gives eternal life (Lee, *Flesh and Glory*, 73–74).

42. "Man is made aware of the unrest in his life, which drives him from one supposed satisfaction to another, never letting him attain the final fulfilment until he finds the water of life" (Bultmann, *Gospel of John*, 188).

43. See, however, Lynn Cohick, who argues that the woman is not presented as an "immoral sinner" but rather as a "seeker of truth" ("'Woman at the Well,'" 249–53).

44. Marianne Thompson, *John*, 103.

45. See Coloe, *God Dwells with Us*, 99–105.

disciples, the Samaritan forgets her water jar and rushes back to the village to announce her discovery (4:28). She has apparently accepted Jesus's disclosures, recognizing her need for the "living water" that Jesus alone can give, through the Spirit (cf. 7:37–39). This dual awareness of her own need and Jesus's identity is articulated in the question to her fellow villagers: "Surely this can't be the Christ, can it?" (4:29).[46]

On the basis of her testimony, the villagers (whom we assume to be male and female) set out for the well, and observing them, Jesus speaks of the fields as "white . . . for harvest" (*leukai . . . pros therismon*, 4:35). They acknowledge the woman's role in their conversion and their joy that they have come to discover the same thing for themselves (4:42a). This comment, along with Jesus's earlier affirmation of those who have labored in mission before the disciples (4:38), is an affirmation of the woman's apostolic role in bringing a village to discover Jesus as the giver of living water. The disciples, who will inherit the same mission, are still uncomprehending at this point, without any idea of the enormous gender and racial barriers that have been overcome in this conversation. They do not as yet comprehend that Jesus does not regard the woman as unclean but rather as worthy of an apostolic calling. Although the level of the woman's faith is disputed, the likelihood is that she has reached true faith, a faith sufficient for her to act as an authentic witness to Jesus.[47] The consequence is the Samaritans' conversion to faith and their declaration that Jesus, though Jewish, is "the Savior of the world" (4:42b).

Mary Magdalene

The second example of women's apostolic calling is that of Mary Magdalene in the resurrection narrative (20:1–18). Like the Samaritan woman, Mary has to pass through misunderstanding to reach Easter faith; unlike the Samaritan woman, she is already a believer, having been among the women at the foot of the cross (19:25b).[48] Once again, she is nowhere associated with a sinful past, nor does she anoint Jesus.[49] She is a faithful disciple who does not desert him in his hour of need (note his thirst, 19:28–30)—which is also,

46. The construction suggests either "caution or wonder" on the woman's part (Marianne Thompson, *John*, 102); Teresa Okure sees it as open ended, inviting a response (*Johannine Approach to Mission*, 174).

47. See Okure, *Johannine Approach to Mission*, 168–81; Lincoln, *Gospel according to Saint John*, 179–82; for the view that the woman's faith is partial, cf. Moloney, *Gospel of John*, 132–33, 146–47.

48. It is possible that there are four women at the cross; it is difficult to know why Mary and her sister would both have the same name, and from a dramatic point of view, the four women parallel the four soldiers. See Hoskyns and Davey, *Fourth Gospel*, 2:630–31.

49. See Wilson, "Mary Magdalene and Her Interpreters," 531–35.

for John, his hour of glory (13:31–32; 17:1)—and she is a key witness of the crucifixion. Mary and her companions bear witness to the cross as saving, as overcoming the "ruler of this world" (12:31).[50]

Mary's narrative begins with her discovery of the stone moved from the tomb and her assumption that the body has been stolen (20:2). She turns to two disciples for assistance, believing the tomb has been assaulted, and they run at once to see for themselves. The story of Peter and the beloved disciple's visit to the tomb is a strange one and seems to interrupt the narrative (20:3–9). The beloved disciple reaches it first—indicating either his more youthful physique or his spiritual ascendancy over Peter—but allows Peter to enter first.

In turning to these disciples for assistance, Mary must be disappointed. Though they hasten to the tomb, the effect of their discovery does nothing to help Mary's bewilderment and grief. What happens to them inside the tomb? There are no angels present, only the grave clothes neatly folded. The following verses are difficult. At sight of the "headcloth" rolled up separately, the beloved disciple "believed" (John 20:8), yet immediately after, we are informed that neither of them believed "the Scriptures that it was necessary for him to rise from the dead" (20:9). The two then depart from the tomb, making no contact with Mary (20:10). But what exactly is it that the beloved disciple, on the basis of the rolled-up headcloth, believes? Various attempts have been made to explain what appears to be a contradiction.[51]

Many interpreters set aside the reference to not believing Scripture in favor of the beloved disciple as the first to attain Easter faith, a faith that is superior to that of all the other disciples, including Mary Magdalene and Thomas.[52] In a variation on this view, the beloved disciple, while grasping Easter faith, does not yet understand the biblical dimension: that the resurrection is foretold in the Old Testament Scriptures.[53] Yet the conjunction "for" (*gar*) at the beginning of 20:9 is explanatory, here as elsewhere: it is not a further factor to be taken into account but an explanation of the response of the two disciples to the emptiness of the tomb and grave clothes, suggesting that they have not arrived at full faith in the resurrection.

A third possibility is that the text is ambiguous on the question of the beloved disciple's faith. If he is only convinced that the tomb is empty and that Mary has spoken the truth, it is a minimal reading of the verb *pisteuein*

---

50. On this theme see Kovacs, "'Now Shall the Ruler,'" 227–47.

51. A possible explanation is the Johannine addition of the beloved disciple into the Easter narrative; Lincoln, *Gospel according to Saint John*, 490–91.

52. See, e.g., B. Byrne, *Life Abounding*, 329–31; Lincoln, *Gospel according to Saint John*, 490–91; Zumstein, *L'Évangile selon Saint Jean*, 2:272–73.

53. Moloney, *Gospel of John*, 518–23. In a similar vein, Marianne Meye Thompson regards the Scriptures at 20:9 as indicating "further testimony" to Jesus's resurrection (*John*, 413).

(to believe). In John believing always signifies faith in Jesus—though that faith may be partial and incomplete (e.g., 8:31).[54] The beloved disciple knows that something mysterious has happened because of the grave clothes: that Jesus's body has somehow passed through them.[55] This is in contrast to the emergence of Lazarus from the tomb, who is still bound in his grave clothes, with the headcloth covering his face (11:44b).

A strange feature is that the beloved disciple fails to communicate his faith to Peter and Mary, and instead returns home: "It is not enough to see like Mary, to enter like Peter, or believe like the beloved disciple if all we do is go home afterwards and carry on regardless."[56] All this suggests he has an inkling of faith, an intimation of the resurrection, but one not sufficient enough to proclaim it. Unlike in the fishing narrative, he does not speak (cf. 21:7). It may be that he reaches a "signs" faith, which is "not the ultimate level of faith."[57]

If this is the case, the beloved disciple is not unlike Martha at her first meeting with Jesus; in reproaching Jesus for his absence, she adds: "But even now I know that whatever you ask God, God will give you" (11:22). Martha does not yet realize that Jesus will raise her brother, but she has a wild hope, a glimmering, that lies open to faith even when the reality seems beyond the power of faith. So also, it can be argued, with the beloved disciple. His faith will not be fully clarified until Jesus's appearance beside the Sea of Galilee, where John is the first among seven disciples to recognize the Risen Christ: "It is the Lord" (21:7a). Authentic faith in Jesus crucified and risen, which leads to proclamation and confession of faith, comes from Magdalene and Thomas, the first narrative leading into the giving of the Spirit (20:19–23), and the second flowing from it a week later.[58]

John's Gospel makes no explicit reference to other women at the empty tomb, although Magdalene says, "*We* do not know where they have laid him" (20:2), implying the presence of other women, as in the Synoptic tradition. In John her witness stands out from among those of the other disciples, men and women alike. Yet, as with other characters in the Gospel, her faith needs to develop through misunderstanding. When we meet her for the second time at the tomb (20:11), we find her weeping—tears that most likely signify

54. There are things the beloved disciple does not know (e.g., 13:25), and he is not expecting the resurrection any more than anyone else; on his literary role, see Culpepper, *John the Son of Zebedee*, 57–72.

55. This is not, strictly speaking, "faith without seeing"—as will be the lot of future believers (20:29b)—since, unlike them, the beloved disciple does see the empty tomb and the folded burial clothes.

56. Burridge, *John*, 229.

57. Keener, *Gospel of John*, 2:1184.

58. On the parallelism between the two, see Lee, "Partnership in Easter Faith," 37–49.

as much frustration as grief and distress. She continues to weep as she peers into the tomb.

Mary's distress screens her from the signs that now confront her. For the first time, angels are present in the tomb, at the head and foot of the stone slab on which the body of Jesus lay; she fails to perceive their significance. Strangely, the angels do not proclaim the message of the resurrection but only ask the cause of her distress. Their stance is suggestive symbolically of the divine presence in the ark of the covenant, with the cherubim on either end of the mercy seat, their wings overshadowing it—a numinous place of presence-in-absence (Exod. 25:17–20; Heb. 9:5).[59] Tears have blinded Mary's eyes, and she does not recognize them for who they are or what they might represent.

Misunderstanding continues in the narrative as the signs intensify. Now Mary encounters Jesus himself, but again the pattern is repeated: she misses the signs and fails to perceive the Risen Christ. The simplest explanation occurring to her is that this must be the "gardener," who may be able to assist in her quest for the stolen body (John 20:15). Her inability to identify this, the greatest of all the resurrection signs, is caused by the overwhelming nature of her distress, which conceals the vibrant signs of life and divine presence all around her.

Jesus's response to Mary leads her forward in her understanding. The first thing he does is to name her, "Mary!," evoking her immediate awareness of his identity (20:16). She responds with joy, discerning the voice of the Good Shepherd, who knows his sheep by name (10:3). Apart from Lazarus and Simon Peter, she is the only other disciple in John whom Jesus calls by name.[60] Second, as she responds in love and worship, he asks her not to continue holding him, as this is not the way he is to remain with her: "Do not hold on to me" (20:17).[61] The narrative implies she is embracing him or prostrating herself at his feet (see Matt. 28:9). Her understanding is progressing but still has some way to go. Finally, Jesus "reorients Mary's joy from reunion to proclamation";[62] he gives her the commission to proclaim to the other disciples ("my brothers and sisters")[63] the message of the resurrection. The theological language is of vital significance: "My Father and your Father, my God and your God."

---

59. See Léon-Dufour, Lecture de l'Évangile selon Jean, 4:217–18; Brant, John, 268–69. Against this, cf. Moloney, Gospel of John, 528.

60. Brant, John, 275.

61. Schneiders, Written That You May Believe, 197–98. Against this, cf. D'Angelo, "'I Have Seen the Lord,'" 108–9.

62. Brant, John, 271.

63. It is hard to know why the NRSV and NIV translate adelphoi as "brothers," unlike the CEB; see Schneiders, Written That You May Believe, 199.

With its covenant overtones,[64] the imagery draws both a distinction and a unity between Jesus's relationship with God and his disciples' relationship with God. They are drawn into his sonship, his filiation, to become children of God.[65] Mary receives the commission in faith and immediately obeys it by proclaiming the resurrection (John 20:18). She has reached full Easter faith, and her profound distress gives way to exultant proclamation.

On the basis of this narrative, the early church accorded Mary Magdalene the title *apostola apostolorum*, "apostle of the apostles," in recognition of the apostolic role she plays in John's account, as well as in Matthew's Gospel (Matt. 28:1–10) and the longer, added ending of Mark (Mark 16:9–11). She is the first to meet the Risen Christ and fully believe, the first to be given the commission, and the first to announce Jesus's triumph over death. Her joyful announcement "I have seen the Lord!" (*heōraka ton kyrion*, John 20:18) is the formal Christian proclamation of the resurrection that distinguishes the official, apostolic witnesses of the resurrection.[66] It is not just an utterance based on personal experience. Because of her vibrant testimony—and later that of Thomas, Peter, and the beloved disciple—and because of the abiding presence of the Spirit-Paraclete (who is Jesus's presence-in-absence), future believers can make her faith their own and are blessed (20:29). Here a woman represents the apostolic community and leads them in the proclamation of Christ's risen presence. Whether she is believed or not is another question (cf. Mark 16:11). Though the text says nothing either way, the following scene shows the group of disciples hiding in the upper room when Jesus appears before them (John 20:19–23).[67]

Confessing Faith in Word and Action

Two other women occupy the central narrative of the Gospel, confessing their faith in word and deed. At the turning point between the two main parts of the narrative, between the public ministry of Jesus (1:1–12:50) and his private ministry to his disciples (13:1–17:26), is the story of the raising of Lazarus (11:1–12:11). Apart from Lazarus himself, the two main characters in this drama are the sisters, Martha and Mary, who play key roles in eliciting the true, inner meaning of this, the climax of the Johannine signs within Jesus's public ministry. The story includes the aftermath in the believing response of

64. Schneiders, *Written That You May Believe*, 199–200.
65. For more on this theme, see Byers, *Ecclesiology and Theosis*, 49–71.
66. Schneiders, *Written That You May Believe*, 200–201.
67. Most likely the narrator at 21:14 is only counting appearances to the group of disciples (Marianne Thompson, *John*, 439–40).

many of the mourners and in the determination by the religious authorities in the council to dispose of Jesus for good (11:47–53).[68]

Martha's story is a characteristic tale of misunderstanding leading, through clarification, to understanding. She is a woman of faith from the beginning, inviting Jesus to her brother's sickbed, and she is one who is loved by Jesus (along with the rest of her family, 11:5). After Lazarus's surprising death she meets Jesus only to reproach him for his absence (11:21) and is encouraged to believe. The quality of Martha's faith, in Johannine terms, is ambiguous at this juncture. She believes in resurrection as a future promise but not a present possibility (11:24), and she fails to grasp the encompassing scope of John's Christology. Jesus clarifies her misunderstanding: the resurrection is not just a future eschatological hope but a present reality for those who believe, because Jesus himself lies at the heart of it. "I am the resurrection and the life," he assures her (in the fifth of the seven "I am" sayings of the Gospel). "The one believing in me, even if they die [physically], will live [eternally], and the one living [eternally] and believing in me will never die [eternally]" (11:25–26).[69] Death, in other words, has no power over the believer, whose grasp on eternal life overcomes all forms of decay and loss, both in the present and in the age to come.

It is significant that Jesus confronts Martha with the question of whether she believes, whether she is convinced that eternal life begins in the here and now for the one who is beloved of Jesus and that it ultimately overcomes death. Her answer is a resounding yes. Like Peter in the Synoptic Gospels, Martha is the one in this Gospel to declare that Jesus is the Christ/Messiah, the central Christian conviction. She makes the core confession of faith in the central scene of the Gospel: "Yes, Lord; I have come to believe that you are the Christ, the Son of God, the one who was to come into the world" (11:27; cf. Mark 8:29). At the same time—also like Peter—Martha does not seem as yet to understand the implications of her own faith and confession.[70] Just as Peter tries to turn Jesus from the path of suffering following his confession of faith (Mark 8:32), so later in the story, when Jesus reaches the tomb of Lazarus, Martha attempts to prevent Jesus from opening the tomb because of the stench of death (John 11:39). Both of these leading disciples have still to grow in their faith and understanding, yet for all that, they embody Christian

---

68. On this extended structure, see Lee, *Symbolic Narratives of the Fourth Gospel*, 191–92.

69. Assuming that this example of Hebrew parallelism is "synthetic parallelism," where the second line not only repeats the first but also advances it; see Lee, *Flesh and Glory*, 217–18.

70. So Marianne Thompson, *John*, 246–47. For the view that Martha's faith is complete here, cf. Schneiders, *Written That You May Believe*, 159; Conway, *Men and Women in the Fourth Gospel*, 141–43. For a more negative appraisal, see Moloney, *Gospel of John*, 327–29.

faith. They make the principal proclamation, even though they struggle to grasp its breadth.

Whereas Martha's confession of faith is in word, Mary's confession is through symbolic action (12:1–8).[71] The narrative of the anointing belongs within the Lazarus story; John has already indicated Mary as the anointer at the beginning, as if it has already happened (11:2). At the banquet organized to celebrate Lazarus's return to life, at which Jesus is the guest of honor, both sisters are present. Martha, incidentally, is serving, and the verb is again *diakonein*, which connotes the activity of ministry (12:2). Mary does not speak but instead pours expensive perfumed oil over Jesus's feet, much to the dismay of the rapacious Judas (12:5–6). As we have already seen, this story cannot easily be harmonized with either Mark's version of the anointing, where an unnamed woman prophetically anoints Jesus's head at the beginning of the passion narrative (Mark 14:3–9 // Matt. 26:6–13), or with Luke's story of the sinful woman who anoints Jesus's feet in gratitude for sins forgiven (Luke 7:36–50). John's account has nothing to do with sin and is carried out by a known and named disciple of Jesus, who anoints his feet, not his head, in gratitude for the raising of her brother to life.

The Johannine Jesus defends Mary's action in strongly worded terms, interpreting her action, in rather compressed language, as a recognition of his forthcoming death and burial (John 12:7–8). Here is a parallel with the Markan and Matthean story of the anointing of Jesus's head by an unnamed prophetic woman, which likewise points to Jesus's death and during which Jesus defends the woman who anoints him (Mark 14:8 // Matt. 26:12). While there is no reference in John's account of this act as a proclamation of the good news, its function is significant for the narrative to follow: "Mary . . . is the first person to understand the significance of the death of Jesus."[72]

There are several significant points of contrast in John's account. The exquisite odor of the perfumed oil that pervades the house (John 12:3) contrasts with the stench of death at the tomb (11:39), pointing symbolically to life replacing death.[73] Mary's action also contrasts starkly with the critical response of Judas—the true disciple against the false, the one who acclaims against the one who betrays. Here Mary joins hands with the "myrrh-bearing women" at the tomb of Jesus in the synoptic tradition, who intend to anoint his beloved body in death. She stands alongside Joseph of Arimathea and Nicodemus in John, who cover Jesus's crucified body with a mountain of oils and spices fit

71. Lee, "Martha and Mary," 207–10.
72. Moloney, *Gospel of John*, 349.
73. Lee, *Symbolic Narratives of the Fourth Gospel*, 222; O'Day, "John," 299; also Lee, "Gospel of John," 124–25.

for a king (19:38–42). At the same time, Mary foreshadows the foot washing at the beginning of the Last Supper (13:1–5), so that Jesus, who will the wash the feet of his disciples in an act of love, union, and cleansing (13:8)—as well as an act to be replayed in the Christian community (13:13–17)—has already had his own feet "washed" by Mary's act of devotion.[74]

There is a further aspect to John's story of the anointing. Not only does Mary display gratitude for her brother's restoration and awareness of Jesus's impending death; she also parallels Jesus's action with her own. There is a huge cost to Jesus's raising of Lazarus. His presence in Judea, where the authorities have already tried to stone him (8:59; 10:31) and arrest him (10:39), is dangerous. When Jesus decides to go to Lazarus, now deceased, Thomas rightly points to the danger of this journey: "Let us also go and die with him" (11:16). The consequences of Lazarus's release from death and his emergence from the tomb are ambivalent: on the one hand, many come to faith in Jesus as a result of his life-giving act, but on the other hand, the religious authorities form their plot to kill Jesus (11:47–53). The cost of what Jesus does in raising Lazarus is paralleled, in a symbolic way, by the costly oil that Mary lavishes on Jesus. Cost is met with cost, and the mutual nature of discipleship is reinforced. Mary stands as the authentic model of discipleship and the costliness it calls forth, in response to the costliness of Jesus's journey to the cross and the laying down of his life.[75] In John's account, Mary of Bethany is a paradigm of true faith that gives its all to the one who gave his all for the salvation of the world.

Other Women

We should also note the presence of two other women at the cross: Jesus's mother's sister and Mary the wife/mother of Clopas (19:25), who are standing alongside the mother of Jesus and Mary Magdalene. We have already noted that they are most likely two separate women rather than one and the same, since it would be odd for two sisters to have the same name.[76] Of Jesus's aunt we know nothing, not even her name, though it has sometimes been speculated that she is Salome, the mother of James and John.[77] However, her presence

74. Mary L. Coloe recognizes the parallels with traditions about anointing the tabernacle, emphasizing the Johannine theme of Jesus as the temple of God ("Anointing the Temple of God," 105–18).

75. Lee, *Flesh and Glory*, 203–11.

76. Unless, of course, they are cousins, stepsisters or sisters-in-law rather than full-blood sisters, which is less likely.

77. Hoskyns and Davey, *Fourth Gospel*, 631.

here indicates her discipleship and courageous following of her nephew. She, too, is "kin" both literally and metaphorically in the new community. In the same way, we know of other relatives of Jesus who played a significant role in the early church—notably, James the Just and Jude, both of whom are described as "brothers" of Jesus. But his aunt is given no further mention in the New Testament, despite her daring and intrepid presence at the cross of a condemned criminal. Her memory is worth preserving, along with that of other members of Jesus's family. In contrast to his siblings, this woman is a believer within Jesus's lifetime, along with his mother.

The other Mary is difficult to identify in terms of her relationships. John connects her to Clopas, who is probably her husband, or possibly her son. Clopas is most likely the same as "Cleopas" at Luke 24:18, where Cleopas and a companion journey to Emmaus and are brought back to Jerusalem through their meeting with the Risen Christ (Luke 24:33). If they are one and the same, Clopas/Cleopas is also a disciple of Jesus along with his wife/mother, Mary. She may also be identified with the Mary of the other Gospels: the mother of James and Joses/Joseph in Mark and Matthew (Mark 15:40, 47; 16:1–8 // Matt. 27:56, 61; 28:1–10) and the mother of James in Luke (Luke 24:10), who replaces Susanna in Luke's catalog of three (Luke 8:3). If so, this Mary is part of a family of believers who have followed Jesus from Galilee. Her discipleship contrasts with the rest of her family, who are present neither at the cross nor the empty tomb. For Luke, Cleopas does not even believe the testimony of his own wife/mother. In John he is not present at the cross, but Mary's presence in the Fourth Gospel is dauntless and worth remembering.[78]

CHART OF WOMEN DISCIPLES IN THE FOURTH GOSPEL

NAME	RELATIONSHIPS	TEXT	IDENTIFICATION	NOTES
[Mary]	Mother of Jesus	2:1–12; 19:25–27	Mother also of Jesus's siblings	Key role at beginning and end of Jesus's ministry
Samaritan woman		4:1–42	Villager; in relationship with a man	Outsider, comes to faith and leads others to faith; contrast with Nicodemus
Martha of Bethany	(Eldest) sister of Mary and Lazarus	11:1–12:11	Disciple of Jesus	Confesses faith in Jesus as resurrection and life by word
Mary of Bethany	(Youngest) sister of Martha and Lazarus	11:1–12:11	Disciple of Jesus	Confesses faith and gratitude in Jesus through anointing
Mother's sister	Jesus's aunt, unnamed	19:25–27	Disciple of Jesus	Second woman at cross, part of fictive family

78. The story of the woman caught in adultery is not part of the Johannine text. For an analysis of it, see O'Day, "John 7:53–8:11," 631–40.

NAME	RELATIONSHIPS	TEXT	IDENTIFICATION	NOTES
Mary	Wife/mother of Clopas	19:25–27	Disciple of Jesus; Clopas = Cleopas; mother of James and Joses/Joseph?	Third woman at cross, part of fictive family
Mary Magdalene		20:1–18	Disciple of Jesus (first mention)	Fourth woman at cross; first to meet and believe in risen Jesus

Father-Son Language

An important aspect of assessing John's perspective on women is the predominantly male language and imagery that is used of God throughout the Gospel. The core symbolism of the relationship between God and Jesus is that of Father and Son, which, beginning in the "musical overture" of the prologue, reechoes across the Gospel.[79] For some, this makes John's Gospel patriarchal, despite its liberating impulses for women: "At the end of the Gospel, patriarchal structures remain intact: believers reside within the house of the Father, and Jesus remains God's obedient Son."[80]

We can respond to this critique in at least two ways. First, we need to remember that the Gospel is an ancient text, arising from a culture very different from our own—one in which the father-son relationship is unmatched within the family. The eldest son must remain obedient to his father, learning his trade and caring for him in old age until the latter's death, when the son will inherit the property, the family business, and power over the family. The parable following the healing of the disabled man reflects the same context, with the son learning from the father in the workshop, receiving authority from him, and sharing in the father's honor (John 5:19–23).[81] John's Christology is grounded in ancient family configurations.

Second, John's language reflects the authentic vulnerability of love. The prologue's abstract language of *theos* (God) and *logos* (Word) becomes personalized in familial imagery so that it expresses warmth of relationship rather than distance and aloofness.[82] Honor is aligned with the idea of glory in John—as we would expect in the ancient world—but this language overturns cultural expectations. The glory of the Father is evident not in stockpiling power but in other-centered, self-sacrificing love. It is the love enacted in the foot washing (13:1–20), which adumbrates the passion, exhibiting "God at

79. Schnelle, *Das Evangelium nach Johannes*, 29.
80. Brant, *John*, 84.
81. Dodd, "Hidden Parable in the Fourth Gospel," 30–40.
82. Byers, *Ecclesiology and Theosis*, 50–52.

our feet" as the genuine marker of "divinity expressed in lowliness and humble service."[83] The divine identity manifests itself in the shame of the cross, which is paradoxically the pinnacle of the mutual glorification of Father and Son. Far from holding on to power within the family, the Father of John's Gospel shares power and demonstrates a vulnerable love that is open to rejection (1:10–11).[84]

Admittedly, within the mutual codependence, there is also subordination of the Son to the Father, but that is pictured in the Gospel as a temporal state of affairs, associated with Jesus's earthly life.[85] The circle of love between Father and Son is harmonious and free of jealousy or power play. It is constantly expanding, drawing others into its orbit, together with creation itself (17:2). The Father's love is an encompassing love that grants authority (*exousia*) not only to the beloved Son but to all who enter its domain (1:12). The Johannine Jesus speaks of his disciples as "no longer slaves" but friends (15:15), who become participants in the intimate dialogue between Father and Son, generated by the Spirit. As Gail O'Day points out, the nomenclature is not about a masculine God (despite the way the tradition has used it), but rather "Jesus calls God Father in John in order to evoke a new world in which intimate, loving relations with God and with one another are possible."[86]

In the prologue, moreover, the language of "flesh" precedes that of gender in divulging the incarnation. Jesus's humanity is not tied to maleness in the Gospel. The focus of the Father-Son connection is relational before it is male, and it expresses a divine reality that transcends human categories, including gender.[87] Relational life freely bestowed and freely shared—this is the chief characteristic of the Father-Son symbolism in the Gospel, and it challenges many of the conceited assumptions of patriarchal power.[88]

Correspondingly, feminine images throughout the Gospel complement the androcentric language for God. These images are not as distinct or prominent, but they lie within the contours of the text. Mothering imagery is to be found, for example, in the Wisdom background to the Gospel.[89] The Spirit is presented in maternal metaphors as giving birth to believers (1:12–13; 3:1–8); believers feed on living flesh in the sacramental language of John 6:51–58, suggesting an infant feeding at the mother's breast; Jesus's departure is epitomized in the parable of the laboring mother giving birth to her child (16:21); and the flow of blood and water from the crucified Christ is redolent of birth

83. B. Byrne, *Life Abounding*, 228, 230.
84. See Lee, *Flesh and Glory*, 110–34.
85. Akala, *Son-Father Relationship*, 109–18.
86. O'Day, "John," 530.
87. Akala, *Son-Father Relationship*, 219–23.
88. Soskice, "Can a Feminist," 81–94.
89. Ford, *Redeemer, Friend and Mother*, 43–45, 124–31.

(19:34).[90] The maternal images are limited, but they imply a trajectory of language and symbol that can legitimately be drawn from the Gospel.[91]

Conclusion

The Gospel of John is perhaps the most woman friendly of all the New Testament texts, and its female characters are among the most powerful and encouraging in the New Testament. Each of the women in the Fourth Gospel plays a significant role in displaying the meaning of discipleship and what is involved in Christian ministry and leadership within the community of faith: the mother of Jesus in her nurturing of faith, the Samaritan woman in her apostolic role to her fellow villagers, Mary Magdalene as the primary witness to and proclaimer of the resurrection, and Martha and Mary of Bethany in attesting to Jesus's identity and mission in word and deed. All these women play a prominent role in the Gospel story. Together they form a trajectory, a future pathway, for women as disciples and leaders in the ongoing life of the community. On the basis of John's narrative, it is hard to justify the exclusion of women from leadership in its many forms, whether lay or ordained. Once again we discover that women have biblical grounds for the authoritative forms their ministry will take, proclaiming the crucified, Risen Christ in word and deed.

---

90. Ford, *Redeemer, Friend and Mother*, 193–99.
91. Lee, *Flesh and Glory*, 135–65.

Chapter Five

Paul's Letters

Historical and Thematic Issues

FROM THE GOSPELS and their related writings we turn in this chapter to the Pauline Letters. Paul, in the popular imagination, is the misogynist of the New Testament and the source of later Christian misogyny, forbidding women's ministry and expecting them to remain silent, submissive to men, and obedient.[1] This picture is found within the church as well as outside it. Jesus is widely viewed as an admirable figure, while Paul is portrayed in forbidding colors as fanatical, obsessive, and antiwomen.[2] Showing that this is far from being the case will be, in part, the purpose of this chapter.

Paul's letters overlap with Acts, which also portrays his mission, as we have seen. But here we go back in time: Paul is writing several decades earlier than Acts (the earliest writing in the New Testament is most likely 1 Thessalonians). Paul's perspective on himself and his ministry presents a rather different outlook from that of Luke, as we might expect: the fact that they are letters in his own hand, written perhaps a generation before the account by Luke, makes a considerable difference. Alongside Luke's writings the letters provide a more intricate picture of Paul and his missional activity, from inside as well as from outside, from one generation to another, and from an autobiographical as well as a biographical perspective.

---

1. See Giles, *What the Bible Actually Teaches on Women*, 94–129.
2. Giles, *What the Bible Actually Teaches on Women*, 94–151.

Authorship

Particular controversy exists around the matter of authorship. A significant number of scholars argue that not all the letters in Paul's name were written by Paul himself.[3] This view is based on perceived differences in theological perspective across the body of writings, diversity in the style of writing and vocabulary used,[4] and potentially different contexts behind each letter. Some of these, in this view, may have been written by disciples of Paul beyond the 50s and 60s (when Paul was writing), and still others by a generation further on. The "authentic" letters—that is, those considered genuinely of Pauline composition—include (in chronological order) 1 Thessalonians, Galatians, 1 Corinthians, Philippians, Philemon, 2 Corinthians, and Romans. In this scenario, Colossians, Ephesians, and 2 Thessalonians belong in the second category, written by a disciple of Paul, while the other three (1 and 2 Timothy and Titus) belong in the third category: part of a later generation of Pauline enthusiasts.

Not all scholars who accept the basic principle recognize this precise division of the Pauline writings; some argue instead for a wider authentic corpus that might include Colossians, Ephesians, 2 Thessalonians, and even 2 Timothy.[5] On this subject the arguments go back and forth, dependent largely on context. Do the letters reflect different contexts, some of them late in the first century, when Paul was already dead and his absence might have been most keenly felt among his followers? The underlying concern is that of the change in context following the Jewish War (66–70 CE), when Christians felt the need to tone down the radical edge of the gospel. If so, which letters reflect the earlier and which the later context?

The literary genre proposed for the later letters, in this interpretive model, is that of pseudepigrapha ("assumed writings") on the basis of a tradition in which ancient writers would use not their own names and identities but those of a revered figure from the past on whom their work depends. This genre reflects a context in which individualism, as we experience it, is practically unknown, and plagiarism is considered not a writer's crime but a due acknowledgment of an older authority within the community. In the biblical world, for example, later sages in Israel would compose their sayings in the name of Solomon rather than broadcasting or publishing them in their own name; the consequence is a large body of Wisdom writings in his name that span generations. The Old Testament prophets might write in the name of

---

3. See, e.g., R. Collins, *Letters That Paul Did Not Write*.
4. See Harrison, *Problem of the Pastoral Epistles*, 18–66.
5. See, e.g., Malherbe, *Letters to the Thessalonians*, 349–75; Bruce, *Epistles*, 26–33; and Murphy-O'Connor, *Paul*, 356–59.

an illustrious predecessor; Isaiah is generally regarded as having at least three authors—the second two possibly descended from the original prophet himself. The same is true for Moses, "author" of the Pentateuch, a collection that we now believe was edited centuries after Moses's death and brought together several different sources. If this genre is to be applied to the writings of Paul, and they are not to be regarded anachronistically as forgeries,[6] it suggests the existence of a group of dedicated disciples of Paul who gathered his letters together and continued producing them beyond his death, remaining faithful to his teaching and adapting it, writing in his name and with his persona. This might include close associates of Paul such as Timothy, Sosthenes, and Silvanus. A variant on this view is that fragments from actual letters of Paul may have been used as the basis for newer compositions within the Pauline community.[7]

By contrast, a significant minority believes that all thirteen letters come from Paul's own hand and that a good case can be made for their authenticity, including the Pastoral Epistles.[8] The personal details of the later letters, such as the affectionate greetings, are seen to convey a sense of individual Pauline authorship and presence that is too vivid to be constructed, while the thirteen letters arguably convey an overarching consistency. Any theological or linguistic variation between the letters, in this view, can be ascribed to differences of context, especially since most of the letters are addressed to specific situations, requiring very different responses. On the one hand, Paul's complex theological perspective on the law and its ongoing relevance are considered consistent across the letters.[9] On the other hand, ideas such as freedom can be handled differently (even among letters that are widely agreed to be authentically Pauline): to the Galatians, the apostle stresses freedom as integral to the gospel, whereas in 1 Corinthians the apostle endeavors to restrict freedom for the well-being of the community. Any differences in style are attributed to the amanuensis (scribe) who is writing the letter under Paul's direction, to a coauthor who has taken over writing parts of the letter, or to developments in Paul's own style.

We do know that others were actively involved in the production of the letters during Paul's lifetime. The scribe was most likely a Christian, as at

6. Cf. Ehrman, *Forged*, 79–114.

7. See Miller, *Pauline Letters as Composite Documents*, especially 138–58; also Barrett, *Pastoral Epistles*, 4–12.

8. See, e.g., Payne, *Man and Woman*, 184–86 (which is mainly concerned with 1 Timothy); also N. T. Wright, *Paul and the Faithfulness of God* (which concerns Colossians and Ephesians).

9. E.g., Brian S. Rosner describes it as "the tension between Paul's negative critique and positive approval of the law" throughout the Pauline corpus (*Paul and the Law*, 45), which he defines as Paul's rejection of the law as covenant on the one hand, and his reframing of the law's relevance as prophecy and wisdom on the other.

Romans 16:22, where he identifies himself in the greetings: "I Tertius greet you, the one who has written the letter in the Lord." At the end of Galatians, Paul writes in his own hand (rather clumsily), implying that a scribe has written the rest (Gal. 6:11). When it comes to coauthors, 1 Corinthians is written with Sosthenes (1 Cor. 1:1), and 2 Corinthians, Philippians, Philemon, and Colossians introduce both Paul and Timothy as the authors (2 Cor. 1:1; Phil. 1:1a; Col. 1:1; Philem. 1a); the writers of 1 and 2 Thessalonians are Paul, Silvanus, and Timothy (1 Thess. 1:1a; 2 Thess. 1:1a); and Galatians is unusual in that it is authored by Paul and the *adelphoi* (brothers and sisters) with him (Gal. 1:1–2a), implying the involvement of a community in the composition. The problem of authorship is muddled by the presence of these coauthors, who for us remain largely invisible.

At one level, none of this makes much difference, since all the letters are Pauline in one sense or another, and all have a place in the New Testament canon. The problem arises from some of the more difficult passages in later letters about women's place in church and home. The picture that emerges, from this standpoint, is of an increasingly reactionary movement from the original Pauline context to the more restricted setting of a later generation.[10] Christians are now assuming that Christ's return will be delayed and that they need to resign themselves to a long wait and to establishing a Christian lifestyle in the repressive context of empire, surrounded by pagan neighbors. Of particular note are the "household codes" that set out a pattern of obedience and are considered a sign of later adjustment to the political ethos and ethics of the day (Eph. 5:22–6:9; Col. 3:18–4:1; 1 Tim. 6:1–2a; Titus 2:1–10). The seven authentic letters of Paul are perceived as more favorable to women's participation in ministry.

In more recent studies, however, conventional interpretations of the later writings are under attack, challenging the reception of them as reactionary and conformist. This questioning does not seek to deny that Paul's views may have adapted and developed over time or that his address to different communities is geared to their particular contexts. Nor does it deny that the apostle Paul was a man of his time. But the research endeavors to demonstrate that, even in the household codes, the notion of obedience and submission may need to be reconsidered. Could it be that the problem lies more in the way these texts have been read than with the texts themselves? For the purposes of the following discussion the focus is not on authorship but on the canonical texts themselves, with their different contents and contexts.[11]

10. So Crossan, "Search for the Historical Paul."
11. "From the standpoint of exegesis or textual interpretation, it is even more important to know what an author represents than it is to know the name of the author" (R. Collins, *Letters That Paul Did Not Write*, 259).

Paul's Female Colleagues

The best place to begin is to consider not the difficult passages but the women who are named across the thirteen letters. More recent attention has moved from statements about women generically to the individual women with whom Paul ministered. The work of these individuals in mission indicates an openness to the active ministry and authority of women that would surprise those who consider the apostle a misogynist. The list in Romans 16 is not an addendum to the letter but is integral, indicating the Roman Christians whom Paul either knows already or still hopes to meet, making connections especially with significant people in the community.

Romans 16 refers to ten women, eight of them explicitly by name: Phoebe, Prisca (Priscilla), Mary, Junia, Tryphaena, Tryphosa, Julia, Persis, the mother of Rufus, and the sister of Nereus. Some of these women's names, along with a number of others, occur elsewhere in the Pauline writings. In a patriarchal world, where the limelight invariably falls on men and where women are mostly concealed in the shadows, this list is extraordinary. True, it does not compare to the list of Paul's male fellow workers, which is longer still (twenty-four men are named, including Tertius). But in its context and for its time, the fact that more than a third in this one chapter alone are female is of great significance. A number of them may have been slaves or freedwomen, as indicated by names that were characteristic of slaves (e.g., Persis, Tryphaena, and Tryphosa).

Numbers by themselves may not prove much, but more significant is the role these women play and the way Paul describes them. The first mentioned is Phoebe, who has been commissioned to carry the letter to the church in Rome. The commission implies that she is a woman of means, able to pay for the voyage from her own funds. Her name is pagan, indicating she is a gentile who has become a Christian. Phoebe is explicitly commended to the Roman Christians at the head of the list. As Beverly Gaventa points out, Paul's commendation of her signifies that she is to be his ambassador and represent him to the church in Rome.[12] Gaventa also proposes that Phoebe may have had a hand in the composition of the epistle and that, at the very least, Paul would have discussed the contents with her and indicated how he wanted it communicated and understood. It is likely that she is the one to read it aloud to the Roman Christians, explaining and expounding its meaning where needed (Rom. 16:1).[13] This makes her the first interpreter of Paul's Letter to the Romans. It also places her alongside other characters, such as Timothy and Silvanus, who assist Paul in his ministry and letter writing.

12. Gaventa, "Listening to Phoebe Read Romans."
13. Gaventa, *When in Romans*, 9–14.

Not only is Phoebe given this responsibility, but she also is described as a "deacon" or "minister" in the church at Cenchreae, one of the two ports on the Isthmus of Corinth. It is not clear how formal the structures were in the Pauline churches at this stage—although they became more formalized in the following decades—but it is plain that Phoebe has a distinctive ministry over one part of the Corinthian church and that she has sufficient status to support her in the role she is given as Paul's ambassador.[14] Note that the word used of her ministry is *diakonos*, a term closely related to the verb *diakonein*, which refers in the Gospels to Jesus's own ministry and that of the leaders of the early Christian community.

Phoebe is designated as "sister" (*adelphē*) and "benefactor" (*prostasis*). The system of benefaction in the ancient Roman world was a widespread and complex one, in which wealthier people acted as patrons to those less well off, giving them gifts and benefactions in exchange for their loyalty and support, whether political or religious.[15] If Phoebe is a patron to the church in Corinth, her own situation must be one of some wealth. No male is mentioned in relation to her, which is unusual and suggests she may be a widow or a single woman of means. She may well be the leader of a church that meets in her own house, given the practice of the earliest churches; the title "deacon of the church at Cenchreae" does suggest a leadership role in that, probably small, community. The benefactions of her ministry would have benefited not just many in the church but also Paul himself.

The other women of Romans 16 are among the recipients of the letter and hear it read aloud, participating in the wider discussion about its meaning and significance. Gaventa speculates on how these Christian women might have heard Paul's message. For her, "Junia and her sisters" would have found it neither oppressive nor demeaning but, on the contrary, liberating—as much for women as for men. In Romans, she maintains, Paul advocates the divine, redemptive power in Christ for all people, through his death and resurrection and by the creation of the new age—a redemptive power that finally triumphs over the "principalities and powers" of sin and death in which human beings and the whole creation are helplessly entwined.[16] This gives women the hope of transformative freedom from all that excludes and diminishes them. It is a theology that, despite many of Paul's interpreters down through the centuries, is grounded in an affirmation of the body, including the female body,[17] holding

---

14. See Paula Gooder's novelistic account of this Christian leader that is based on historical evidence and knowledge of Pauline theology (*Phoebe: A Story*).

15. On women and the Roman patronage system, see Cohick, *Women in the World*, 285–321.

16. Gaventa, "Listening to Romans."

17. See especially Westfall, *Paul and Gender*, 177–204.

out the hope of a renewal not only of human existence but also of the earth. In this sense, Paul sees the groaning of creation as labor pains that are already bringing to birth a transformed world beyond the power of sin and death.[18]

Priscilla is another important woman named in relation to Paul's ministry. She is familiar to us from Acts, where she is mentioned as the theological teacher of Apollos and the fellow worker of Paul, along with Aquila, her husband (Acts 18:1–3, 24–26). She is also mentioned elsewhere in the Pauline writings (1 Cor. 16:19; 2 Tim. 4:19). It is as clear from Paul's own writing as from Luke's that Priscilla is a close companion and coworker with Paul in the church's mission. Paul generally calls her "Prisca," which is a diminutive form of "Priscilla," and his close, affectionate bond with her and her husband is perceptible, along with their considerable status in his missional work. Second Timothy speaks of the church in their home in Ephesus, implying that both she and Aquila are leaders of the house church there (2 Tim. 4:19). Here again we encounter Prisca as theologian, missionary, and leader in the church. Being mentioned first, before her husband—the opposite of convention in the ancient world—most likely illustrates her eminence in the church.

Another extraordinary figure in the list is that of Junia. In the more recent past, translators and commentators have found it hard to believe that a woman would be named an apostle (*apostolos*), although Saint John Chrysostom, bishop of Constantinople in the fourth century, believed she was particularly honored to be so named.[19] Instead more modern commentators assumed that the original form of the name was "Junias," a male name, rather than "Junia," a female name.[20] The fact that "Junias" is not found elsewhere in the Roman-Hellenistic world and that "Junia" is a relatively common female name has not seemed to deter them.[21] Yet, in the light of the evidence from names, we can no longer doubt that Junia, along with Andronicus (presumably her husband), is an apostle.

Both Junia and Andronicus are described as "prominent/outstanding among the apostles"—it is remarkable that women should be so highly

18. On Paul and ecology, particularly in relation to Rom. 8:18–22, see B. Byrne, "Pauline Complement," 308–27.

19. John Chrysostom, *Homily 31 on Rom. xvi.5*, 554–55.

20. It appears in the accusative form, *Junian*, the nominative of which could be, technically, either a contraction of the male Junianus or Junias. On the textual evidence, see the discussion by the text critic Eldon J. Epp, in *Junia*, 23–80. Commentators tend to support this view: e.g., Dunn, *Romans*, 2:894–95; B. Byrne, *Romans*, 450–53.

21. More recent translations, in company with the KJV, use "Junia" (e.g., NRSV, NIV, REB), although the NJB retains "Junias," along with the RSV and ASV; even the ESV has "Junia," though with a footnote suggesting the name could also be "Junias."

commended.[22] Paul is using the title "apostle" in a more inclusive sense than just the Twelve, since, for him, a wider group also held this office, including Paul himself. Yet it is more than a general name for someone engaged in mission, even in Paul's day. Elsewhere Paul speaks of the role of apostle as an essential form of leadership within the body of Christ, carrying a great weight of responsibility for the spiritual well-being of God's people: "God has appointed in the church first apostles" (1 Cor. 12:28). Andronicus and Junia are designated as "relatives" of Paul, which may indicate a family relationship or, more likely, that they were fellow Jews. Whatever their relationship, Paul regards them as eminent apostles, suggesting not just their commitment but also their authority to proclaim the gospel.

Richard Bauckham has suggested the possibility that "Junia" might be the Roman name for the Hebrew "Joanna" and that Junia can be credibly identified with the Galilean disciple of that name from Luke's Gospel (Rom. 8:3).[23] It was not uncommon for Jewish people to have a Greek as well as a Hebrew name. A good example is a woman we have already encountered whose Hebrew name is Tabitha and whose Greek name is Dorcas (Acts 9:36–43). Bauckham argues for this identification on the basis that "Junia" sounds like "Joanna" and that Joanna, like a number of other early Jewish Christians, might well have adopted a Roman name in her missionary travels. In the ministry of Jesus, according to Luke as we have seen, Joanna is a member of the highly Romanized Herodian court; Andronicus, Bauckham suggests, may be an alternative name for Chuza or her second husband, if she was widowed (Luke 8:2–3).[24] If this view is right, then we have in Junia not only an apostle but an actual follower of Jesus in his earthly ministry and an eyewitness of his ministry, death, and resurrection. This might, in part, underline her (and Andronicus's) prominence among the apostles.[25]

One of the remarkable features of women in the list is the shape of their ministry. Mary, Tryphaena, Tryphosa, and Persis, along with Prisca, are described as workers or hard workers "in the Lord" (Rom. 16:12). The language is not that of women's traditional roles (cooking, cleaning, caring for children) but is used by Paul of his core ministry and that of his companions. He describes himself and other leaders as "God's coworkers" (*theou . . . synergoi*), laboring to cultivate and to build the Christian community as "God's

---

22. An article by M. H. Burer and D. Wallace attempts to argue that the phrase means "outstanding *to* the apostles," implying that she herself is not an apostle ("Was Junia Really an Apostle?," 76–91); against this, cf. Bauckham, *Gospel Women*, 172–80.

23. Bauckham, *Gospel Women*, 186–98.

24. See above, chap. 2, "Women in Discipleship and Ministry."

25. See Peeler, "Junia/Joanna," 273–85.

farm, God's building" (1 Cor. 3:9). The apostolic vocation itself generates the strenuous toil of founding and consolidating Christian communities (1 Thess. 2:9); at one point Paul describes Timothy as "slaving for the gospel" along-side him (*syn emoi edouleusen eis to euangelion*, Phil. 2:22). Timothy and the Pauline women share with Paul in this labor for the gospel, participating fully in mission and ministry.

Women who are active in ministry are also found in other letters in the Pauline corpus. In Philippians, Euodia and Syntyche are described as "co-workers" of Paul whose capacity to cooperate despite differences of opinion is essential for the church's mission in that place (Phil. 4:2–3). He treats the women no differently from male leaders. Indeed, it is likely that they are among the "bishops and deacons" (*syn episkopois kai diakonois*) indicated at the beginning of the letter (1:1b), whom Paul wishes in particular to ad-dress. If the women are leaders of house churches or evangelists and in some kind of dispute, Paul is seeking to avoid a situation of dissension or rivalry among different leaders, as he has done in Corinth (1 Cor. 1:12–13).[26] Once more, Paul assumes the legitimacy of female leadership.

Other women may also be the heads of house churches. The members of Chloe's household have reported to Paul on the problems in Corinth and were most likely sent by Chloe herself in her capacity as head of household (1 Cor. 1:11). Nympha in Colossians, who is engaged in mission and min-istry with others, is explicitly named as the leader of a house church (Col. 4:15).[27] The Letter to Philemon is addressed not only to Philemon but also to Apphia, whom Paul addresses as "our sister" and who is most likely a leader of the church alongside Philemon and Archippus (Philem. 2). Phoebe is the only other woman addressed as "sister," paralleling "brother," which is used of Timothy and other male fellow workers of Paul.[28] Eunice and Lois, the mother and grandmother of Timothy, are not leaders as such, but they are commended for sharing their faith with Timothy, his faith being the basis of the leadership to which Paul appeals (2 Tim. 1:5).

Claudia is of some interest because of speculation over her identity (2 Tim. 4:21). Her name is Roman and is usually associated with aristocratic women living in Rome. It may be that she is linked to both Pudens and Linus, who are named before her in 2 Timothy, all three being leaders in the church.[29] In the traditional list Linus succeeds the apostle Peter as head of the Christian community in Rome and may have been the son of Pudens and Claudia. She

---

26. Marshall, *Epistle to the Philippians*, 108–11.
27. On Thekla, who is not mentioned in the New Testament, see Cartlidge, "Thekla," 1.
28. So Cotter, "Women's Authority Roles in Paul's Churches," 351.
29. Fee, *1 and 2 Timothy, Titus*, 302.

may even be the Claudia Rufina who is praised by the Roman poet Martial, a princess from Briton living in Rome in the late first century CE.[30] Either way, her name suggests a remarkable but hidden story of an upper-class woman who has given up much in terms of worldly power and influence to follow Jesus and become a Christian leader. She is portrayed as a faithful supporter of Paul within the Roman community of believers, in a context when many others have apparently deserted him. Here is another Joanna/Junia who has given up much for the faith.

CHART OF WOMEN WORKERS IN THE PAULINE CORPUS

NAME	TEXT	DESCRIPTION
Phoebe	Rom. 16:1–2	Letter-bearer; deacon, benefactor; Corinth
Priscilla/Prisca	Rom. 16:3–5; 1 Cor. 16:19; 2 Tim. 4:19	Friend and missioner with Paul; worked with him; ministered in Ephesus
Mary	Rom. 16:6	Hard worker in gospel; nothing else known
Junia	Rom. 16:7	Outstanding apostle; eyewitness of Jesus's ministry?
Tryphaena	Rom. 16:12	Worker "in the Lord"; probably sister of Tryphosa
Tryphosa	Rom. 16:12	Worker "in the Lord"; probably sister of Tryphaena
Persis	Rom. 16:12	Worker "in the Lord"; described as "beloved"
Rufus's mother	Rom. 16:13	Has acted as spiritual mother also to Paul
Julia	Rom. 16:15	Unknown
Nereus's sister	Rom. 16:15	Unknown
Chloe	1 Cor. 1:10–11	Informal report to Paul; head of house church?
Euodia	Phil. 4:2	Dispute with Syntyche; coleader of church (bishop or deacon?)
Syntyche	Phil. 4:2	Dispute with Euodia; coleader of church (bishop or deacon?)
Nympha	Col. 4:15	Probably leader of church in her house
Apphia	Philem. 1–2	Letter addressed to "our sister"; coleader of house church?
Claudia	2 Tim. 4:21	Leader in church in Rome; possibilities for identity?
Lois	2 Tim. 1:5	Timothy's grandmother; commended for teaching him faith
Eunice	2 Tim. 1:5	Timothy's mother; commended for teaching him faith

The list of women associated with Paul in his ministry gives immediate pause to the accusation of misogyny. The argument is strengthened when we take seriously the leading roles these women play within the church in Corinth, Rome, Ephesus, and elsewhere. Paul shows no quarrel with the titles given to women in leadership—"deacon," "benefactor," "apostle"—but, on the

---

30. See Vandrei, "Claudia Rufina," 61–62, who shows how the legend of Claudia, the first Christian, serves the claim that Christianity reached the British Isles long before the Roman Church evangelized it.

contrary, commends them in the highest terms. The evidence indicates that Paul has no problem with women's ministry. Other texts should be read in the light of Romans 16 and other signals of women's leadership. It is hard to imagine how these women can exercise ministry if they are required to keep silent and remain submissive within the Christian assembly.

Male Language, Female Imagery

Before examining other texts about women, we need to ask about the language and imagery of the Pauline Epistles, which, even when their intention is patently inclusive, is often androcentric—male oriented, presupposing the secreted presence of women within masculine forms. This linguistic phenomenon is part of a culture where maleness is normative and where males can represent females, though grammatically it does not carry the same weight as it does in English. Not so long ago, English used terms such as "man" and "men" to comprise women as well as men and used "brethren" to indicate sisters as well as brothers.

This convention is particularly striking with the use of the noun *adelphoi*, which expresses the Pauline understanding of the family. Here the Christian community is welded together through a sense of "covenant kinship that is based not on blood or marital ties but . . . on a symbolic sense of mutuality and communion," which constitutes the family of God and is given "theological priority over the natural family."[31] The notion of the fictive family occurs in a world where the individual is embedded in her or his biological family, which confers status, occupation, values, religion, and selfhood. From that perspective the idea of the church as family is radical, binding human beings to one another in Christ beyond biological kinship. This profound relationship begins and ends in the nature of God and the revelation in Christ.

In Greek, there is almost no difference between the word for "brother" (*adelphos*) and the word for "sister" (*adelphē*); only the ending differs, while the stem, *adelph-*, stays the same. While *adelphos* and *adelphē* can be used together in the singular form (e.g., Mark 3:35), the situation changes where the plural is needed, with *adelphoi* (the masculine plural) often being sufficient, as it is at Mark 3:33–34. For that reason, as we have seen in previous chapters, most modern translations use "brothers and sisters" to translate Paul's language, not in order to make an ideological point but to

---

31. This description reflects 1 John but is equally true of the Pauline Letters. See also Aasgaard, "*My Beloved Brothers and Sisters!*," especially 7–8.

translate more accurately.[32] If a text obviously means male siblings only, then "brothers" is the correct translation; if females are included in the Pauline framework, "brothers and sisters" is nearer the intentionality of the text. In contemporary English, "brothers" no longer includes female siblings as well as male. Where *adelphoi* is found in the Pauline corpus, we should translate it inclusively.

There is a similar situation with other examples of androcentric language. Paul speaks of Christians as, literally, "sons of God" (*huioi tou theou*; e.g., Rom. 8:14). He also speaks of our "adoption" as God's children, a word that means literally "sonship" (*huiothesia*, 8:15) and connects directly to Jesus's identity as Son: "God having sent his own Son [*ton heautou huion*]" (8:3; Gal. 4:4–6). It could be argued that the male language here is not fully inclusive, as Paul goes on to speak of Christians as "heirs" (*klēronomoi*) of Christ (Rom. 8:17) in a context in which women could not generally inherit. The radical nature of this message is that women are counted among the heirs of Christ and not excluded by virtue of their gender. This is signaled by the shift from "sons" to "children" (*tekna*, 8:16–17). The ancient world varied in customs, and elite Roman women could inherit to a certain extent. Either way, this is a further example of where "sons" is used in an inclusive way, within a specific cultural context that assumes the company of daughters.[33]

Such usage is no longer current in contemporary English and is only ever found in some parts of the church, though not in common parlance. To translate *adelphoi* as "brothers," as a number of translations still do (e.g., the ESV), has the effect today of doubly disadvantaging women and rendering them even less visible. Ancient women saw themselves encompassed in this terminology; modern women do not. Cultural context needs to be taken into account. As we saw with the Gospels, it is important for us, in our imaginative retelling of the early church and of the language addressed as much to us today as to past readers, that we envisage the presence of women alongside men as sisters and daughters in their own right. Women have firm grounds for claiming their rightful place within the Pauline writings.

In addition to language, we need also to consider feminine imagery that is found, somewhat unexpectedly, in Paul's writings. Paul uses maternal images to describe his own apostolic ministry and mission, images that "are a vital

32. On the issue of inclusive language in general, see Haddad, "What Language Shall We Use?," 3–7.

33. See especially Corley, "Women's Inheritance Rights," 98–121. Corley sees the language as ultimately inclusive but involving women in the further step of having to envisage themselves as male. See also Aasgaard, who argues that Paul works with clusters of familial metaphors rather than one overarching "family" (*"My Beloved Brothers and Sisters!,"* especially 118–36, 306–14).

part of communicating what the apostolic task involves."[34] The imagery functions metaphorically to outline central aspects of Paul's theology, portraying his apostolic ministry in terms of pregnancy, giving birth, and nursing children. According to Gaventa, Paul presents himself in 1 Thessalonians as both an infant and a nurse in the same verse (1 Thess. 2:7)—and later as a father with his children (2:11). This unusual metaphorical combination of infant and nurse portrays the apostle as "childlike, in contrast to the charlatan," and equally as "the responsible adult . . . the nurse who tends her charges with care and affection."[35] To the Corinthians Paul portrays himself in vivid color as a nursing mother, who knows how and when to feed her infants with milk and solids (1 Cor. 3:1–3a).[36]

The apostle elsewhere describes himself as a woman in labor (Gal. 4:19), indicating his own struggle with the Galatian community and their theology. Ironically, he does not give birth to them directly as their mother but rather gives birth to Christ in them; he uses the maternal metaphor without driving it to its logical conclusion, turning instead to the apocalyptic image of Christ as the goal of creation.[37] This parallels the groaning of creation in labor (Rom. 8:22)—though again, it is not creation that will produce new life, any more than Paul can, but rather God working in and through Christ.[38]

By use of this rich, maternal imagery, Paul effects two things. On the one hand, he underlines the symbolism of the people of God as family, closely related to each other in Christ. On the other hand, far from colonizing female experience, Paul shows his sensitivity to the world of women in a countercultural way. He is prepared to lose honor and esteem in the eyes of his world, revolutionizing cultural values with his conviction that power is revealed not in domination but in vulnerability. In this sense, his use of such imagery "compromises his own standing as a 'real man.'" This ability on his part arises from his preaching of the cross (1 Cor. 1:18–2:5), "his proclamation of the crucified Jesus, who is no more a 'real man' by the world's standards than is a nursing Paul."[39]

Two other Old Testament figures, Sarah and Hagar, are used in Galatians allegorically to contrast the freedom and slavery of Paul's message. The apostle is arguing passionately for the freedom of the gospel as against

34. Gaventa, *Our Mother Saint Paul*, 7.

35. Gaventa, *Our Mother Saint Paul*, 27, reading "infants" instead of "gentle" at 2:7 (see Metzger, *Textual Commentary*, 561–62).

36. Gaventa, *Our Mother Saint Paul*, 41–50.

37. For an overview of Paul's apocalyptic thinking, which lies at the center of his theology, see M. Gorman, *Reading Paul*, especially 57–64.

38. Gaventa, *Our Mother Saint Paul*, 29–39, 51–62.

39. Gaventa, *Our Mother Saint Paul*, 50.

the slavery of the law, into which he sees the Galatian Christians falling. The sons of the two wives of Abraham represent for Paul the descendants of a free woman on the one hand and a slave woman on the other (Gen. 21:1–21). Paul is not speaking literally here, as Ishmael is not a slave nor are his descendants enslaved. However, Paul uses typology to draw the contrast between the two mothers, understood symbolically (though Sarah's name is implied rather than given).[40] Paul inverts the usual understanding of these figures in relation to the Jewish people "by placing the origins of the two covenants geographically,"[41] so that Hagar now becomes associated with Mount Sinai and the covenant associated with the Mosaic law, while Sarah symbolizes the freedom and grace that, as Paul argues elsewhere, precedes the giving of the law and points forward to the new covenant in Christ (Rom. 4:1–25). For Elsa Tamez, while Hagar may be the socially marginalized figure in this trope, it is more likely that Sarah is socially marginalized because of her infertility.[42] The imagery tips the scales somewhat toward feminine language for God's people; instead of the more dominant "children of Abraham" (e.g., Gal. 3:29), they are here, in this one context, effectively designated "children of Sarah."

Conclusion

In this initial chapter on Paul and his letters, we have seen something of the way in which he worked alongside women in leadership within the church. The best place to begin any discussion of Paul is with his actual practice and with the women whom he encouraged and supported in mission and who in turn supported him. Romans 16 gives us an impressive list of these women and their mutual and cordial relationships with him. In particular, Phoebe stands out as the bearer, and also possible interpreter, of the Letter to the Romans, Paul's greatest writing and one of the finest texts in the New Testament. Already what we have seen casts serious doubt on the accusation of Pauline misogyny. From here, however, we turn to examine some of the key texts within the Pauline corpus, some of them distinctly problematic.

---

40. Tamez, "Hagar and Sarah," 267–68.
41. Tamez, "Hagar and Sarah," 268.
42. For a different feminist reading, see Sheila Briggs, who argues that the text endorses the inequality of slavery and is sectarian ("Galatians," 223–25).

Chapter Six

Paul's Letters
Key Texts

IN THE LAST CHAPTER, we saw the significant role played by women in the Pauline churches and the apostle's support of their ministry, along with his awareness of their gifts for mission and evangelism. From that general view of Pauline practice, this chapter looks briefly at some texts within the Pauline world that raise serious questions around the leadership of women. More recent study of these texts has suggested new ways of interpreting Paul and his heirs that reread him in the light of fresh knowledge. In this short overview of some contentious texts, we need to retain awareness of the authorship dispute over the Pauline corpus, which is itself an interpretive conclusion from the complexity of these writings.

Baptism into Christ (Gal. 3:26–29)

The most famous and widely quoted passage relating to women's place in the church occurs in Galatians 3, coming from the hand of Paul himself—a text that challenges ancient values, where "ethnic background, economic standing, and gender were three of the major barometers for social standing and privilege":[1] "For you are all sons and daughters [literally, "sons"] of God through faith in Christ Jesus. For as many of you as were baptized into

---

1. Payne, *Man and Woman*, 57.

Christ have put on Christ [as a garment]. There is no longer Jew or Greek [i.e., gentile], there is no longer slave or free, there is no longer male and female; for you are all one in Christ Jesus. If you are of Christ [i.e., belong to Christ], then you are seed of Abraham, heirs according to the promise" (Gal. 3:26–29). The immediate setting is a discussion of the law and its limitations (3:16–18), which is centered on the core question of "who exactly constitutes the children, the seed (*sperma*) of Abraham?"[2] There is no absolute distinction between law and grace, because the law has its God-ordained place (3:19–22), but salvation depends on the divine promise given to Abraham in the covenant and not on his keeping of the law.[3] This promise is fulfilled in Christ, whose obedience takes him to the cross and to whom Christians are united in baptism (3:22).

In the verses immediately preceding, Paul uses the image of the *paidagōgos*, the slave who takes children to and from school in the Roman-Hellenistic world and is responsible for their safety and good behavior (3:23–25).[4] The role is symbolic of the law and its limited power and restrictions, whereas the coming of Christ brings true freedom. There is a new selfhood in belonging to Christ, a new status as adult children of God, which is symbolized above all in baptism. It is baptism that makes us children of God, and it is baptism through which we also become children of Abraham. For Paul, our new status as the free children of God depends on our entry into Christ and our taking on his identity as Son. In this way we become heirs of the divine promise of salvation, given first to Abraham.[5]

The key matter in Paul's theology lies in the first pairing, that of Jew and gentile, particularly concerning circumcision, which the apostle regards as no longer needful for entry into the people of God. Paul is exercised throughout Galatians at what he sees as the community's reversion to the Jewish ritual law, its denial of its own heritage of freedom in Christ. His chief concern is with the inclusion of the gentiles as gentiles, so that they do not have to become Jews first. The Christian gospel, for him, involves by definition "a distinctiveness and diversity of the people of God."[6] If Paul is quoting from a baptismal liturgy that includes all three categories,[7] his emphasis on the first group has significant implications also for gentile women. Baptism is inclusive

---

2. Wright, *Paul and the Faithfulness of God*, 2:2035; on Gal. 3 and the theological argument that moves toward 3:29 as its conclusion, see 2:2034–68.

3. On the role of the law in relation to the greater covenant and promise, see Cousar, *Reading Galatians*, 62–67.

4. See Young, "Figure of the *Paidagōgos*," 80–86.

5. B. Byrne, *Paul and the Christian Woman*, 1–14.

6. Westfall, *Paul and Gender*, 171.

7. Loader, *New Testament on Sexuality*, 390–91.

of gender, whereas circumcision is not; baptism confers a new freedom and belonging for Christian women within the community. The connection to the third group is thus vital, if indirect. The same may be said for slaves, many of whom are women. Paul understands baptism in a symbolic way as bestowing a new freedom that is as pertinent for women as for men; it is "a powerful voice articulating God's new creation, a creation that liberates both women and men from their worlds of achievement and identity."[8]

At the same time it is ironic that this text, which has been at the root of contemporary feminism's call for female leadership and ordination, appears in a letter that is concerned with a male procedure (circumcision) and that mentions no women, apart from the name of Hagar (4:21–5:1).[9] Gaventa, who points this out, unpacks the theology of Galatians, with its sense of God's apocalyptic entry into the world and the radical overturning of all the measures of human identity. Paul's concern is with "the world-obliterating character of the gospel,"[10] which has profound ramifications for women, challenging the destructive gender values under which they struggle: "Like the other pairs in this verse, 'male and female' functions as a metonym for places in which we live, the spheres in which we name ourselves and find our identity. Those who are 'in Christ' cannot be in the identity business of being first of all female or male."[11] In this sense, Gaventa argues, Galatians 3:28 is not fundamentally a political manifesto for equality—the full humanity of women as coequal with men—but rather for the new identity in Christ that is given to us by grace and that outplays and outmaneuvers every other attempt at self- and other-definition, whether patriarchal or not. It does undermine patriarchy, just as it undermines any other privileging of one group over another, but it does so in a way that reaches down to the deepest levels of our need of, and utter dependence on, Christ: "In an act of new creation, God invades our several worlds of meaning and claims us as part of Christ's own body."[12] The challenge is not only to patriarchy, racism, colonialism, and other forms of oppression and discrimination but also to any false and superficial meaning we endeavor to place on our own lives and those of others outside our fundamental identity in Christ—an identity that is gained not by our own efforts or achievements but by grace.[13]

8. Gaventa, *Our Mother Saint Paul*, 74.
9. See Gaventa, "Galatians," 267–78; Gaventa, *Our Mother Saint Paul*, 63–66.
10. Gaventa, "Galatians," 272.
11. Gaventa, "Galatians," 275.
12. Gaventa, "Galatians," 277.
13. Against a feminist reading of this text, cf. Wayne A. Grudem, who argues it declares that all Christians are united but do not necessarily play the same roles (*Evangelical Feminism*, 521–29).

It is noteworthy that a similar set of pairings is found in 1 Corinthians but this time without reference to male and female: "For in one Spirit we were also all baptized into one body, whether Jews or Greeks, whether slaves or free people, and we all were caused to drink of one Spirit" (1 Cor. 12:13). Paul is speaking of the oneness of the body of Christ, formed first in baptism. Why then the exclusion of gender? It is possible, given his disapproval of sexual abstinence in marriage (7:2–5), that he is reluctant to add a category that might encourage some in the community to think marriage is now irrelevant.[14] Or he may think it complicates the core metaphor of the body, which dominates the passage.[15] The other two categories include women, as noted with Galatians—many of whom are gentiles and/or slaves. In this context, for Paul, "the identity of the individual is now relative to the type of gift that the Spirit has distributed rather than to ethnicity, social status, or gender."[16]

Colossians confirms a similar vision, though in a less stylized form, that there is "not Greek or Jew, circumcision and uncircumcision, barbarian, Scythian, slave, free, but Christ is all things and in all people" (Col. 3:11). Here again, there is not an explicit reference to male and female but a discussion of the racial divide that separates one human being from another, emphasizing that "national and cultural differences and inequalities are overcome in the new humanity of Christ."[17] Though being a Jew and a male, and from a specific socioeconomic class and geographical region, Jesus embraces all human beings through the resurrection, beyond any human categories. Baptism, therefore, signifies a "new creation" (2 Cor. 5:17) as baptismal candidates enter into Christ's identity, where they embark on a journey to transformation.

Keeping this in mind makes sense of our passage from Galatians. Baptism means entry into a new, eschatological order of things through faith, an order of freedom and goodness brought into effect through Christ's death and resurrection. It is not simply a ritual act but, being grounded in faith, is symbolic of the pattern of Christian living, where believers daily die to the old order of things and rise to the new (Rom. 6:3–4). The new identity no longer depends on the three core divisional hierarchies and demarcations of race, class, and gender: they are not lost but relativized as signs of the old age rather than the new age.[18] There is a mutuality of entry into Christ that, in a real sense, restores the foundational character of women and men as mutually created in the divine image. The slight difference in wording makes the

---

14. Hays, "Paul on the Relation," 139–40.
15. Loader, *New Testament on Sexuality*, 392–94.
16. Westfall, *Paul and Gender*, 235.
17. Schüssler Fiorenza, *In Memory of Her*, 252.
18. Giles, *What the Bible Actually Teaches on Women*, 110–12.

point: not "male *or* female," as with the other two distinctions, but "male *and* female," reflecting the Genesis text as it appears in the Septuagint, the Greek translation of the Old Testament (*arsen kai thēly*, Gal. 3:28; Gen. 1:27 LXX). Jesus's identity is a cosmic one in Pauline thought; it is as definitive for, and as inclusive of, gentiles, females, and slaves as it is of Jews, males, and free people. This affinity generates a fundamental solidarity between all who are in Christ, not because they are like-minded in the human sense but because they share a common kinship in Christ.

Women and Veils (1 Cor. 11:2–16)

Given the contours of the Galatians text, and its extraordinary potential for social and personal transformation, we turn to other, more difficult and ambiguous passages within the Pauline corpus. One such example is 1 Corinthians 11, which in general concerns matters of worship and practices of which Paul disapproves; it moves from the lesser (women's dress styles in worship, 11:2–16) to the greater (abuses at the Lord's Supper, 11:17–34). The passage is generally recognized as complex in its logic and unclear about the cultural practices lying behind it:[19]

> I want you to understand that the head of every man is Christ, and the head of a woman is the man, and the head of Christ is God. Every man praying or prophesying having something on his head shames his own head. And every woman praying or prophesying with uncovered head shames her own head; it is one and the same as being shaved. For if a woman is uncovered, then let her also cut her hair short; and if it is shameful for a woman to have short hair or to have it shaved off, let her be covered. For a man ought not to have his head covered, being the glory and image of God; but woman is the glory of man. For man is not from woman but woman from man. For man also was not created from woman but woman from man. For this reason the woman ought to have authority on her head on account of the angels. Except that neither is woman without man nor man without woman in the Lord; just as woman is from man, so also man is through woman; and all things are from God. Judge for yourselves: Is it appropriate for a woman to pray to God uncovered? Does not nature itself teach us that for a man to wear his hair long is dishonorable for him, but if a woman has long hair it is a glory to her? For long hair is given her as a covering. If anyone wants to be argumentative, we have no such custom, nor have the churches of God. (1 Cor. 11:3–16)

19. See Fee, *First Epistle to the Corinthians*, 542–50. According to Richard Hays, "It is impossible to give a fully confident interpretation of the passage" (*First Corinthians*, 183).

This passage has three statements about women and men and their inter-relationship, with implications for conduct in worship particularly on the part of women; the first two are the most difficult and contentious. The main issue at stake is that of head coverings for women. Paul speaks of long hair as a woman's "glory," as against the custom of men wearing their hair short (11:14–15). If this is indeed the issue being discussed,[20] Paul is pointing to the appropriateness of women's hair being long and covered, as well as tied up and not loosely flowing over their shoulders. Long hair for him signifies women's femininity, while the hairstyle and head covering may indicate control of their sexuality, acknowledgment of their gender difference, or protection from the male, lascivious gaze.[21]

In the first statement (11:3) Paul speaks of a descending or extending pattern between God, Christ, man, and woman (although *gynaikes* can mean "women" or "wives," depending on the context, just as *andres* can mean "men" or "husbands"). Each relates to the succeeding one as *kephalē*, meaning "head," which can signify either authority or source. On this point, commentators are divided, some arguing for "source" and others for "head" in the sense of authority (both meanings are also present in English). Those who opt for "source" argue that Paul's meaning is not one of subordination but rather of origin, recalling the second creation account, where Eve is created from Adam. Those who see some notion of headship argue that it is part of the order of creation or that it indicates patriarchal assumptions on Paul's part. Both sides point to examples in Greek literature that support their interpretations.

What is at least clear is that Paul is using *kephalē* metaphorically because of its connection to the issue of veils, so it is best to retain the image in translation—however we might understand it. It may even be, as Anthony Thiselton suggests, that the term is ambiguous in Paul and can be used with either meaning.[22] This makes it particularly difficult to discern what Paul is actually saying in his use of the metaphor. In the ancient world, all women were under the *kephalē* of a man (husband, father, brother), which mostly included authority. Even if "source" is the dominant meaning here, it still implies at least a sense of dependence,[23] whether or not it includes submission.

---

20. By contrast, some argue that the issue is hair length and hair style rather than veils or head coverings; e.g., Payne, *Man and Woman*, 92–112.

21. Thiselton, *First Epistle to the Corinthians*, 823–33. George Montague sees the absence of a veil as signaling "sexual availability" within the culture (*First Corinthians*, 189).

22. Thiselton, *First Epistle to the Corinthians*, 812–23.

23. Westfall, *Paul and Gender*, 80–91.

In the second statement (1 Cor. 11:7–9), Paul retains a similar pattern but changes the metaphor from *kephalē* to *doxa* (glory) to outline the interrelationship of man and woman (or husband and wife). These verses are dependent on the creation narrative, where Eve is formed as Adam's partner (Gen. 2:4–25). Part of the ambiguity of woman/wife and man/husband is that Adam and Eve are both. For some, this represents a patriarchal ordering of creation in which Eve is the image of God not directly (in contrast to Gen. 1:27) but only indirectly via Adam—the woman/wife being a step further away from God and Christ than the man/husband. For Pheme Perkins, for example, Paul is confirming the patriarchal pattern here for marriage and other male-female relationships by constructing a "hierarchical scheme" that represents an "asymmetry" between men and women and confirms male preeminence and even authority.[24]

By contrast, Cynthia Long Westfall offers an alternative reading, arguing that women bear an additional identity that gives them no less eminence than men: "If every man is the glory of God in the pattern of Adam, then . . . woman in the pattern of Eve is the 'glory of the glory.'" In Long's account, this is a surplus feature of woman's identity, not a reduction of it: "It is something more, or something in addition, that is included in her multiple identity rather than something less, secondary, or missing."[25] Paul has an intricate understanding of creation, she argues, where Eve is both the image of God alongside Adam (Gen. 1:26–27) and also the glory of Adam because of being created from him (2:21–22). For Westfall, that additional glory lies in her desirability on account of her hair, which, in a liturgical setting, needs to be covered.[26]

Before moving on to the third statement, we need to pause to consider 1 Corinthians 11:10, which is a key verse. The central question we are asking is whether these verses in the first two parallel statements imply a level of submission for women/wives or are simply an acknowledgment of the secondary order of their creation and the gift and companionship they bring to men/husbands, as Eve does to Adam. Yet, although we cannot rule out the possibility that Paul sees some level of wifely obedience as inevitable—perhaps as reflecting the pattern of the old age—it does not make any serious difference to women's authority and leadership in the church. The point of 11:10 is all too easily bypassed or ignored, yet it is integral to the passage and to the

---

24. Perkins, *First Corinthians*, 138, 140.
25. Westfall, *Paul and Gender*, 65–66. Westfall also notes the narrative in 1 Esd. 4:14–17, where women are said to bring glory to men and are therefore more powerful, not less (*Paul and Gender*, 66–67).
26. See the full discussion in Westfall, *Paul and Gender*, 61–105.

possibilities it opens for women's ministry. Some years ago, Morna Hooker pointed out, over against more traditional readings, that nowhere in Greek does the word that is translated "authority" (*exousia*) mean the authority under which a person acts; it always refers to the person's own authority in acting.[27] This means that, however we might interpret the configurations around *kephalē* and *doxa*, their only implication is the need for covering over a woman's head when she is engaged in leading worship. This is a point that cannot be lost in the debate over the significance of these two words. With this addition to her dress, she has indeed her own authority.

Prophecy, moreover, holds a high place in the gifts given by the Spirit to the church (see 1 Cor. 12:28–29). It is close to what we would consider preaching or teaching today: "The public proclamation of gospel truth as applied contextually and pastorally to the hearers. . . . [It] may include *applied theological teaching, encouragement, and exhortation to build the church.*"[28] Whatever we make of these ambiguous verses, Paul unequivocally recognizes the right of women to play a leading role in the assembly, though their veiled head may signify their derivative place in the order of creation (noting that Adam's existence is also derivative: from the earth). Thus the woman's *kephalē*, when appropriately veiled, symbolizes both her dependence of origin and, more importantly, her authority to proclaim God's word in the assembly.[29]

The third statement occurs at 1 Corinthians 11:11–12 and is rather different from the first two. In verse 11, the apostle seems to make an about-face to assert the mutual interdependence of woman and man in the new order of things. The telling phrase "in the Lord" (*en kyriō*) indicates that Paul has in mind the new age, which relativizes the accepted order of male-female relations. Along with verse 12, verse 11 confirms between men and women a paradoxical "mutuality in origin,"[30] which moves in counterpoint to Paul's previous two statements. Now it is apparent that while women are in one sense dependent on men as their origin of existence, in another sense men are dependent on women for their very lives. Here Paul perhaps has in mind the relationship between mother and son, another aspect of the male-female relationship.

When we take all three assertions together, however tangled they may seem, Paul in the end is confirming a new order, which is already operative in the authority women have to pray and prophesy in the assembly. In the

---

27. Hooker, "Authority on Her Head," 410–16; see Montague, *First Corinthians*, 187.

28. Thiselton, *First Epistle to the Corinthians*, 826 (italics original).

29. On the puzzling reference to the angels and the possible range of meanings, see Perkins, *First Corinthians*, 139–40. The most likely explanation is that angels function as the guardians of liturgical order; see Fitzmyer, *First Corinthians*, 417–19.

30. Westfall, *Paul and Gender*, 72.

end, he sees women and men as both differentiated by virtue of creation yet also interdependent in the new order, their ministries jointly needed for the building up of the church.[31] At the same time, he insists on the acknowledgment of women's status in creation through the wearing of the veil, perhaps wishing to confirm their gender identity or else to avoid misunderstanding in the pagan world.[32] He may seem to some readers to give with one hand and take with the other, but what he gives far outweighs what he takes in relation to women's ministry.

It may be that Paul in this whole passage is attempting to restrict the Corinthian women prophets because they have grasped hold of their new freedom in Christ—in terms of Galatians 3:28—to a degree that Paul finds disturbing: "The Corinthians woman prophet has experienced a surge of status in wisdom, power, and honor and has reshaped her ethnic identity, caste, and gender in ways that give her more scope."[33] Paul does not deny women this freedom, but as always (and particularly with the Corinthians), freedom is relative to other issues, such as love and concern for the whole community. Paul sees the abandonment of the veil as a hindrance to the church's well-being. Whatever we make of the first two statements, they do not inhibit women's ministry except in the matter of dress. Furthermore, it is the third statement that is most radical, because it is "in the Lord" from which the new creation comes, through Jesus's death and resurrection.

Contradiction? (1 Cor. 14:34–36)

Paul's teaching on women's ministry in 1 Corinthians 11 seems contradicted by a later passage in the same letter that seems to assert the opposite, forbidding women's voices to be heard in the assembly (14:34–35): "[As in all the churches of the saints] let the women in the churches be silent; for it is not fitting for them to speak, but let them submit, just as also the law says. But if they want to learn anything, let them at home ask their own men; for it is shameful for a woman to speak in church."

It is possible that the words immediately preceding "let the women in the churches be silent"—"as in all the churches of the saints"—are part of the

31. For the view that 11:4–5, 7–10 represents the Corinthian view, while 11:2–3, 6, 11–16 is Paul's riposte to correct the Corinthians, cf. Peppiatt, *Rediscovering Scripture's Vision*, 66–68.

32. Hays, however, sees the veil as women's acknowledgment of their inferiority in relation to men (*First Corinthians*, 183–84).

33. Wire, *Corinthian Women Prophets*, 181–88. Wire believes that "Paul unquestionably sees himself having lost status" (65, 67), but that seems an exegetical leap from what the text says or implies.

same sentence, implying that the command for women's silence is a universal mandate for the church. But it makes better sense in the preceding sentence, where it bolsters the main point of the chapter: "God is not a God of chaos but of peace, as in all the churches of the saints" (14:33). The fundamental concern is that of order versus disorder and the pacific and decorous nature of Christian worship and community.

This injunction to silence can be read in a number of ways. Some argue that the three verses do not belong but were added later to the text of 1 Corinthians, as demonstrated by their somewhat uneasy position within the textual tradition, some manuscripts placing them later in the same chapter. Not only might the external evidence (the manuscripts) suggest a post-Pauline addition, but the internal evidence could point to an interpolation; the flow of the argument seems less confusing without these verses, which, in any case, stand in contradiction to Paul's teaching in 1 Corinthians 11.[34] While this is possible, the manuscript evidence is not strong.

Others accept the verses as integral to the text, arguing that they are a quotation from the Corinthian letter to Paul or a summary of the Corinthian position in which they are arguing for the silencing of women in the assembly.[35] This is a literary feature of 1 Corinthians where Paul addresses specific topics raised by the Corinthians in their prior letter to him; for instance, he quotes them as saying, "It is good for a man not to touch a woman" (1 Cor. 7:1) or "We know that all have knowledge" (8:1). If this is another such example, the apostle would again be endeavoring to qualify or refute the Corinthian view and support the authority of women to speak and prophesy in the assembly. In that case, there would be no contradiction with chapter 11. Yet there is no literary indication of a Corinthian quotation, as there is in other examples.[36]

Both are possible responses to a difficult injunction. Yet it is equally possible, and the simplest explanation, that the words are authentically Pauline and that the apostle is criticizing certain types of speech within the assembly. The injunction to silence in the same section is addressed equally to those who would speak in tongues where there is no interpreter present (14:28) and to prophets who all want to speak at the same time (14:30). In the case of the women, it may be that because they are far less educated and live a more secluded life than their menfolk, they do not understand the level of

34. See especially Fee, *First Epistle to the Corinthians*, 789–92.

35. See Peppiatt, *Rediscovering Scripture's Vision*, 76. See also R. Collins, *First Corinthians*, 513–17, 521–22.

36. The quotations in 1 Cor. 7:1 and 8:1 are both preceded by the words, "Now concerning" (*peri de*), indicating that Paul is addressing an explicit concern of the Corinthians in their prior letter to him.

conversation and consequently talk or question among themselves during worship. The instruction to learn at home from their men would make sense if they require an understanding of something that is beyond their education, including beyond their knowledge of Greek.[37] If, for example, they are also responsible for serving the communal meal, conversation among them is likely.[38] Or it may be that women are interrogating their menfolk (husbands, fathers, brothers, sons) in front of others, bringing shame on them according to the values of the ancient world.[39] In either case, it is not prophetic or prayerful talk that is discouraged in these speech ethics but rather conversation or questioning that disrupts the good order of the Spirit's utterances.[40]

What is clear is that if the verses are genuinely Pauline, some level of contextual practice is at stake, a practice that is local and now lost to us. In all cases throughout the chapter, Paul is addressing himself to those who might disturb the decorum and dignity of worship. It is already clear from the previous passage that female prophets (whether married or unmarried) have the right to speak in the assembly and not remain silent. Taking the context into account makes it clear that there need be no contradiction between the two texts in 1 Corinthians.

Silent or Quiet? (1 Tim. 2:11–15)

A passage similar to this, with its apparent injunction to silence, is located in one of the later letters within the Pauline collection. This passage from 1 Timothy is a key text in the question of women's leadership in the church, responsible for providing "a lens or exegetical grid through which all other Scripture is applied to women";[41] almost every word has been disputed in recent years. Here is the NRSV's translation: "Let a woman learn in silence with full submission. I permit no woman to teach or to have authority over a man; she is to keep silent. For Adam was formed first, then Eve; and Adam was not deceived, but the woman was deceived and became a transgressor. Yet she will be saved through childbearing, provided they continue in faith and love and holiness, with modesty." The overarching concern of the letter to Timothy

37. See Bailey, *Paul through Mediterranean Eyes*, 412–16.

38. Westfall makes this point in relation to the home context of worship as opposed to a more formal gathering (*Paul and Gender*, 230–33).

39. So Thiselton, *First Epistle to the Corinthians*, 1131, 1150–62.

40. Montague sees this as reference to Paul's wish to preserve marital relationship so that wives are instructed to refrain from questioning and thus embarrassing their husbands in public (*First Corinthians*, 255–57).

41. Westfall, *Paul and Gender*, 279.

is that of asserting sound over against false teaching (1:3–4; 6:3–4), guarding the mystery of faith (3:9, 16), and confirming its fruitfulness in godly living and in the proper ordering of the church. Within that framework, instructions are given on a number of levels to ensure the passing on of proper teaching to the Christian community in Ephesus. The passage immediately follows instructions for men to pray together without contention (2:8) and for women to dress appropriately, clothing themselves above all in "good works" (2:9–10).

Those who argue that only seven letters are the direct product of Paul do not necessarily see the problem of this passage as an acute one. The Pastoral Letters are interpreted as reflecting a later situation in the church in the late first century CE, when Christians felt the need to tone down the revolutionary edge of the gospel on a number of fronts, including that of women's participation in worship.[42] With the receding of hope for the immediate return of Christ, the conviction of having to live for an appreciable time in a world dominated by the Roman Empire took hold of Christian consciousness and caused a softening of its attitudes and behavior, with the result of restrictive implications for women's ministry.[43] It might even be described as a "backlash" against Paul's earlier teaching: "In the name of Paul the letter writer teaches his community that in order to have a place of any value within the church, in order to be 'saved,' women must participate within the structure of the patriarchal household."[44] Deborah Krause, who rejects Pauline authorship, sees the letter's baleful posthistory resulting in "the limitation of women's political power throughout Christendom and the perpetuation and legitimation of the hatred of women in the guise of maintaining the true church and the proclamation of the gospel."[45]

If Paul wrote 1 Timothy (with or without the help of a secretary or colleagues), the immediate question is that of the consistency of his teaching across the corpus of his letters. Reactionary scholarship asserts that this text is a teaching for all time, excluding women from leadership and teaching authority.[46] Luke Timothy Johnson, who accepts Pauline authorship of the letter, takes a different view and struggles with its meaning for the contemporary world. His hermeneutical solution is to recognize the contextual nature of Paul's teaching and to question whether it is normative, given the harm that such teaching has inflicted. He speaks instead of the need "to engage the

42. So Schüssler Fiorenza, *In Memory of Her*, 245–84, 288–91.
43. This assumption may explain the NRSV's translation, which shows no awareness of interpretations of the passage other than the traditional one.
44. Krause, *1 Timothy*, 64.
45. Krause, *1 Timothy*, 50.
46. See, e.g., Grudem, *Evangelical Feminism*, 89–101, 371–440.

words of Paul in a dialectical process of criticism within the public discourse of the church."[47]

Whether this letter was written by Paul himself or by his disciples after his death makes little difference to the fact of its inclusion in the New Testament canon.[48] Difficult texts within the New Testament—regardless of authorship, as we have noted—need to be reexamined circumspectly from within their own context, as far as we can assess it, without assuming that conventional interpretations are right or the only way of reading them. Part of the damage done to women in subsequent history may have arisen as much from the interpretation of these texts as from their original meaning. This passage from 1 Timothy, in particular, contains a number of semantic concerns that affect its meaning, with the potential to challenge traditional readings. The underlying question is whether this text establishes a "stained glass ceiling" above which women in the church cannot rise.[49]

Silence

More traditional exegesis interprets this literally as the instruction that women remain silent during the Christian assembly. Conservative and liberal scholarship agree on this point. Where they disagree is on the issue of the implications for women today. The more liberal approach argues that the letter reflects a later context where, as we have seen, women are now confined to traditional roles and virtues, including silence in the public arena—an instruction that goes against Paul's own teaching and is no longer relevant for the church today.[50] "Complementarian" scholarship draws the same exegetical conclusion but, by contrast, sees the instruction as genuinely Pauline, non-contradictory, and of ongoing relevance for the contemporary community: women are not permitted to speak in public worship but are to be subservient to their (male) pastors and husbands.

An alternative view argues that the appropriate way to translate the Greek word group here is "quietness" rather than "silence," given that 1 Timothy 2:2 also speaks of living a quiet and peaceful life as citizens (*hēsychion, hēsychia*). This view coheres with the general usage of the word group elsewhere. The context suggests conflict within the community around misleading teaching, therefore giving rise to the appeal for peaceable living. Women are called not to keep silent in the church in this translation but rather to be quiet, avoiding

---

47. L. Johnson, *First and Second Letters to Timothy*, 211.
48. See the helpful discussion in Wall and Steele, *1 & 2 Timothy and Titus*, 4–7.
49. Hutson, *First and Second Timothy and Titus*, 72.
50. See, e.g., excursus 3 in R. Collins, *1 & 2 Timothy and Titus*, 72–75.

disputes and false teaching; they are also permitted to learn in a culture that often frowned on education for women.[51]

Submission

The more familiar reading of the noun "submission" asserts that women are to submit (*en pasē hypotagē*) to their male leaders, whether husbands or church authorities. Although the text does not specify it, the assumption is that this is a directive to women to maintain the normal standards of their society and culture, where their role is to submit to male authority. Yet the lack of indirect object need not imply that women are to submit to men.[52] In the context of the epistle's concern with false teaching, the emphasis may well be on the need for quiet submission to the teachings of the faith rather than to male authority figures: "It is a large leap of logic to assume that [Paul] means here that women are to be submissive to men. To learn tranquility with all attentiveness is to learn that tranquility from God through humility. The obedience is to God, not patriarchy."[53] These days we may not use quite this kind of language about teaching and learning, but we know that without an openness of spirit and a desire to learn on the part of the student, teaching will prove ineffective. In the context of false teaching, the author's concern is that women should learn in a spirit of openness and receptivity. The implication is that, as for the men who are praying contentiously in worship, there is disruptive conflict in the community.[54] But why is the advice for quiet submission to true teaching given only to women? One possibility is that it is the women rather than the men who have listened to the false teaching and may even be perpetuating it. While this may reflect the ancient (if not modern!) opinion that women are in general less rational and more led by emotion than men, it may also originate not from women's supposedly more credulous nature but from their significant lack of education.[55]

To Teach and Have Authority

It is clear that the two infinitive verbs in this verse stand in close relationship to each other, but the contentious question is how they are related. Both infinitives are governed by the main clause, "I do not permit," expressing

---

51. Hutson, *First and Second Timothy and Titus*, 73.
52. Against this, cf. Douglas Moo, who argues that the submission is to husbands and male leaders ("What Does It Mean," 183–85).
53. Oden, *First and Second Timothy and Titus*, 97.
54. Belleville, "Exegetical Fallacies," 4.
55. So Keener, *Paul, Women, and Wives*, 357–71.

authorial embargo. Commentators of different persuasions assume that the writer is giving the instruction that Christian women are forbidden to teach or to exercise any authority within the community. For some, as we would expect, this is a message for all time;[56] for others, it is governed by the local, post-Pauline context, which has moved away from authentic Pauline teaching, which grants women precisely such authority (e.g., 1 Cor. 11:10).

Yet there is another possibility of translation that challenges these assumptions. The second verb (*authentein*) is unusual and, in literature from the ancient Greek world, carries a decidedly negative connotation: not of holding or possessing authority (as most translations have it) but rather of a dominating authority that seeks to gain the upper hand over others.[57] The verbs may relate to each other as two distinct vetoes, as translators and commentators tend to assume.[58] But that hardly accounts for the negativity of the second verb. Another possibility that works well, if not better, grammatically argues that both verbs refer to the one prohibition.[59] Taking into account the contrary meaning of the second verb, the second infinitive expresses purpose: "to teach so as to dominate."[60] This way of reading the text would cohere with the letter's concern for those supporting false teaching. Individual women taking others aside and advocating erroneous views in a contentious spirit are hereby instructed to cultivate a quiet and receptive spirit.[61] In the light of this, a more literal translation for these verses might run as follows: "Let a woman learn in quietness with all submission. But I do not permit a woman to teach with the intention of dominating a man, but she is to go about in quietness."

It is true that gentleness and modesty of demeanor were considered in the ancient world the virtues peculiarly appropriate to women. The fact that a minority of women could play leading roles in ancient society and the early church does not mean that traditional virtues were not also required of them. Modesty, in particular, along with self-control in speech and decorum in dress, is a virtue advocated for all women (1 Tim. 2:9–10). The ancient world

---

56. E.g., Moo, "What Does It Mean," 180–82.

57. On the meaning of the verb, which only appears once in the New Testament, see Westfall, *Paul and Gender*, 290–94.

58. E.g., Moo, who regards teaching and having authority over a man as two distinct yet connected tasks: "Paul prohibits women from conducting either activity, whether jointly or in isolation, in relation to men" ("What Does It Mean," 183).

59. This is called hendiadys and is a common construction in Greek; see Hutson, *First and Second Timothy and Titus*, 75.

60. Belleville, "Exegetical Fallacies," 4–7; Giles, *What the Bible Actually Teaches on Women*, 118–25, 144–51.

61. Giles emphasizes the singular here ("a woman"), arguing that it is not a universal prohibition against all women's teaching (*What the Bible Actually Teaches on Women*, 122–23).

was complex in its value system; although it was patriarchal and had a clear and distinct gender bias, women's leadership, including over men, was not unknown in the ancient world. We need to bear in mind that Paul and his disciples were people of their time and that some of the "feminine" values they assume reflect a very different social order and value system from our own.

Yet enjoining women to show conventional virtues associated with their gender does not mean that they cannot take on leadership positions; rather the cultural norms decree that their leadership should be accompanied by these virtues.[62] Even so, the Pauline writings also connect such values with that of inner serenity and carrying out of good works—and this for all Christians, including Timothy himself (1 Tim. 6:11). The virtues, traditionally female, do not exclude Christian women from leadership in ministry. The authority of Priscilla as a teacher in Ephesus, for example, is not questioned, and she is greeted, along with her husband, Aquila, at the end of the following epistle (2 Tim. 4:19).[63]

Eve and Childbearing

For many readers, 1 Timothy 2:13–15 advocates the return of women to their traditional roles as mothers, depriving them of other roles in the assembly and blaming them for sin—whether this advice is regarded as a realistic and universal calling to women or as an unacceptable (and not genuinely Pauline) form of misogyny that turns back the clock on women's ministry. The reminder of Eve's capacity for being the victim of deception as against Adam is difficult because, at face value, it seems to imply that Adam is not guilty of sin; Eve, created second, is the one to believe the serpent's words. This view of women as the source of sin, leading good men astray, is overtly or covertly present in Christian history. The same notion is widely available not only in patristic but also in rabbinic and other Jewish texts.[64] Yet 1 Timothy does not say that Adam is innocent of sin but that he is not *deceived* (*apatan*). The sense is that Eve is the one who initiates the act of disobedience, being convinced by the serpent's arguments; Adam simply follows her lead. This makes a contrast with other texts in the Pauline corpus, where there is no mention of Eve but only of Adam's sin (Rom. 5:12–21). In 1 Timothy Eve

---

62. See Hylen, *Thecla*, 43–62.

63. Hutson's interpretation takes a middle line between the egalitarian and complementarian positions; he sees the text as somewhat patriarchal and as permitting women to teach but only with the permission of their husbands. He also argues that this passage, given its difficulties of interpretation, should not be used against women's leadership today (*First and Second Timothy and Titus*, 76–85).

64. Oden, *First and Second Timothy and Titus*, 99–100.

may be the one to be deceived, but Adam, by comparison, looks weak and ineffective. Despite his priority in the order of creation, he shows no backbone or moral fiber. Nothing here implies that Eve has usurped the man's authority.[65] Rather the contrast suggests that certain women in the community in Ephesus were influenced by erroneous teaching—not least by virtue of their relative lack of education. The text need not be read, as it sometimes is, as an indictment against all Christian women for all time, still less as a basis for excluding them from leadership.

Westfall reads this passage entirely in relation to married couples, where wives are encouraged to learn about theology and spirituality from their husbands at home in order to rectify the deficiencies of their education and socialization in mixed public contexts. In this reading, the parallels with 1 Corinthians 14:34–35 are patent. At the same time, noting the high rates of maternal mortality, Westfall sees the move from singular to plural ("she . . . they") as referring in the first case to the wife and in the second to the husband as well as the wife, implying that he, too, is to live out of Christian virtue and show responsibility for his wife's well-being in pregnancy and childbirth.[66]

A variation on this view gives greater stress to the Ephesian context of the letter and the influence of the religion of the goddess Artemis (which had already merged with the cult of the Egyptian goddess Isis), whose temple, the Artemision, was one of the Seven Wonders of the Ancient World. Acts tells of the hostility Paul experiences in Ephesus over the worship of Artemis and the emotional reaction of the crowd at any perceived slight against the deity who guards their city (Acts 19:23–41). Her cult was dominant in Ephesus, with a particular focus on fertility and marriage, the goddess acting as the protector of women in childbirth.[67] In this interpretation, Artemis is regarded as the savior of laboring women. The false teaching, the fact that its mythology attracted Christian women, and the earlier injunctions on women to dress appropriately (1 Tim. 2:9–10) all connect to the cult of Artemis/Isis. First Timothy enjoins the women, in this view, not to be drawn back into their previous pagan ways: not to dress or behave as adherents of the goddess, nor to be led astray by the goddess's cultic values and myths (4:7). Instead they are to hold fast to their Christian faith and find salvation in childbirth, not from their old belief in the protective power of the goddess but from the saving God of Jesus Christ (1:15; 2:3).[68]

---

65. As some complementarians have argued—e.g., Moo, "What Does It Mean," 185–86; against this, cf. Giles, *What the Bible Actually Teaches on Women*, 126–28.

66. Westfall, *Paul and Gender*, 305–12.

67. See Peppiatt, *Rediscovering Scripture's Vision*, 145–48.

68. Peppiatt notes the parallels with the contemporary Greek novel *Ephesiaca* (or *Ephesian Tale of Anthia and Habrocomes*), which concludes after the dramatic adventures of the lovers

Another possibility is that 1 Timothy 2:15 continues an explicit reference to creation, with Eve as the subject (of *sōthēsetai*, "saved"), as she is of the previous clause. The verse would then point to Eve as the "mother of living" (Gen. 3:20), revealing divine grace in the face of human fallenness: "God's salvation of a fallen woman, who experiences God's faithfulness in the act of giving new life, is exemplary of humanity's realization of God's redemptive purpose."[69] This reading can be pushed further. If the subject is Eve, then the reference to the bearing of children may well be to the birth of Jesus—not just any childbearing but *the* childbearing (*dia tēs teknogonias*, 1 Tim. 2:15a).[70] In this reading there is a parallel between Eve and Mary so that Mary's child-bearing will save Eve in an eschatological sense and thus all women in and through Christ. It coheres with the second part of the verse, which speaks of Christian women abiding "in faith and love and holiness with wisdom" (2:15b)—that is, entering into solidarity with the faith of Mary. In line with the issue of theological deviation in 1 Timothy (which certain women in the community may have embraced), Mary's obedience contrasts with Eve's disobedience, Mary's spiritual equilibrium with Eve's spiritual waywardness.[71]

Whether this theory concurs with 1 Timothy more broadly may be disputed, but the letter's emphasis on Jesus as Savior (1:15; 6:13–16) and its explicit reference to the incarnation ("who was revealed in flesh," 3:16) strengthen the case for a contrast between Eve and Mary, with the second part of 2:15 referring to Christian women, daughters of Eve by birth and of Mary by faith. In that case, the translation of 2:13–15 might run as follows: "For Adam first was formed, then Eve. And Adam was not deceived, but the woman, being deceived, came into transgression. But she [Eve] will be saved through the Child-bearing, if they [Christian women] abide in faith and love and holiness with wisdom."

Women in Leadership? (1 Tim. 3:2–12)

A further disputed text in 1 Timothy is 3:2–12, which raises the question of whether women are included among those designated as bishops/overseers and deacons/servers. Here the problem lies, once more, in the way the Greek text is translated. Is it possible that the text does not confine itself to men in

---

with their return to Ephesus and their sacrifice to Artemis, acknowledging her protective power (*Rediscovering Scripture's Vision*, 146–52). On the Isis cult and its belief in the equality of women and men, see Belleville, *Women Leaders and the Church*, 36–38.

69. Wall and Steele, *1 & 2 Timothy and Titus*, 158.

70. Oden, *First and Second Timothy and Titus*, 100–102.

71. Against the figurative reading, cf. Hutson, *First and Second Timothy and Titus*, 78–80.

these roles? There is an argument that it may not exclude women at all—not, at least, for deacons. The references to "he," "his," and "him" in most translations are not present in Greek, as they are not needed. Yes, the forms may be in the grammatical masculine, but that in itself is not significant: the masculine is used generically for both male and female in Greek. But the real objection revolves around the requirement that the bishop and deacon in each case be a "one-woman man/men" (*mias gynaikos andra/andres*, 3:2, 12). According to Philip Payne, the phrase is a generic saying, an example of androcentrism, where the nearest English equivalent might be "monogamous."[72] The issue is not so much that of polygamy (which was illegal in any case in the Roman Empire) but rather fidelity to the one partner as opposed to adulterous behavior. Nor could it imply that only married men could aspire to these offices, since Paul himself was not married—of which even his successors would be aware. And the section on deacons contains a specific reference to women, which could mean the wives of deacons but is much more likely to refer to female deacons, who are instructed to show the same ethical attributes as the male deacons.[73] Admittedly, there is no explicit reference to women as bishops, but that in itself does not mean 1 Timothy sees bishops as exclusively male.[74] Translating this passage with a more inclusive lens would yield the following:

> Therefore, it is necessary that bishops be above reproach, monogamous, sober, prudent, ordered, hospitable [literally, "loving strangers"], able to teach; not a heavy drinker, not violent, but gentle, not quarrelsome, not loving money, managing their own house well, having their children submissive and reverent . . . not a neophyte [newly baptized Christian] lest, being puffed up, they might fall into the judgment of the devil. . . . Deacons likewise should be reverent, not two-faced, not given to much wine, not seeking dishonest gain, holding to the mystery of faith with a pure conscience. And let them first be examined; then let them minister, being blameless. The women deacons also should be reverent, not dividers, clear-minded, faithful in everything. Let the deacons be monogamous, managing their children and their own households well.

The same may also be said for Titus 1:7–9, which speaks of the moral attributes needed for presbyters and bishops using similar language. These instructions do not, and need not, exclude women from ministry roles any more than they would exclude single or widowed men.

72. So Payne, *Man and Woman*, 277–79.
73. As argued by R. Collins, *1 & 2 Timothy and Titus*, 90–91; against this, cf. Wall and Steele, *1 & 2 Timothy and Titus*, 109–10.
74. See Peppiatt, *Rediscovering Scripture's Vision*, 132–34.

If these attempts to read 1 Timothy in new ways have exegetical merit, it follows that the letter is not prohibiting women from engaging in teaching or leadership ministry. Rather it is concerned that women (whether leaders or not) display traditionally feminine virtues, some of which are given, paradoxically, a new impetus in Christian faith—especially the challenge to reject the competitive and aggressive amassing of honor, a traditional masculine virtue. The commending of modesty and good works may seem obnoxious to contemporary feminism with its admiration for outspoken, feisty women who can claim confidently their gifts and abilities. But today's context, for most Christians, is very different from that of the early Christians, whose faith and community life was socially and politically precarious and vulnerable. The context today gives the possibility for women to be more forthcoming and assertive than they have been in many places and over many generations in the past.

The Household Codes

The group of texts commonly known as "household codes" present a particular set of problems. They set out the respective obligations and responsibilities of paired groups within the family: husband-wife, parent-child, master-slave. These codes have their origin, at least in part, in the Greek philosopher Aristotle (384–322 BCE), who was concerned to promote moral harmony and cohesion in the home.[75] Aristotle's vision is patriarchal, and he has no qualms about slavery or the subordination of women. Within the Pauline corpus several passages set out these codes for not only husbands and wives but also slaves and masters, as well as parents and children. Although this is a familiar pattern in the ancient world and reflects household values in pagan as well as Judeo-Christian circles, there is a particularity to them in Christian hands. Christ is set at the heart of them, and his redemptive work underlies them, making them unique in the ancient world.

The first of these passages, from Colossians, gives instruction on the relationship between wife and husband (Col. 3:18–19). F. F. Bruce points out that the church, being a new institution, could afford to be more radical in reflecting the new creation in Christ than the family could, whose structures were old and venerable and not easily re-formed: "It was no part of the business of early Christianity to destabilize society, which would have been the effect of radically changing the family structure."[76] Instead the attitudes within the established

75. Balch, *Let Wives Be Submissive*, 33–38.
76. Bruce, *Epistles*, 163.

structures were to be overturned from within and based now on values of self-giving love and respect from the more to the less powerful. Indeed, the phrase "as is fitting in the Lord" (3:18) would prove "to be more revolutionary in its effect than was generally foreseen in the first Christian century."[77]

In Ephesians, the discussion is more extensive and draws on, by way of comparison, the relationship between Christ and the church. Wives are to submit to husbands as if to Christ and are also to show them respect, while husbands are to love their wives as Christ loves the church, serving their wives and seeking their well-being as they seek their own (Eph. 5:22–33). Ephesians as a whole is concerned theologically with unity through Christ and his self-giving death, a unity that entices strangers into community and outsiders into intimate relationship (2:12–13). Ephesians has in mind the alienation between Jew and gentile that is now overcome in Christ so that, in place of division, there is reconciliation and peace, creating "one new humanity" (2:15).

It is essential for us to appreciate, as we have already seen, the gulf that lies between our understanding of the family and that of the ancient world. In the ancient setting, families were extended and included not only other relatives but also the household slaves. In the Roman setting, where laws relating to the family were controlled by the empire, the father of the family (*paterfamilias*) had absolute authority, without the possibility of redress for socially inferior members, including women. The family was the basic means of production and worked together for survival within a context of "cottage industry," while marriages were arranged and based not primarily on romantic love but on the need to produce children and secure the family honor. Religion also was the responsibility of the *paterfamilias*, who acted as the priest in his own home, and all members of the household shared it and participated in its rituals.[78] Husbands, too, were older and much better educated than their very young and inexperienced wives, marking out a gender division that would be hard to envision in the Western world today.

We need also to note the qualifying aspects of the household codes in Ephesians on marriage. The submission of wives to husbands is one aspect of the submission enjoined on all Christians to one another (Eph. 5:21). Submission—generally a quality for women, children, and slaves in the ancient world—is seen here as a virtue for all members of Christ's body, regardless of age, status, or gender. Furthermore, the husband is to show his love in self-giving care for his wife, and her well-being is now paramount for him. His role is not to use her as an unpaid servant to fulfill his domestic needs

77. Bruce, *Epistles*, 163.
78. See Fee, "Cultural Context," 5–7.

and requirements, nor is it to exploit her as a sex object. Rather, he is to be attentive to her needs—indeed, to serve her as Christ has served the church. Moreover, the passage concludes by quoting the creation account in Genesis: "For this reason a man will leave behind his father and mother, and cling to the woman, and the two will be one flesh" (5:31; Gen. 2:24). Here the normal male-centered pattern is reversed: it is not the woman who is to abandon her familial identity and cling to the man, but it is the man who does so for her. The passage, in other words, is bounded on either side by qualifying statements that open possibilities for new ways of envisioning marriage in the Christian community.

At one level, the household rules in Ephesians and elsewhere in the New Testament do not attempt to change the basic outline and structures of marriage in the ancient world. Marriage is injected, however, with an entirely new dimension that challenges many of the patriarchal and hierarchical values of the ancient Greco-Roman world. Christ himself, love, and self-giving service now lie at the core of marriage and family—not the building up of honor, especially for the household males, but rather the giving and receiving of mutual love and service. This would have been particularly challenging for the male head of the house, who, in the ancient context, as we have seen, had an extraordinary level of authority over the members of his household, including the freedom of sexual exploitation and the power of life and death.[79] It is within the wider context of mutual Christian service that the household codes are reframed, with self-giving love at their heart.

Gordon Fee's study of this passage argues that taking into consideration the theology of Ephesians and the very different world of the Greco-Roman family, it is not the structures themselves that are to be imitated but rather the spirit that animates them. Fee argues that the structures are, in one sense, of much less relevance than the Christocentric reinterpretation of all relationships within the family. The placing of Christ and his atoning death at the heart of the family, whatever the structures may be in their different cultural contexts, is what really matters. To demand that wives obey husbands in a context where couples marry with identical status as citizens and with equivalent standards of education and life experience makes no sense in today's context. What does make sense is the injunction that the radical, self-giving love of Christ stands at the heart of married relationships, transforming them from within, whether the structures are those of the ancient world or are the very different ones of the modern world.[80]

---

79. Peppiatt, *Rediscovering Scripture's Vision*, 93–94.

80. Fee, "Cultural Context," 7–8. See Payne: "If Paul were writing today, he would probably give different commands to uphold the same principles" (*Man and Woman*, 172).

The parallel scenario is the institution of slavery in the ancient world, which the household codes do not explicitly challenge. On the one hand, the relationship between master or mistress and slave is transformed so that slaves can no longer be physically abused; on the other hand, the structure itself remains. What seems repugnant to us, that one human being should own another, body and soul, with absolute obedience to be rendered, with no freedom to make decisions, and without payment for labor,[81] was part of the fabric of the ancient economy. The institution is mollified but not obliterated for Christian slave owners and their Christian slaves in the New Testament's domestic codes.

When certain Christians in the nineteenth century were confronted once again with slavery, they opposed it on biblical grounds, convinced that it contravened the spirit of the gospel. John Newton, the writer of the hymn "Amazing Grace," had himself been a slave trader, and his conversion led him to view with repugnance his previous employment ("that saved a wretch like me") and to support William Wilberforce in his campaign to outlaw slavery. At the same time, ironically, Christian slave owners felt they could justify the practice from the household codes of the New Testament without reference to theological and ethical principles.[82]

Today, Christians universally oppose slavery, and do so in the confidence that biblical teaching supports them. Yet patriarchal authority within home and marriage continues to exist and be promoted in some sections of the church on so-called biblical grounds.[83] Such Christians appeal to the "letter" of the domestic codes while ignoring the gospel principles underlying them. If we oppose the one, we ought by definition to oppose the other: if slavery is tolerated in the short term but falls away before a higher gospel principle, so should patriarchal marriage. The two belong together and are part of the old order of things, which can be for a time reformed but which in the end are to be turned on their heads and revolutionized. For Paul, in the new age inaugurated by Christ's death and resurrection, "the structure of this world is passing away" (1 Cor. 7:31).

81. This was the case for the majority of slaves in the ancient world, who worked on farms or in mines or by rowing ships. They were either born into slavery or captured in war. Some could buy their own freedom, and some had positions of authority, even owning slaves. But this was not the general story, and many lived in misery and servitude, their bodies the property of their owners and available to be used and abused without compunction. See, e.g., Edmondson, "Slavery and the Roman Family," 337–61.

82. See Giles, *What the Bible Actually Teaches on Women*, 180–94.

83. A similar argument might be employed for injunctions to children to be submissive and obedient to parents. While the obedience of children is still expected today in the West, particularly of young children, there is not the same expectation of submissiveness. And no adult son or daughter would feel themselves in any way bound by parental dictates.

The intention of these codes in the New Testament is not to create new, revolutionary social models but rather to enable Christians to "live out the gospel message and convey the message to the larger society."[84] There is a complex message in these codes, a seeming adoption of community standards yet a subtle recoding of the benchmarks beyond anything in the Greco-Roman world. Thus women and slaves receive a new standing in relation to Christ because they belong to him and to other members of the Christian household. Unlike in the biological family, in the fictive family of the church, they are not enslaved but set free, not subordinate but equal, not subjected but able to participate fully, including in leadership. This has implications for the biological families to which they return. Their loyalty shifts from the *paterfamilias* to Christ so that their conformity to the household system is given a new focus that relativizes all their other relationships.[85] Women and slaves now have the freedom to choose their own faith and to do everything with a new allegiance and a new motivation.

Conclusion

In the Pauline Letters, there is a conscious attempt to change not the structures of the world but rather the church itself, which is a small and powerless entity within the Roman-Hellenistic world, an entity lacking political influence or power. This transformation represents a conversion of identity in the eschatological community in relation to all identity markers that human beings construct for themselves or for others, including race, class, and gender. Slaves and free people, gentiles and Jews, women and men now live alongside each other in the household of faith as sisters and brothers, each gifted with gifts from the Spirit along with the authority to exercise those gifts.[86] The point is clear from the Letter to Philemon (also addressed to Apphia), where master and slave, Philemon and Onesimus, are now joined together in *koinōnia*, Christian fellowship, as brothers: it is a radical gospel with far-reaching relational and social implications.[87] Whether the later writings follow through on this vision is not so clear. But what is apparent is that male-oriented scholarship has made unwarranted assumptions about some of these texts, interpreting them in ways that deny women's leadership. These interpretations represent a betrayal of the Pauline vision—whether by his canonical successors and/ or by his succeeding readers, influenced by a culture in which "appeals to

---

84. Lu, "Woman's Role," 13.
85. Lu, "Woman's Role," 12.
86. Westfall, *Paul and Gender*, 166–72.
87. Peppiatt, *Rediscovering Scripture's Vision*, 35–37.

the weak nature of women and to the necessity of patriarchal control of the household" were all too common.[88]

In every age there is a gap between the promise of the gospel and its full realization, because of the limitations of culture and context. The same gap is present in the New Testament community, as the church seeks to implement the extraordinary vision and freedom of the gospel as proclaimed by Paul: "Here we should . . . draw a distinction between the claim in principle and its realization in given circumstances."[89] In our context, new possibilities arise for implementing that Pauline vision, which goes back to Jesus himself. It seems almost incredible that there are those who wish to hold back the full working out of the gospel in situations where it is suddenly, in the providence of God, made possible. That holds not only for marriage but for other issues in the interpretation of the Pauline Epistles.

88. Krause, *1 Timothy*, 57.
89. Heine, *Women and Early Christianity*, 150.

Chapter Seven

Later New Testament Writings

WITH THIS CHAPTER we come to the end of the New Testament evidence on women and women's leadership. Not all of the biblical books are included here, as some have little if anything to say on the subject, such as 2 Peter or Jude. Even the texts included here are nowhere near as prolific on women as the other New Testament texts we have examined so far. But there are points worth raising in the remaining letters, with their strongly pastoral and practical emphasis, that connect to women's ministry. The book of Revelation is quite distinct from these letters, but it also has several intriguing portraits of female characters that are worth examining.

Hebrews

We come first to the Letter to the Hebrews, which was traditionally ascribed to Pauline authorship until more modern times.[1] The style of writing and the theology of Hebrews have made it universally clear that it is not a Pauline epistle. It may even be not a letter at all but a treatise or homily.[2] Hebrews has an epistolary ending, with the usual mutual greetings and benediction (13:22–25), but oddly enough no epistolary beginning. The author launches into the central theme of the epistle without preamble of any kind, in a sublime prologue to Christ (1:1–4): "In various ways and by various means God of old having spoken to the ancestors in the prophets, in these last days has

---

1. Gray and Peeler, *Hebrews*.
2. Witherington, *Letters and Homilies*, 20–21.

spoken to us in a Son" (1:1–2). On balance, it is more likely that the beginning, with the author's name, was lost than that the ending with its traditional greetings was added.[3]

Despite the recurring passages of encouragement all through the epistle, as well as in the final chapter, Hebrews is not concerned with details about the shape and form of ministry. Toward the end, the epistle offers instructions, enjoining the audience to imitate the faith of leaders (13:7), to obey them (13:17), and finally to greet them (13:24). There is no indication of the gender of the leaders in these instructions, and no reason to assume that they are all male. The audience is called to "submit" to them as well as to obey them: "Trust those leading you and submit, for they are keeping watch over your souls as those rendering an account, so that they may do so with joy and not with groaning; for this is harmful to you" (13:17). The focus here is on willing cooperation and a sense of mutual ministry with leaders, which "is to be the hallmark of the Christian community in every way."[4]

In the commendation of the saints in Hebrews 11, the list comprises male figures from the Old Testament (Abel, Enoch, Noah, Abraham, Isaac, Jacob, Joseph, Moses, and others), but a number of females are also listed, either overtly or by implication.[5] Although there is a textual problem, Sarah is probably mentioned alongside Abraham as one who demonstrates faith in God's word that she will produce a child, despite her age and inability to conceive: "By faith also Sarah herself, being barren, received power for the establishment of seed, even though being beyond the right age, since she considered faithful the one promising" (Heb. 11:11; Gen. 18:1–15).[6] Moses's parents are extolled for their faith in courageously concealing their child (Heb. 11:23; Exod. 2:1–4), and he himself gains the status of "the son of Pharaoh's daughter." Rahab is commended for her hospitality to the Israelite spies in the exodus story and for her faith in God: "By faith Rahab, a prostitute, was not destroyed with those who disobeyed, welcoming the spies in peace" (Heb. 11:31; Josh. 2:1–21). Where the catalog becomes more general, it is conceivable that the references are to women in leadership who endured suffering and showed courageous faith alongside men: Deborah, Jael, Judith. The letter explicitly mentions women who "received their dead by resurrection" (Heb. 11:35), implying faith on the part of women convinced that death is not the end—the mother of the seven tortured and martyred sons under Antiochus Epiphanes comes to mind

3. Ellingworth, *Epistle to the Hebrews*, 59–62.
4. DeSilva, *Perseverance in Gratitude*, 509.
5. Hoppin, *Priscilla's Letter*, 35–48.
6. D'Angelo, "Hebrews," 610. See also Gray and Peeler: "Sarah is a key player in the drama of faith" (*Hebrews*). Against this, cf. Attridge, *Commentary*, 324–26.

(2 Macc. 7:20–23), but most of all, Mary of Nazareth, who in a metaphorical sense "receives" her son, Jesus, back from the dead.

An important feature of Hebrews is the kinship symbolism,[7] which we have also encountered in John and Paul. The pattern begins with Jesus himself, who as the unique Son of the Father, forms kinship with God's sons and daughters through the incarnation and atonement in order to rescue them from the power of Satan/death (Heb. 2:14, 17):[8] "Since then the children had in common blood and flesh, he too likewise shared the same things. . . . Therefore he had to become in every way like his brothers and sisters [*adelphoi*], so that he might become a merciful and faithful high priest in the matters relating to God to make expiation for the sins of the people." The context is the covenant, which is profoundly relational, so much so that Hebrews advocates Christians meeting together regularly as essential "for the solidarity of a group understanding itself as a household . . . , as social bonds and belief structures are mutually reinforcing."[9] This powerful sense of the fictive family is located in Jesus as Son, a major title throughout the epistle. It emphasizes the close bond between God and God's people through the covenant made in Christ's sacrifice. This is not the language of a demanding and authoritarian God but the language of intimacy and love, emphasizing the ongoing and gracious self-communication of God.

There is a further aspect to Hebrews that warrants attention. In 1900, the German New Testament scholar Adolf von Harnack proposed that Prisca (Priscilla) was the author of the Epistle to the Hebrews. This view has been picked up by several other scholars.[10] The argument is that the context of the epistle coheres with the experience of Prisca and Aquila. If Hebrews is addressed to Christians in Rome who have endured recent suffering (Heb. 10:32–34), this reference to suffering may well incorporate not only the persecution of Christians under Emperor Nero (64 CE) but also the earlier expulsion of Jews from Rome under Emperor Claudius (ca. 49 CE) as a result of internal disputes, most likely over Christianity. Prisca, along with her husband, Aquila, is one of those expelled from Rome (Acts 18:1–3). They are probably included among "those from Italy" who have been forced to leave but retain their links with the Roman Christians (Heb. 13:24).[11]

7. Peeler, *You Are My Son*, especially 140–78.
8. This view of the atonement is that of *Christus Victor*: that Christ suffered on the cross in order to defeat Satan (evil, sin, and death) (Gray and Peeler, *Hebrews*).
9. Gray and Peeler, *Hebrews*.
10. See, e.g., Hoppin, *Priscilla's Letter*, 11–34; Kittredge, "Hebrews," 2:430–34; also Bilezikian, "Beyond Sex Roles," 37–38.
11. Hoppin, *Priscilla's Letter*, 80–122.

Prisca is portrayed in Acts as the theological teacher of Apollos along with her husband, as we have already seen (Acts 18:24–26), which means that she is capable as a theological teacher. She is associated with Paul, to whom the authorship of Hebrews was traditionally linked. She is, in other words, a serious contender for the role of author, and while it cannot be proved from the text itself, there are strong arguments to support it and few that would in themselves exclude it.[12] If so, her name at the beginning is suppressed for good reason, in terms of the ancient world, which could hardly conceive of a woman penning so sophisticated a text. Even if Apollos is the author rather than Priscilla, Acts makes it clear that he has been taught by Priscilla.[13] In either case, we encounter a woman engaged in the ministry of teaching—including the teaching of men.

James

The Epistle of James, with its strongly Jewish-Christian character, is not a particularly significant text for understanding women's ministry in the New Testament. Having an uneasy place within the canon, it is one of the "Catholic" or "General" Epistles, which are not obviously addressed to a single community. It begins as a letter but lacks an epistolary ending and employs sophisticated but somewhat androcentric language and imagery. The only explicit reference to a woman is in the parallelism between Abraham and Rahab, who both embody the power of works (and particularly the ministry of hospitality to the needy) to illustrate faith—a key theme of the letter—demonstrating by their actions that "faith without works is dead" (James 2:26): "In the same way also, was not Rahab the prostitute justified by works, having received the messengers and having sent them off by another route?" (2:25).[14]

One contentious text is found at 3:1, where James speaks of *adelphoi* as teachers: "Not many should become teachers, my *adelphoi*, knowing that you will receive a greater judgment." Is this inclusive of women teachers, or does it refer only to males? The letter uses the Greek word *adelphos/adelphoi* (brother/brothers) eighteen times, and the feminine singular form, *adelphē* (sister), only once. Greek can add the separate word "sisters" after "brothers" but more often does not, especially in the plural, given that the stem is identical (*adelph-*). And androcentric usage means that females can be included in

12. One argument is the masculine participle used at 11:32; for a defense of female authorship on this issue, see Hoppin, *Priscilla's Letter*, 49–52.

13. On Apollos as author, see Witherington, *Letters and Homilies*, 21–24; for a list of the candidates, see Hoppin, *Priscilla's Letter*, 55–79.

14. L. Johnson, *Brother of Jesus*, 178–79.

male nouns. In every other context in James, *adelphoi* is an address to the whole community (brothers and sisters),[15] which is part of the imagery of the fictive family—the term being most often accompanied by the possessive pronoun "my" and on two occasions by the adjective "beloved":

adelphoi (plural)	my adelphoi	my beloved adelphoi	adelphos (singular)	adelphē
4:11;	1:2;	1:16;	1:9;	2:15
5:7, 9	2:1, 14;	2:5	2:15;	
	3:1, 10, 12;		4:11 (2x)	
	5:12, 19			

The NIV is the most accurate of modern translations in this regard, rendering *adelphoi* fairly consistently as "brothers and sisters," except at two occurrences where it translates it as "(fellow) believers" (James 1:9; 3:1). The NRSV moves between "brothers and sisters" (in most cases), "believer" (once), and "beloved" (six times), which somewhat weakens the image of the family. The ESV and NJB translate "brothers" throughout, either giving the impression of a male audience or assuming, against all current usage, that "brothers" is itself inclusive today. In terms of accuracy of translation, "brothers and sisters" is correct, suggesting that the phrase "my *adelphoi*" at 3:1 is no different from its other uses in James. Therefore this verse is most likely addressed to male and female teachers, and there is no indication that women are excluded from teaching in this community.[16]

Drawing its inspiration from Jewish Wisdom traditions, James commends a righteousness that is the opposite of rivalry, egotism, pride, ambition, and the pursuit of wealth and status and is associated more with female virtues in the ancient world than with male ones: purity, peace, gentleness, submission, justice, and mercy (2:13–18; 3:6–10). James commends a form of patience that is active, hopeful, focused on good works, and prayerful.[17] Once again, there is an implicit challenge here to the patriarchal values of the ancient world, particularly in relation to the male pursuit of honor, power, and self-promotion. The Letter of James, moreover, with its emphasis on social justice, has much to offer women today in their work of ministry, with its "many resources for exploring contemporary injustices against women and children, as well as other injustices emanating from inequitable distribution of resources . . . that continue to affect women across the globe."[18]

15. Byron, "James," 613.
16. Scot McKnight generally sees *adelphoi* as inclusive but thinks it difficult to be conclusive about whether 3:1 refers to male teachers or male and female teachers (*Letter of James*, 70–71, 266–68).
17. Tamez, "James," 389.
18. Byron, "James," 613.

1 Peter and Household Codes

Of the two Petrine Epistles, only the first has relevance to our question.[19] First Peter is written with an awareness of what it means for Christians to live in a context of adaptation to life under the Roman Empire, because of its vigorous suppression of any form of religious or political sedition.[20] A key virtue for the community is to display moral uprightness of character to the gentile world so that "looking on your good deeds, they may glorify God on the day of his visitation" (1 Pet. 2:12). This agenda serves as an introduction to 1 Peter's version of the household codes, which begin with the duties of Christians to other people, and especially to those in the family of faith: "Submit to every human institution on account of the Lord" (2:13).[21] The duties concern those of citizens to the emperor, slaves to their masters, and wives to their husbands, with a final note to husbands about the way they treat their wives (2:17–3:7).

We note that these household codes according to 1 Peter, here as elsewhere, say nothing about leadership in the church but are concerned with the household. Here the letter advocates that slaves and wives follow Roman social practices of household management in order to bear witness to the world around them and provide assurance that Christians do not posit a danger to society: "Household slaves, submit with all respect to masters. . . . In the same way wives, submit to your own husbands" (2:18; 3:1). Following the instructions, Christian behavior should provide a stark contrast to some of the more violent and enthusiastic religious cults, which, for the Romans, present an ominous challenge to social order. Christian women are to dress modestly and appropriately, following Sarah's example of wifely submission (3:3–6). Christian slaves are called to endure suffering without protest (2:21–25). The open attitude of the Christian community in including women and slaves is already a subject of criticism from the pagan world around it, which perhaps explains the need for them to submit and not make trouble for the fledgling church.[22] Yet both texts have been used to compel those enslaved in oppressive structures or trapped in violent marriages to endure abuse patiently rather than escape or resist.

---

19. On authorship, compare Donald P. Senior, who believes it is pseudonymous (*1 Peter, Jude and 2 Peter*, 4–7), with Ben Witherington III, who believes it was written/dictated by Simon Peter (*Letters and Homilies*, 51–54).

20. Cynthia Briggs Kittredge sees this as cultural "accommodation" rather than "resistance" ("1 Peter," 617–18).

21. On the household codes in 1 Peter, see Balch, *Let Wives Be Submissive*, 81–121.

22. Kathleen Corley argues that women and slaves are forced to bear the burden of the cultural accommodation on behalf of the church ("1 Peter").

First Peter does not advocate a simple following of patriarchal practice. Everything here concerns the gospel and its proclamation in word and deed, with Christ at the center, and there is a subtle challenge throughout the epistle to the values of the pagan world. Thus wives are to be held in honor by husbands precisely because of their new identity in Christ, an honor not necessarily accorded them elsewhere in Greco-Roman society. They are elect members of the church, an integral part of a priestly people, servants of Christ himself, "coheirs of the grace of life" (3:7).[23] The submission required of them, as of slaves, is not based on their lesser rationality or inferior humanity but rather on the need to live peaceably within the dominating context of empire. Showing the ability to conform makes wives a greater witness to unbelieving husbands (3:1b). Women have some access to true freedom in Christ and render to their husbands a relative obedience in comparison to the final obedience for God alone, which is their primary responsibility. Here the level of license permits wives to follow their own religious path, in deference to Christ, rather than that of their households, where husbands act as the religious head, the priestly authority for the family. This is potentially an act of defiance (doubtlessly costly) against patriarchal power.[24]

The context of 1 Peter is needed for understanding this version of the household codes. The household is the main symbol for the church, where the identity of the community is to be strengthened in a setting of hostility and persecution.[25] At the deepest level, from our perspective, we can see how the gospel's core principles, glimpsed here but found more explicitly elsewhere, make for the undermining of the dyadic pairs and their pattern of subordination. In the end, it is Christ who determines identity, whatever and wherever the social context. There is a kind of pragmatism to 1 Peter, an implicit awareness that Christian behavior needs to conform in some contexts, even while the principles of faith lead to a new way of being in relationship to one another. The instructions are addressed to people whose situations are powerless. First Peter is about the church living with a profoundly world-changing identity as a priestly people, while also respecting the current social mores in order to survive oppression and more effectively proclaim the gospel. The instructions on women's appearance, however distasteful to modern

---

23. Lu, "Woman's Role," 9–15.

24. This kind of sympathetic, though not uncritical, reading of 1 Peter is contested by Jennifer Bird, who sees the instructions as disturbingly patriarchal: "The very fact that part of the problem was mistreatment at the hands of spouses or masters makes the command to quietly submit themselves to the *paterfamilias* an abusive command. What we see here is a primary level of silencing of the most vulnerable in those communities" (*Abuse, Power and Fearful Obedience*, 91).

25. Kittredge, "1 Peter," 615–16.

sensibilities, challenge the expectation of wives to be ornaments for their husbands, status symbols whose value lies in their physical attractions. For 1 Peter, their true value is an ethical and spiritual one, grounded in their actions for love and justice.

While the central principle stands firm, the particularity of the mores assumed in 1 Peter (just as is the case with Ephesians) cannot be binding on future generations, and still less today, when marriage is no longer overtly patriarchal in its structures. Obedient submission to (unjust) male authority is no longer required, particularly with the widespread opposition to slavery and the liberation of women from patriarchal marriage. Significantly, the two belong together. As we have seen previously, it is not possible to argue against slavery in the modern context while still supporting female submission in marriage. The ending of one type of oppressive relationship extends to all others. Yet there is a message for us in 1 Peter. It points to the need in some situations for endurance and slow growth rather than revolutionary action, which sometimes does more harm than good. It assures people whose situations are genuinely powerless that Christ identifies with them in their suffering, no matter how lowly they are in the world's terms. There is a powerful word in 1 Peter, but how we communicate it needs to be sensitive to the context, both then and now.

The Johannine Epistles

The Johannine Epistles contain little or nothing that connects them directly with women's ministry.[26] The only reference is to "the elect lady and her children" (*eklektē kyria kai tois teknois autēs*) and "the children of your elect sister" (*ta tekna tēs adelphēs sou tēs eklektēs*) in the second epistle (2 John 1, 13). While it is possible that the language refers to specific women, perhaps the leaders of house churches, it is more likely that it functions as metaphor. Sibling imagery is a key component in the kinship model of Christian community in 1 John, where the new family is made up of members of the church who are united not by ties of blood but by a common love of and belief in Christ.

Yet there is another issue, particularly in 1 John, that has to do with women's identity within the household of faith—namely, the strongly masculine slant of the language. First John speaks literally of male family members within this metaphorical construct without explicit reference to females: brothers, fathers, sons. Yet this language is not as masculine as at first appears.

---

26. On the question of authorship, see Painter, *1, 2, and 3 John*, 44–51.

The intention of the text is inclusive, for women and men, and "brothers and sisters" is the more accurate translation of *adelphoi*.[27]

Strangely enough, the ESV translation of the Bible, which claims to be a more literal rendition, presents a version of the Johannine Epistles that, far more than the original, marginalizes the female members of the community. Take one example: "Whoever loves his brother abides in the light, and in him there is no cause for stumbling. But whoever hates his brother is in the darkness and walks in the darkness" (1 John 2:10–11 ESV). Compare this to another translation in a similar tradition: "Anyone who loves their brother and sister lives in the light, and there is nothing in them to make them stumble. But anyone who hates a brother or sister is in the darkness and walks around in the darkness" (NIV).[28] The debate here is not primarily a political one but a question of accuracy in translation. In contemporary English "brothers" refers only to male siblings and is no longer employed as an inclusive term. In the ESV, whatever the translators may have intended, 1 John appears to be addressed to men and for men.

The core symbol for God as "Father" raises the issue of whether 1 John unquestioningly endorses the patriarchal structures of the ancient family.[29] The language for God is undeniably masculine throughout the letter, but it is symbolic language, after all, not literal language. The epistle is also capable of drawing on feminine as well as masculine images for God. The notion of rebirth, for example, can be interpreted as masculine or feminine, given the Greek verb *gennaō*, and while the reference includes God's begetting, the form of the verb refers also to God giving birth to believers: "Everyone born of God [maternal] does not continue in sin, because God's seed [paternal] abides in them, and they are unable to sin because they are born of God [maternal]" (1 John 3:9).[30] As in the Fourth Gospel, the Father in 1 John is not a patriarchal deity and does not augment power in an authoritarian way but is presented as a God of communion and relationship, drawing human beings into a kinship that challenges the evil powers of hatred, violence, and death. In the end, the imagery is an essential part of the family symbolism throughout 1 John, emphasizing the deeply personal nature of God in intimate relationship to believers.[31]

---

27. Sloyan, *Walking in the Truth*, 20. Hans-Josef Klauck notes that women are included in the androcentric language by ancient literary convention, which is problematic for us today (*Der erste Johannesbrief*, 277).

28. See Clason, "Feminism, Generic 'He,'" 23–35.

29. Osiek and Balch, *Families in the New Testament World*, 103–55.

30. On maternal imagery in the Gospel of John, see Lee, *Flesh and Glory*, 135–65. Against this, cf. Olsson, *Commentary on the Letters of John*, 317–22.

31. See Lee, "Fictive Kinship," 403–4.

Of all the other writings in the later part of the New Testament, the Johannine Epistles reflect the most overtly pastoral and practical context, in light of recent conflict within the community that has caused a radical split. The family imagery, as it emerges particularly in 1 John, is increasingly powerful throughout the letter, giving the reader access to a profound sense of loyalty and belonging within the believing community. When translated with sensitivity to the language—to reflect female as well as male participation—the Johannine Epistles offer a vision of community and kinship. This vision echoes that of the Gospel of John and reveals the core message of divine love, revealed in Christ, along with the self-giving love to be lived out in practical ways among the siblings.

Revelation

The book of Revelation (or the Apocalypse) is a combination of apocalypse and letter, written by John of Patmos (John the Seer) to the seven churches of Asia Minor in and around Ephesus.[32] Apocalyptic is a genre of literature that is found in Judaism and early Christianity and that sees the world as sharply divided between the present context of suffering and hardship and the future hope of God's beneficent and victorious rule.[33] In the New Testament, the picture is complicated by the conviction that God's future, in one sense, has already dawned on the present in Jesus Christ. The author of Revelation believes that "despite the resistance of the world, what [he] is permitted to see as already fulfilled in the heavenly world is already beginning to assert itself in the present, and to prevail."[34] This conviction has turned the direction of Revelation from speaking only of a divine future and the end of all things (as was traditionally thought) to speaking of the current suffering and struggles of the Christian community as it is shaped by God's future.

Even with its focus on mission, Revelation has little to say about women's ministry or gender in relation to ministry, although several female references appear within the text. The most prominent are the allusions, in later sections, to the two opposing cities: Babylon and Jerusalem. The evil city, full of luxury and abuse, is named the "whore," whereas the good city, with its beauty and sanctity, is pictured as the "bride." Feminist writers have been rightly critical of the division of women into two extreme categories: either pure and virginal

---

32. It is highly likely that the author of Revelation is different from the author of the Gospel and Johannine Epistles, due to significant differences in style, although some of the imagery overlaps with the Fourth Gospel. See Aune, *Revelation*, xlvii–lvi.

33. On the apocalyptic nature of Revelation, see Boring, *Revelation*, 35–59.

34. Schnelle, "Revelation," 769.

or sexually promiscuous, where the one is set up on a pedestal and the other despised.[35] Yet it is unlikely that such bifurcation is of particular significance in the personification of the cities. The Greek word for city, *polis*, is in the feminine gender, and the language is fairly conventional, deriving from the apocalyptic and prophetic traditions.[36] Although the language for Babylon is initially sexual (Rev. 17:1–2) and buys into paternalistic stereotypes, with Old Testament overtones of idolatry in the background, it is not actual women that the reader primarily thinks of as the descriptions of Babylon and Jerusalem unfold but rather the characteristics of cities. The one city is built on the self-aggrandizement, materialistic power, idolatry, and oppression of empire, whereas the other city is constructed with a sense of architectural harmony between past and present, beauty and goodness, nature and civilization.

In the lament over the fallen city, Babylon is pictured as "the great city which has rule over the kings of the earth" (17:18), whose merchants are grief-stricken at her fall since they no longer have buyers for their luxurious list of wares: "Cargo of gold, silver, precious stones, pearls, linen, purple, silk, scarlet cloth, every kind of scented wood, every vessel of ivory, every vessel of precious wood, bronze, iron, marble, cinnamon, spice, incense, myrrh, frankincense, wine, olive oil, fine wheat flour, corn, cattle, sheep, horses, chariots, and bodies and human lives" (18:12–13). The lavish lifestyle this merchandise services includes immense suffering—for the slaves, for example, and for those who dare to oppose it—and it is idolatrous as well as oppressive. By contrast the new Jerusalem, which is also depicted with jewels on its foundations, radiates the illuminating presence of God and the Lamb at the center, and the city, with its river and avenue of trees, provides salvation and healing to all and an end to suffering and death. The gifts of this city are not for sale but are given freely to all: "Let anyone who wishes take the water of life as a gift" (22:17). As ideal readers, we might need to move beyond the superficial stereotypes of women as whores or virgin brides to the political theology that lies behind them, a theology that challenges empire and its satellites. This is admittedly not easy for all women.

Of more immediate import in Revelation is the portrait of two female characters, both with symbolic characteristics. In the first place, a prophet in the community at Thyatira is given the name "Jezebel," a symbolic name recalling the Canaanite queen of Israel in the time of Elijah who promoted the worship of Baal and persecuted the poor in Israel (1 Kings 16:31; 19:1–3; 21:1–16; Rev. 2:20). The main complaint against Jezebel of Thyatira is that she

---

35. See Pippin, "Revelation/Apocalypse," 628–29.
36. See Schüssler Fiorenza, *Revelation*, 13–14.

encourages "fornication"—that is, idolatry—by teaching that it is permissible for Christians "to eat meat offered to idols." The dispute is essentially theological and ethical, and though the language is sexual, it works as a common metaphor for the worship of pagan deities. John of Patmos takes a strong line against Christians eating meat that has been slaughtered and sacrificed in pagan temples, believing that the church needs to be uncompromising in its opposition to idolatry. Craig Koester speaks of "Jezebel's encouragement of the kind of religious accommodation that would ease tensions with society" while the Seer is "calling for more rigorous commitment to God and Jesus."[37] Note that Paul in 1 Corinthians takes a more lenient view, concerned more with the danger of vulnerable Christians being led back to idolatry than with Christians eating such food per se (1 Cor. 8:1–13), although he opposes Christians participating in banquets held in pagan temples (1 Cor. 10:14–11:1). The real issue with Jezebel, for Revelation, is the nature of her teaching rather than her gender, as there were clearly precedents for women as prophets in Christian communities.[38]

The second female character of significance in Revelation is the celestial woman who appears as a "great sign" in heaven (Rev. 12:1). The woman is pregnant, about to give birth, while the fiery red dragon waits to devour her child (12:2–4).[39] The immediate contrast is between the forces of life and fertility, embodied in the woman, and the forces of destruction represented by the dragon. Both figures are symbols of power. The dragon has seven crowned heads and a destructive tail, signifying his assumption of sovereignty as he destroys the heavens and waits to consume the newborn child. By contrast, the heavenly woman is "clothed in the sun" with "the moon beneath her feet, wearing on her head a crown of twelve stars" (12:1, 3). She is associated with the celestial powers that control life on earth and bring forth its fruitfulness. Yet her power contrasts with her vulnerability at this point in the narrative, as she labors to give birth to her child, leered over by the terrifying dragon. As the story progresses, the child is rescued, snatched up to the throne of God (12:5), and there is war in heaven that ejects the dragon (12:7–12). The woman, meanwhile, escapes, fleeing into the wilderness, where she is protected by God (12:6) and then by the earth itself, which comes to her aid as the dragon pursues her and attempts to destroy her children (12:13–17).

This mythological narrative has raised for many the question of the woman's identity.[40] Some traditions have identified the woman with the Virgin

---

37. Koester, *Revelation*, 308.
38. Koester, *Revelation*, 298–99.
39. On the dragon/serpent in Revelation, see Bauckham, *Climax of Prophecy*, 185–98.
40. For more details, see Beale, *Book of Revelation*, 624–43.

Mary, the mother of Christ, with suggestions of the flight into Egypt (Matt. 2:13–15), the crucifixion of Jesus, and his ascension into heaven (Luke 24:51). The details, however, do not cohere. The woman is a symbolic figure (as is the fiery red dragon) not of an individual woman but of Israel. She represents Zion, through whom God's people are nurtured, depicted in the Old Testament as a mother comforting her children (Isa. 66:7–13). What is significant is that a female figure is portrayed with such vibrant symbols of life-giving power and authority.

One text in Revelation that is particularly challenging is the reference to the 144,000 who have not "polluted themselves with women." Yet the chaste "virgins" (*parthenoi*) are female, representing the firstfruits of a harvest of faithful followers for the Lamb (Rev. 14:4–5).[41] However offensive the idea of being polluted by women seems to the modern reader, the language is both inclusive and metaphorical, since "such a misogynist stance appears nowhere else in Revelation."[42] If so, the text is speaking of Zion and symbolizing idolatry as sexual adultery: it signifies those, whether male or female, who have not given in to the worship of empire and who are therefore worthy to enter the new Jerusalem.

Though an enigma for many readers, the book of Revelation has extraordinary riches to be mined, if read aright in relation to other apocalyptic writings. Its symbolic language is more bizarre than that of the Fourth Gospel, and its female characterizations seem initially problematic today. But understood within its own worldview and its own context, it presents symbols that address the struggle, vulnerability, and longing for justice of the Christian community then and now, together with symbols of the life-giving way authority can be wielded in female as well as male hands.

Conclusion

These texts, coming toward or at the end of the New Testament canon, do not at first glance have much to say about women's leadership. Yet on closer inspection, challenging points emerge. The issue of translation and how to render androcentric language comes very much to the fore in the Johannine letters. The possibility of female leadership is represented in Hebrews, along with a reminder of the teaching role of Priscilla elsewhere in the New

---

41. Koester takes this to refer to females, as the word is almost never used of males (*Revelation*, 609–11). See also King, *Opening the Scroll*. Against this, cf. Aune, *Revelation*, 2:811–12; Pippin, "Revelation/Apocalypse," 629–30.
42. Schüssler Fiorenza, *Revelation*, 88.

Testament. The importance of context in understanding and interpreting texts is evident from 1 Peter, with its likely setting in the struggle against empire. And the images of female figures from Revelation present, on the one hand, conflicting and ambiguous models but also, on the other hand, positive representations of female authority that are life giving and fruitful. In general terms the interpretation of these texts, allowing for awareness of their original setting, offers a challenge to male-only images of authority and allows the biblical text to be understood in new ways that speak directly to the contemporary context.

PART 2

WOMEN'S
MINISTRY
IN THE
TRADITION

Chapter Eight

History and Texts

FOR SOME CHRISTIANS, it is enough to explore the biblical witness to decide the issue of women's ministry. It is a kind of sure bet on the question, and nothing more needs to be said once the exegetical work of forbidding women's leadership is done. This view often goes alongside the conviction that the witness of Scripture is univocal and transparent.[1] Thus there are no passages, in this view, that might be confined to specific situations, nor is there diversity of viewpoint or texts whose meanings are difficult, if not impossible, to decipher. There is, in short, no need for any interpretive theories to be explored, since the meaning of Scripture is plain, including its opposition to women's ordination. For other Christians, the story of the church has greater significance on the question of women's ministry. Here, too, there can exist a kind of fundamentalism, this time around tradition. The church has never had women in ordained ministry throughout its history, so the argument goes, and to move from the unanimity of tradition would be to place the church's identity in jeopardy. Ordaining women, or giving them leadership responsibilities as laity, would break decisively with an otherwise unbroken historical tradition.[2]

Both views might seem to represent extreme positions, "straw men" to knock down the patriarchal argument, but they are precisely the reasons given to keep women from leadership in the church and to deny them authority. We have already seen something of the complexity of Scripture and the

1. The view is encapsulated in Mark Thompson, *Clear and Present Word*, 143–70.
2. See, e.g., John Paul II, *Ordinatio Sacerdotalis*.

need for dynamic reinterpretation in the light of new knowledge and new contexts. This chapter turns now to look at the historical tradition beyond the Scriptures, asking the question, Do we have so unanimous a witness and so unbroken a historical practice as some have claimed?

Scripture, Tradition, and Context

Throughout the church's history, Scripture has been interpreted in the light of the various contexts in which Christians have found themselves. This is not to say that there has been no coherence or continuity of belief. Even in all the disagreement and painful schism, the church has held for the most part to its understanding of who God is, as revealed in the Scriptures and in the life, death, and resurrection of Jesus, and has maintained some kind of grasp on what the community of faith is, as it lives and grows around these central affirmations.

The claim is sometimes made that those who advocate for women's ministry are giving in to a liberal agenda arising from Western secularism that is implicitly alien to the Bible and the traditions of the church. Yet both the Bible itself and its interpreters down through the ages have addressed their own time and culture in their readings of Scripture, and they in turn have been influenced by those cultures. There is nothing inherently problematic in the dynamic between text and culture, except where dialogue breaks down. To take one example, the gospel itself, according to J. C. Beker, is made up of two aspects in Paul's writings: its core, which Beker calls its coherence, and its contingency or engagement with culture.[3] It is not a question of making a great effort to bridge the gulf and relate the gospel to context, but rather it is that the gospel itself contains both a universal and a contextual dimension. This is a helpful model for interpreting the New Testament as a whole. Biblical interpretation has the capacity to articulate the coherence of the gospel, as well as the capacity to speak powerfully into specific contexts. In this way, the Scriptures are able to reach across boundaries of age, culture, gender, and ethnicity. Context is part of the gospel itself and not something extraneous to it. In this sense, we can say that the gospel has both a universality and a contextuality to it.[4]

This is an important point apropos of the context of women in the contemporary world. As we saw in previous chapters, women in the patriarchal setting of the New Testament world were much less educated and had little public profile or power in comparison to men. Marriage was different in shape and character from what we know today. Women were vulnerable to death

---

3. Beker, *Paul the Apostle*, 23–35; see also Beker, "Authority of Scripture," 376–82.
4. See Mostert, "Catholicity of the Church," 123–36.

in childbirth—and in some places to divorce that could leave them disgraced and without access to their children. Leadership fell to males, with their much greater social and educational power, though elite women, married or single, could also take on limited roles in civic society. Today by comparison, women, at least in the Western world, are educated to the same level as men, and sometimes higher. They have an autonomous identity and wide experience in the external world, with access to social power, and pursue careers within and beyond the home according to their gifts. Patriarchy and gender bias may still exist, but it is nothing like the level and intensity of the ancient world.

To include reference to women's contemporary context is not in itself a betrayal of the gospel nor a denial of its universal scope and claims. We are obligated to speak to and from our social contexts by the imperative of the gospel, just as we have to take seriously the gulf that separates us from women in the biblical world and from ancient culture generally. Dialogue with culture on women's place in church and society need not mean selling out to secular and antibiblical values. On the contrary, the gospel calls for such collaboration by virtue of the incarnation and God's radical engagement in Jesus Christ with human life in all its breadth and diversity. The tradition of the church at its best has always engaged with culture.

Context is not just a series of historical events and cultural expressions that have no connection to each other across the generations. Although contexts do change—and sometimes change often—practices and beliefs accumulate from one generation to another. Without this accumulation, the church would be reinventing itself de novo in every generation. This underground stream of custom and convention flowing beneath the surface of the church's daily life, though not always apparent to it, can be named "tradition," a word that may be viewed as either blessing or curse. In a brief but cogent essay on biblical authority, Kevin Giles argues from his vantage point as an evangelical that tradition plays an important role in interpreting Scripture. He distinguishes between "church traditions" (styles of music, liturgical vestments, and so on) and "tradition," understanding the latter to be the community's ongoing decisions on what the Scriptures mean. Thus, for example, there is a vital place for the ecumenical creeds in his discussion, since they gather together and clarify what the diversity of scriptural texts actually says on the identity of Jesus and the nature of God as Trinity.

Giles does much to break down the hard-and-fast delineation between those who affirm the authority of Scripture and those who see "tradition" as having a role in revelation. In fact, the interrelationship is more of a spectrum than a strict division of either-or. The early creeds and confessions were debated on scriptural grounds. Part of the issue lies in discerning the difference between church teaching that goes beyond Scripture—moving into areas that the Bible does not envisage—and teaching that goes against it. New problems that have no direct word from Scripture require new answers, guided by theological principles that derive ultimately from the Bible. Giles believes that the issue of women's ministry is still awaiting a doctrinal consensus across the church to draw together the biblical witness into a clear theology of affirmation.[5]

In Catholic and Orthodox churches, in both the East and West, tradition has a much clearer place, running alongside Scripture as authoritative in the life of the church. Here again is the distinction between tradition and traditions, the former signifying the core ecumenical councils of the church, as well as the early texts that established the life of the church and its core teachings. Of particular significance are formulations of the Trinity and the nature of Christ that are drawn from the Scriptures and elucidated by the church. In this sense, tradition in the formal sense emerges from the life of the church through the Holy Spirit as it is led "into all truth" (John 16:13). Note that Scripture and tradition do not stand in opposition in this perspective but are seen as working cooperatively.[6] Tradition has its roots in Scripture and is to be distinguished from human-constructed traditions that contradict biblical teaching. It is tradition that "at the same time treasures and transcends both context and culture."[7]

The task of discernment is to differentiate between tradition—in the formal sense of trajectories emerging from Scripture—and traditions, which are ephemeral, eccentric, or antithetical to biblical teaching. This is a common task across denominational boundaries. There is no wide gulf between Giles's understanding of the church's task and the Orthodox understanding of it; it is more a question of emphasis. Scripture does not exist in a vacuum, and the church believes that the Holy Spirit is the one who both inspired and inspires the sacred text in the task of interpretation. In this sense, "Tradition and traditions are not to be confused,"[8] yet the task of untangling them is complex and controversial, and they are not easily separated.[9]

Early Trajectories: Texts outside the Canon

Alongside the biblical books that became the canon of the New Testament, a large number of other texts from the history of the early church belong on the spectrum between tradition and traditions. These texts demonstrate

---

5. Giles, *What the Bible Actually Teaches on Women*, 17–18.
6. Chryssavgis, *Way of the Fathers*, 63–69.
7. Chryssavgis, *Way of the Fathers*, 21.
8. Behr-Sigel, *Ministry of Women*, 94.
9. As Behr-Sigel points out (*Ministry of Women*, 93–99).

something of how the early communities beyond the first century understood the New Testament witness and the trajectories they saw arising from it. These noncanonical writings pose a particular challenge on the issue of women's ministry because of the texts' ambivalent status within the church. Some of these stand on the border of, or even outside, what emerged as orthodox Christian faith and present a view of the world and matter as negative, if not actually evil. This view is often associated with various forms of Gnosticism or Marcionism in the second century, which held spiritualized worldviews that gave no place to the Old Testament or the God of creation. Some writings are somewhat ambiguous in their relationship to the wider church. Other noncanonical writings belong firmly within Christian faith, even if they were not accepted into the New Testament canon.

One example of the latter is that of the late-second-century apocryphal writing The Acts of Thekla.[10] The figure of Saint Thekla was immensely popular among Christians in the ensuing centuries. Her biography tells of a wealthy woman who gives up riches, status, and fiancé for the sake of the gospel, which she first hears from Saint Paul. As a consequence of her conversion and commitment to celibacy, she endures the persecution of her family and the Roman Empire, since her disdain of marriage and motherhood makes her a threat to its values.[11] Following her conversion, Thekla proclaims the gospel, even baptizing herself in the arena when threatened with death, from which she miraculously escapes. Her greatness is associated with her heroism and willingness to face a martyr's death, her passionate love of the gospel, her disregard for Roman cultural values, and her chosen vocation of celibacy for the rest of her life. Because she is a disciple of Paul and commits herself to a life of danger, and because of her attachment to the gospel message, Thekla is considered equal to the apostles. She is "a well-educated, intelligent and independently minded woman" who also knows "herself to be called by God to a ministry of teaching (men and women) and initiating (men and women) in the church."[12] In revering her, early Christians also praise her "feminine" virtues, alongside her countercultural conduct, particularly that of modesty, through which she demonstrates the capacity both to stand alongside male leaders and to submit to the qualities required of females in their own contexts.[13]

10. Thekla's biography constitutes sections 1–43 of the biography of Paul and often circulated independently; see "Acts of Paul and Thecla," 364–72. See also Cohick and Hughes, "Thecla," 1–25.

11. See Cartlidge, "Thekla," 1–14.

12. Dr. Geoffrey Jenkins, personal communication, January 19, 2020. There is a lesser-known and longer biography, *The Life of Thekla*, which portrays Thekla as an apostle; see Kateusz, *Mary and Early Christian Women*.

13. Hylen, *Thecla*, 73–81.

There have been claims that certain groups, some of them later considered heretical by the church, were more favorably disposed toward women's ministry than the groups within developing orthodox or proto-orthodox circles.[14] Much of the discussion about this revolves around the figure of Mary Magdalene, who is extolled in several "Gospels" of the early period that lie on the fringes or outside Christian orthodoxy. Mary has a whole Gospel dedicated to her—although a key part of the original manuscript is lost—which depicts her having a special relationship with Jesus as his disciple, with an equivalent status to the apostles. Jesus, indeed, gives her secret teaching to deliver to them. The Gospel of Mary is not considered orthodox theologically because it shows "a generally pessimistic view of the world and also the body," although these are not seen as evil in themselves.[15] There is also, correspondingly, no sense of a future return of Christ or of the redemption of creation. Mary has already achieved eternal rest even before her death in this Gospel, though her death will complete it. This perspective arises from a docetic view of the world, in which created matter has little or no place and the body has no ultimate, eschatological significance. Mary receives revelation from the Risen Christ yet experiences misunderstanding and hostility from the male disciples, who struggle to comprehend and resent the relationship she has with Jesus, especially given that she is a woman. Why would special revelation be given to her that is not given to them? In defending her against the criticisms of Peter, Levi speaks with authority: "If the Savior made her worthy, who are you then, for your part, to cast her aside?"[16]

The Gospel of Philip—so named because the apostle Philip is the only male apostle to be mentioned—is one of the Nag Hammadi documents discovered in 1946 and should probably be dated somewhere between the second and fourth centuries. It reflects the views of Valentinian Gnosticism. Here Mary Magdalene is one of the three closest female companions of Jesus, the other two being his mother and her (or his?) sister. Jesus loves Magdalene above all the other disciples in this text and kisses her, much to their annoyance. While this is sometimes seen as the basis for the view that Jesus married Mary Magdalene, the point of his preference for her has more to do with her superior access to the light of understanding than with any sexual motive.[17] In another of the Gnostic texts, Pistis Sophia, discovered in 1773 and dating

14. Pagels, *Gnostic Gospels*, 48–69.
15. Parkhouse, "Matter and the Soul," 222.
16. "Gospel according to Mary," 599. This Gospel was discovered in 1896 in Coptic; originally it was written in Greek, probably in the second century CE.
17. "Gospel of Philip," 141–60.

back to the third or fourth centuries, Mary Magdalene is portrayed as one of the main disciples in asking questions of Jesus, and she is highly commended by him for her insightful questioning.[18]

The positive presentation of Mary Magdalene coheres with the New Testament picture of one of the main Christian witnesses to Jesus's death, burial, and resurrection who, in John's Gospel, is the first to be given the commission to proclaim the resurrection, as we have already seen.[19] What exactly is added by these noncanonical texts to the biblical portrait of Mary Magdalene is perhaps the explicitly favorable comparison between her and the other disciples in Jesus's estimation. But it is worth noting that there is sometimes a price to be paid for this prominence. In the Gospel of Thomas, another of the Nag Hammadi texts, whose dating is probably early, Jesus assures the disciples in relation to Mary that "every woman who makes herself male will enter into the reign of heaven."[20] At the very least these noncanonical texts confirm the presence of women as leaders in the community beyond the first century, particularly the figure of Mary Magdalene. She is generally portrayed as a devoted disciple of Jesus and revered for her role as the primary witness to the resurrection; as a consequence, she is depicted as a leading figure of faith.

Also significant is the role of Mary the mother of Jesus in early Christian understanding, where she is portrayed as both mother and leader. The Proto-Gospel of James, an orthodox Christian rather than Gnostic Christian text, narrates the story of Mary's birth, her childhood in the temple (including entry into the holy of holies), the annunciation to her at a well, and her giving birth to Jesus in a cave.[21] Note the parallels here with the story of the child Samuel in the temple (1 Sam. 2–3). The work is purportedly written by James, who is portrayed as the stepbrother of Jesus.[22] In the Gospel of Bartholomew (or Questions of Bartholomew), which also contains the tradition of Mary dwelling in the temple, it is Mary rather than Peter who leads the Twelve in prayer, though only after a debate in which her preeminent authority is asserted by those present.[23] The additional elements in these early noncanonical Gospels, though in some respects legendary, underline the importance of the mother of Jesus as a prophetic figure and a leader in the early Christian community.

18. "Pistis Sophia."
19. See above, chap. 4, "Mary Magdalene."
20. Gospel of Thomas 114 (Aland, 530).
21. For an overview of the Proto-Gospel and its significance in regard to Mary, see Gaventa, *Mary*, 249–93.
22. "Proto-Gospel of James."
23. "Gospel of Bartholomew." See Kateusz, *Mary and Early Christian Women*.

Hidden History in the Early Church

Texts

These and other texts indicate that there was considerably more diversity among Christian communities in the early period than is often assumed and that women played a much larger role than the texts we have suggest: "When you hear the witness or even the quoted voice of a woman in an Early Christian text, including the Bible, it is often the tip of the iceberg in terms of what it actually represents about women's contributions."[24] There is emerging evidence of women exercising leadership within the church during these early centuries, though alongside the history of women's pastoral and priestly ministry is another tale of resistance to their ministry. What is now becoming clear is that the story of women's involvement in teaching, preaching, and sacramental ministry in the early church has been concealed by later attempts on the part of scribes and church authorities to hide or deny the evidence of the early centuries. We need to reconsider what constitutes tradition in the light of this reality.

Women's leadership in the earliest period is associated with the two key New Testament women already mentioned in this discussion: Mary Magdalene and Mary the mother of Jesus. The title "apostle of the apostles," given in the early church, is confirmed in the medieval church for Mary Magdalene.[25] The Catholic Church, which has transformed her memorial day to a feast day (July 22), now regards her as an evangelist and the primary witness (*prima testis*) of the resurrection.[26] In the East, where she is not usually confused with the penitent sinner who anoints Jesus's feet (Luke 7:36–50), Mary is given the title *isapostolos*, "equal to the apostles."[27] Like the mother of Jesus, Mary Magdalene can also be seen as a second Eve, retrieving what Eve lost in the garden of Eden in her meeting with the Risen Christ and her obedient proclamation of his resurrection in the Easter garden (John 20:1–18).[28]

The mother of Jesus is commemorated in these sources not just for her motherhood, as we have noted, but also for her leadership in the early church. In the Dormition traditions ("dormition" means the death of Mary), which

24. McCarty, "Glimpse into the Wisdom," 2.

25. Hippolytus of Rome speaks of Martha and Mary as "apostles of the apostles" (identifying Mary Magdalene with Mary of Bethany) but otherwise shows no particular support for women's ministry; so Y. Smith, "Women's Ordination," 311–35.

26. The title appears to arise in late antiquity and the medieval West (Rabanus Maurus and Thomas Aquinas); see "Apostle of the Apostles."

27. See M. Green, "Mary Magdalene," 27.

28. Camery-Hoggatt, "Images of Mary Magdalene," 23.

narrate the story of Mary's death (some of them dating back to the early centuries), Mary incenses the tomb of Jesus, and at her death, women swing censers over her body, suggesting that this liturgical function was generally practiced by women as well as men in the Christian assembly.

According to Ally Kateusz, there is an important textual issue in this evidence that points to hidden traditions about the depiction of Mary and other women leaders in the church. In assessing the differences between manuscripts, modern textual critics tend to prefer the shorter reading in any disputed manuscript as reflecting the more original reading. This preference ignores the fact that sometimes sections might be omitted by scribes who find them improbable or offensive. This is most apparent in passages outlining women's liturgical leadership, where the longer narratives are more explicit than the shorter ones and, in Kateusz's view, earlier in dating. For example, Kateusz argues that one of the Dormition manuscripts, written in a form of Aramaic in the second century, preserves a much longer narrative that includes Mary acting with considerable authority: preaching, performing miracles, and leading in prayer. This material suggests that "later scribes did not *add* scenes of Mary's leadership, they *excised* them."[29]

As with a number of other issues, it is not unanimously agreed, as is sometimes claimed, that women had no access to the ordained ministries in orthodox Christian circles. Women deacons existed not only in the New Testament period but also beyond it.[30] In 112 CE, Pliny the Younger, the Roman governor of Bithynia, writes to the emperor Trajan about how to deal with Christians, describing two female *ministrae*, probably deacons, whom he has questioned under torture (they are slaves and can therefore be treated this way) and who have held fast to their faith.[31] The role of deacons may have meant a specific ministry *to* women—teaching and baptizing—but there is no reason to assume it was *confined* to women, especially in the early period. Female deacons were more prevalent in the East, but in the third century, the office of deaconess, with a ministry directed to women, emerged; it existed alongside that of (female) deacons into the sixth century.[32] Even so, their precise roles are not easy to discern, and it is likely that there was considerable diversity across different communities within the Orthodox tradition.

29. Kateusz, *Mary and Early Christian Women* (italics original). For an overview of the contents of The Six Books Dormition Apocryphon, see Stephen Shoemaker, who disagrees on a number of points connected to Mary's priesthood (*Mary in Early Christian Faith*, 212–67).

30. See Madigan and Osiek, *Ordained Women*.

31. Pliny, *Letters II* 10.96.

32. On the relevant texts and inscriptions that reveal a remarkable and widespread number of women serving the church in an official diaconal capacity, see Madigan and Osiek, *Ordained Women*, 25–105.

Writing of ordained women in the Western church, Gary Macy has found evidence in texts and funerary inscriptions that illustrate the ordination of a small number of women as bishops and priests. He names Brigid of Ireland in the ninth century, who was consecrated bishop by a kind of accident but still went on to function as a bishop.[33] And a handful of inscriptions refer to women presbyters from the fourth to the sixth century;[34] we can only imagine their struggle against constant criticism and opposition. Women played other roles in the liturgy as well, and the evidence suggests that "the practice of women serving at the altar persisted long after legislation had forbidden it."[35]

Also extant are biographical fragments of women leaders in the early church. One such leader named Mariamne, most likely Mary Magdalene, is said to be the apostle Philip's sister and appears in the Acts of Philip as an apostle, preaching and baptizing throughout her life.[36] Another biography depicts Irene of Macedonia, called an apostle, who is baptized by Timothy and goes on to perform miracles, teach, and baptize. Nino, a female saint of the Georgian church, has a biography written of her that includes reference to her ordination in Jerusalem by the patriarch there and narrates her ministry as an apostle who baptizes, preaches, performs miracles, and travels around engaging in mission.[37]

In the light of this biographical evidence, it is hardly surprising that Tertullian in the third century rails against women in public ministry. In his austere view, women should not teach or baptize and, even in private, should not evangelize pagans; silence, modesty, and chastity are to be their virtues, without ostentation of any kind, confined exclusively to the domestic sphere, and without formal ministry of any kind in church or home: "But the impudence of that woman who assumed the right to teach, surely she is not going to arrogate to herself the right to baptize as well."[38] To Tertullian's outrage, Thekla is being used as a model to justify women's apostolic ministry.

There is a certain irony to this: Tertullian himself admired the Montanists, who, following the teaching of Montanus (fl. second century CE), believed in ecstatic revelation from the Spirit-Paraclete and lived scrupulously moral and ascetic lives. Two women were associated with Montanus as prophets, Priscilla and Maximilla, coleaders of the movement. Nothing remains of the

33. Macy, *Hidden History*, 54.
34. Macy, *Hidden History*, 60–63. See also Madigan and Osiek, *Ordained Women*, 163–202.
35. Macy, *Hidden History*, 63.
36. Kateusz, *Mary and Early Christian Women*; see also Bovon and Matthews, *Acts of Philip*, 31–108.
37. Kateusz, *Mary and Early Christian Women*.
38. Tertullian, *De baptismo* 17.4 (Evans, 97); see Torjesen, *When Women Were Priests*, 159.

Montanists' views, except for the orthodox tradition that eventually declared them heretical.[39] Yet Tertullian, without abandoning his Catholic faith, was influenced by the "New Prophecy" in his later years, which included (though he had some reservations) authoritative female prophets.[40]

Another significant and slightly later text is the Life of the Virgin, a seventh-century (though the date could be later) biography of Mary from birth to death, purportedly written by Maximus the Confessor.[41] In this account Mary is present with Jesus throughout his ministry of teaching and healing, giving leadership to the women followers, who are explicitly named "disciples," and teaching and supervising the apostles (both male and female) in their dissemination of the good news after Jesus's resurrection. The narrative elevates not only Mary but also the women disciples with whom she is associated, who are present at the Last Supper, where Mary officiates alongside Jesus. Men and women live and work together in equality in this biography, with paired ministries.[42] Whatever we make of the Marian theology, the biography testifies that women ministered coequally with men in some Christian communities. The practice may reflect the kind of Christian assembly that Epiphanius of Salamis (315–403 CE) rails against in his *Panarion* (his "medicine chest" of heresies), an assembly in which female bishops and presbyters use Galatians 3:28 to justify their ministry.[43]

The same tradition of women's participation in the Last Supper is found in the Apostolic Church Order, a text arising from the third or fourth century. The author does not dispute the tradition of women's presence but does deny that Jesus gave them eucharistic authority alongside the men. He gives a number of reasons to discount women's ministry at the altar, including that Mary laughed during the ritual (cf. Gen. 18:12–15), thus discrediting her authority, and that women, in any case, should pray seated rather than standing. The text not only confirms the tradition of female presence at the Last Supper but also reveals that in the early centuries the question of women's ministry was debated. There was "a raging ideological conflict" in which one side was "using Mary to justify women officiants, and the other faction . . . was going to great lengths to try to undermine Mary's authority."[44]

39. Eusebius, *Ecclesiastical History* 5.14–19 (Lake, 1–5:470–71).

40. Coakley, *God, Sexuality, and the Self*, 124–26.

41. Maximus the Confessor, *Life of the Virgin*. Kateusz is critical of Shoemaker's translation, arguing that it obscures the authority of Mary and the women disciples (*Mary and Early Christian Women*).

42. Kateusz, *Mary and Early Christian Women*.

43. Epiphanius of Salamis, *Panarion* 2.2.3 (Williams, 23).

44. Kateusz, *Mary and Early Christian Women*.

Art and Artifacts

Written texts take us some distance, revealing the ambiguous story of the reception of women's ministry and the cultural bias against them in many—though not all—quarters of the church. What needs also to be taken into account are the art and artifacts from the early period, which tell a less ambivalent story and furnish evidence of women's continued ministry. From paintings we find imagery and symbolism associated with women deacons, priests, and even bishops—not necessarily from fringe parts of the church whose orthodoxy might be suspect. The key feature of these depictions lies in the clothing the women wear and the particular liturgical offices that the clothing designates.

In some portrayals, the mother of Jesus is depicted directly below Jesus, surrounded by the apostles and with her arms raised to lead in prayer and bless the assembled throng. More significantly, she is shown wearing the episcopal garb of the church in the West from the sixth century (including the pallium, a long white cloth decorated with a cross and worn over a chasuble by bishops for the Eucharist); such depictions may include Elizabeth in similar array. In one such portrayal, Mary is surrounded by twelve women who are pictured as apostles and leaders (and they include Thekla, Perpetua, and Felicity). These depictions make clear that Mary is not unique in this respect; the depictions support the ministry of both women and men. A mosaic from Rome places her above the altar with arms raised, wearing a pallium and surrounded by Peter, Paul, and a number of bishops, the center of eucharistic worship. This picture of Mary as bishop, and even archbishop, persists in early Christian art. Another garment associated with priestly office is a fringed cloth, later called a maniple, that is worn by a person presiding at the Eucharist and is associated with depictions not just of Mary but also of other women.[45]

Despite artistic records of women celebrating the Eucharist from the second century onward, some of the early fathers were highly critical of churches that had male and female clergy. Saint John Chrysostom (ca. 349–407 CE), for example, in speaking of Simon Peter's commission by the Risen Lord (John 21:15–19), exclaims, "When one is required to preside over the Church, and to be entrusted with the care of so many souls, the whole female sex must retire before the magnitude of the task."[46] Later in the same treatise, he notes that though prevented by Scripture from teaching, some women have pushed themselves forward, shouldering an authority that is against their nature:

45. Kateusz, *Mary and Early Christian Women*. Note the irony of the Vatican decree of 1916 that Mary is not to be depicted in priestly garb.
46. John Chrysostom, *Six Books on the Priesthood* 2.2 (Neville, 17).

"The divine law excluded women from the ministry, but they forcibly push themselves in. . . . They have got such power that they can appoint and dismiss priests at will. Topsy-turvy (you can see the force of the proverb borne out) 'the followers lead their leaders.' . . . Women, the very ones who are not even allowed to teach. . . . But I have heard it said that they have assumed such freedom of speech that they even rebuke the prelates of the churches and upbraid them more bitterly than masters would their slaves."[47] Ironically, the arguments against women's ministry point to its persistence in the early church.

The history of art presents us with an alternative and more positive perspective on women's ministry. Pope Paschal in the ninth century is pictured in a mosaic with his mother, Theodora, in the chapel of San Zeno. The depiction is damaged and the name slightly defaced, but the woman is portrayed as a bishop in her own right.[48] It is also likely that evidence of other women leaders was hidden or effaced: one fresco from the fifth or sixth century in the funereal catacomb in Naples, now restored, depicts Cerula as a bishop near the picture of Bitalia, who is also arrayed in episcopal attire. Both have the telling depiction of the four Gospels around their heads, which is typical symbolism for bishops.[49] Elsewhere there is pictorial evidence of gender pairing at the altar, with a male and a female priest concelebrating.[50]

In these and other ways, the true story of women's participation in leadership in teaching, evangelizing, and celebrating the sacraments has been hidden and, in some cases, distorted. It is often assumed that words like *presbytera* and *episcopa* mean the *wife* of a priest or bishop, but again this is an assumption that should be questioned, especially when the women concerned are arrayed in presbyteral or episcopal attire. One church father complains that a woman bishop (*episcopa*) is not in submission to her husband.[51] The retelling of these censored stories from ancient texts and Christian art needs to be heard anew. They reveal the ways in which "our false imagination of the past impedes our interpretation of ancient artifacts that depicted Christian women as ministerial and Eucharistic leaders."[52] The evidence is strong that, on the one hand, women continued to engage in pastoral, sacramental, preaching, and teaching ministry in parts of the early church and that, on the other hand, this ministry was seen as an embarrassment and shameful in others parts of the church.

47. John Chrysostom, *Six Books on the Priesthood* 3.9 (Neville, 78).

48. Macy, *Hidden History*, 53.

49. Kateusz, *Mary and Early Christian Women*.

50. See, e.g., the third-century fresco in the Calistus Catacomb in Rome (Kateusz, *Mary and Early Christian Women*).

51. Kateusz, *Mary and Early Christian Women*.

52. Kateusz, *Mary and Early Christian Women*.

Early Church Mothers

This narrative of a hidden history in relation to women's ordination needs also to be set alongside the many women in the early centuries of the church who did not aspire—or were prevented from aspiring—to ordained ministry but whose ministries in their own spheres were extensive. We often speak of the writings of the church *fathers*, but it is important to remember that there were also mothers, though considerably fewer in number and with fewer writings. These women either wrote themselves or influenced profoundly the men who did. It may also be that in the number of early Christian writings now lost to us, there were also women writers.

Of the female writers, perhaps the best known is Perpetua of Carthage. The *Passion of Saints Perpetua, Felicity and Their Companions* is written in part by Perpetua herself in the early years of the third century.[53] She writes a kind of diary of the events leading up to her martyrdom in the arena, where she dies along with Felicity, her slave, and several other catechumens (candidates for baptism).[54] Both women are recent mothers, Felicity giving birth to a daughter immediately before her martyrdom, and their equality in the arena testifies to the leveling effects of Christian community. Perpetua's narrative is that of an educated woman who is deeply immersed in Christian faith;[55] she places her love of Christ and her desire not to disown him above the deepest of family ties.

In the *Passion*, Perpetua recounts how she stands out against her father, defying his authority and his tearful pleas that she sacrifice to the emperor and renounce her allegiance to Christ. In one of her visions, Perpetua dreams of a ladder she must climb, avoiding the terrifying serpent at its base. She succeeds by standing on the monster's head and climbing onto the ladder, an allusion to the promise that Eve's descendants will strike the serpent's head (Gen. 3:15). Perpetua's passion can be interpreted in a number of different ways, including in relation to Montanism, but one of these is surely the way in which the believer's relationship with Christ not only transcends all other relationships but also challenges the patriarchal and authoritarian world of Greco-Roman culture. She defies father and emperor to stand in solidarity with the other catechumens, among them slaves, in devotion to Christ.

Egeria is another female writer of the early church. Little is known of her origins and status, but she recounts the story of her long pilgrimage to the

---

53. Heffernan, *Passion of Perpetua and Felicity*, 100–134.
54. Cohick and Hughes, "Perpetua and Felicitas," 27–64.
55. On the marginalization of Perpetua, including in terms of her authorship, see Tilley, "Passion of Perpetua and Felicity," 832–36; see also Heffernan, *Passion of Perpetua and Felicity*, 1–8.

Holy Land, writing in letter form (in Latin) to the women at home.[56] These "sisters" may possibly be members of her family, but they are more likely fellow Christians and perhaps consecrated women in religious community. The parts we have of Egeria's journey (*Itinerarium Egeriae*)—the earliest manuscript is partial and late—display her courage in traveling alone; her deep spirituality and connection to God; her lively, inquiring mind; and her profound love of the church. Not only does she spend three years in Jerusalem participating in the liturgical life of the church there and describing it for future generations, but she also visits the shrine of Thekla to pay homage to an early woman leader and hero of the faith.[57]

A third woman writer of this period is Empress Eudocia (ca. 401–460 CE), who became a Christian on her marriage to Theodosius II, emperor of the Eastern empire, the center of which was in Constantinople. Eudocia was brought up in Athens and given an excellent education in the classics by her philosopher-father. Rumors of adultery and even murder surround Eudocia's life, but she lived in a context of political intrigue that itself makes the rumors questionable. She helped to found the University of Constantinople but fell out with her powerful sister-in-law, Pulcheria. Pulcheria, who was herself a theologian of some prominence and a noted ascetic, organized with her younger brother, Theodosius II, both the Council of Ephesus (431) and the Council of Chalcedon (451). Unlike Eudocia at first, Pulcheria supported strongly the title *Theotokos* (God-bearer) of Mary in an effort to promote what became orthodox Christology: that Christ has two natures, divine and human, not one. Eudocia and Pulcheria never reconciled their rivalry or differences.[58]

In exile in Jerusalem, where she spent the last years of her life, Eudocia wrote a number of literary works as a Christian scholar, not all of which are extant and few of which have been translated into English. In addition to a poem commemorating the martyrdom of Cyprian of Antioch, she wrote using the genre of the Homeric cento (pl. "centones"). The centones she wrote are poems on Christ and the Bible woven together like a patchwork quilt from familiar lines taken from Homer's *Iliad* and *Odyssey*. These epic tales were considered in late antiquity as the height of literary sophistication. In all, Eudocia wrote more than three thousand lines of poetry, uniting her love of Christ and Scripture with her impressive classical learning. Perhaps because of their eccentric quality (to our eyes) and because they are penned by a

---

56. McGowan and Bradshaw, *Pilgrimage of Egeria*.
57. Cohick and Hughes, "Egeria's *Itinerary* and Christian Pilgrimage."
58. Cohick and Hughes, "Aelia Pulcheria."

woman whose theology, if not morality, was at points suspect,[59] these poems have been neglected and are rarely studied.[60] Yet they testify to the impact of educated women in the church and their capacity to articulate theology and spirituality—even if their writings are often ignored. They testify also to a highly educated scholar who wanted to find a way to integrate her literary learning from paganism with her Christian beliefs.

Women of Influence

In addition to women associated with theological texts, many women were martyrs for their faith, and still others took on the ascetic life, either in communities together or as hermits. The period of the desert mothers (*ammas*), in particular, from the third to the sixth centuries, saw many women leave behind the security of home and family to embrace a countercultural way of living in response to the gospel.[61] Significantly, none of these women are accorded the level of interest received by their male colleagues. Yet their testimony to Christ and to the life of faith is every bit as committed and heroic, serving others with spiritual insight and radical self-giving.[62]

Not all female theologians were actual writers; some, instead, influenced the men closest to them who did write. Most impressive among these are the Cappadocian Mothers in the fourth century: the women associated with Gregory of Nyssa, Basil the Great, and Gregory of Nazianzus.[63] These three great champions of orthodoxy in the battle against the Arian heresy (they understood the Trinity at a deeper level as the equal union and interrelationship of the three divine Persons) were greatly influenced as theologians by the women of their families. Gregory and Basil's mother, Macrina the Elder, and their sister, Macrina the Younger, are both saints.

Gregory of Nyssa regarded his sister as his theological teacher and the successor to Saint Thekla; he wrote an account of Macrina's life after her death (*Vita Sanctae Macrinae*). In this deeply moving account, Macrina is depicted as a Christian philosopher, teacher, woman of prayer, and miracle worker.[64] With her mother and their female servants she established a monas-

---

59. Apart from the rumors about her personal life, which make no sense given her continued prestige and status within the empire, Eudocia had an initial theological preference for Monophysitism (the idea that Christ has only one nature) but conceded to what became orthodox Christology later in life. From Palestine she also had a significant influence on the Council of Chalcedon.

60. Note the forthcoming study by Sowers, *In Her Own Words*.

61. Chryssavgis, *Way of the Fathers*, 45–51.

62. Swan, *Forgotten Desert Mothers*, 5–31.

63. See especially Sunberg, *Cappadocian Mothers*.

64. Gregory of Nyssa, *Life of St. Macrina*.

tic community on egalitarian terms, each woman sharing the work in equal measure; she had already given away all her possessions. Gregory also wrote a dialogue on the resurrection in which Macrina is the teacher, setting out the Christian understanding of the resurrection of the dead and the life of the soul (*De anima et resurrectione*).[65] Doubts may be cast over whether this is really Macrina or Gregory speaking, but these are false alternatives. His portrait of her life and death coheres with this teaching, and although Gregory was a consummate theologian in his own right, he maintained an acute awareness of how much of his theology derived from his sister. In a patriarchal context, it would be unusual in any case to boast of a woman as theological mentor and educator. On the basis of Macrina and her influence, Gregory believed in the equality of the sexes and the ending of sexual differentiation in the life to come. It is not without cause that Macrina has been described as "the fourth Cappadocian."[66] Here again we encounter the hiddenness of women as theologians. We can also recognize the need to draw women into the spotlight in our reading of a Christian past that is often male centered and marginalizing of women's contribution to the ministry of the church.

These women and the roles they play, along with supporting evidence from texts and artifacts, need to be taken into account when we discern the authentic shape of tradition. It is true that a number of these women are already considered saints in the church's calendar. But their contribution to the theological and liturgical life of the household of faith is still downplayed, if not ignored or discredited in many communities, especially those most concerned with delineating the character and contents of tradition.

Conclusion

There is no single, unanimous voice on women's ministry throughout the history and experience of the church. From the early days, women engaged in leadership and ministry in various communities and in different ways. The suppression of that ministry was not total in the early centuries and not universally forbidden for over a millennium. In some contexts, women's ministry flourished and was valued, despite opposition. Women held office in the church, preaching, teaching, and administering the sacraments, a ministry that was slowly eroded in many areas. These activities continued in religious life and in other ways, exercising considerable influence through later periods. But not until the Reformation of the sixteenth century and its aftermath did

65. Gregory of Nyssa, *Soul and the Resurrection*.
66. See Pelikan, *Christianity and Classical Culture*, 7–21.

women's ministry and leadership begin to reemerge, again slowly—both in spontaneous expressions such as ad hoc preaching and in more formal orders of ministry. History, in other words, needs to be rewritten—and is already being rewritten—to remove the bias of male historiography and to make visible the dim or hidden figures of women in the church's story, including the astonishing roles they played in leadership. This gives us a basis for understanding the tradition in new and exciting ways that open doors for women's gifts to emerge.

Chapter Nine

Theology

A SOLID THEOLOGICAL CASE can be made, on the basis of the tradition, as we have seen it in previous chapters, for women's ordination and authority in the life of the church. This chapter moves from history to theology (inasmuch as they can be separated) to discuss some of the theological objections often given to restrict and delimit women's ministry. Many of these discussions focus on theological themes that are biblical in origin, either explicitly or implicitly, and draw on what we have already seen of the New Testament evidence, as well as the witness of the early history of women's leadership. Thus this chapter draws out issues already touched on in previous chapters.

Women's Ministry and the Twelve

One theological argument that claims the authority of the tradition is that the Twelve are the inheritors of Christ's ministry and that no woman, however worthy, is included among them and therefore cannot function in formal ministry. Once again, we are up against the distorted and excluding power of gender. The twelve apostles undeniably play a critical function in the New Testament, particularly in the formation of the Christian church. The Lukan story of Pentecost is predicated on the presence of the Twelve (Acts 2:1–13), a number that needs first to be completed due to the demise of Judas Iscariot and which is made up by Matthias, an eyewitness of Jesus's own ministry (1:15–26). In the book of Revelation, the heavenly city has walls adorned with precious stones that have inscribed on their foundations the names of the twelve apostles, just as the gates are inscribed with the names of the twelve tribes of Israel (Rev. 21:12–14). No woman is included in either group.

Neither is the apostle Paul included among the Twelve, despite his significance for the future shape of the church, which emerged from his missional work among gentiles. Nor are gentiles included among the Twelve: they are all Jewish males. Their function is primarily symbolic, connecting the church both to Israel as a community and to Jesus himself and his ministry.[1] Despite the Twelve's key place within the formation of the church, they are not alone in holding authority or proclaiming the gospel in apostolic ways. Indeed, Paul speaks of other apostles in Romans 16, male as well as female, including the apostle Junia, and Luke names Barnabas as an apostle (Acts 14:14). That Paul and others held a status in teaching authority that was the equivalent of the Twelve, even if their symbolic value is different, can hardly be doubted.

Some ecclesial traditions speak of Jesus's choosing of the Twelve as if that action in itself indicates that women cannot be priests.[2] In this view, Jesus's command at the Last Supper, "Do this in remembrance of me," is addressed not to all Christians but specifically to the gathered apostles (Luke 22:19; 1 Cor. 11:23–25).[3] The same is argued for Jesus's washing of the feet of the Twelve: that it speaks of their union with him in priestly ministry and enjoins them to follow his example as they pursue their vocation (John 13:8, 12–15).[4] This priestly ministry is then passed down through tradition via the role of the bishops, the rightful successors to the Twelve, who only ever ordained males thereafter.

There are a number of unquestioned assumptions in this formulaic reading of the Last Supper. For example, it is not at all clear from the Gospels that only the Twelve were present at the Last Supper. There is some evidence, particularly in the Johannine account, to suggest that other men, as well as women, were also present on this solemn occasion.[5] Some later church traditions, as we have seen, also preserve a memory of the presence of Mary the mother of Jesus and other Galilean women.

Nor is it clear that any sense of ordination is exegetically present in the narratives of the Last Supper as we have them. It is not enough to claim that Jesus's words of remembrance have the effect of ordination and are addressed with that meaning to the twelve apostles. This feature is not explicit in the

---

1. Wijngaards, *Ordination of Women*, 92–99.
2. On recent Catholic teaching from the Congregation for Doctrine, see Wijngaards, *Ordination of Women*, 91–92.
3. The words are absent from Mark's and Matthew's accounts (Mark 14:22–24 par.) and only appear once in Luke's Gospel, over the bread.
4. See, e.g., Broussard, "Did Jesus Make the Apostles Priests."
5. Lee, "Presence or Absence," 1–20.

text and does not allow for the presence of other participants in Jesus's mission, such as Cleopas and his companion (Luke 24:13–32). There is even a question over whether anyone is "ordained" in the formal, lifelong sense of an office as we understand it today in the New Testament community. It is a case of *eisegesis*: reading into the text something that is not there and that reflects later church assumptions.

There is a further factor, which we have already touched on in previous chapters and which relates directly to this point. In the Synoptic Gospels, Jesus has a special relationship with a group of men whom he particularly calls and appoints to share and carry on his ministry (Mark 3:13–19; 6:7–13). But these are not the only people with whom he has a distinctive connection; others, too, are called and sent out on mission. Luke tells of a successful mission by seventy disciples whom Jesus sends out to proclaim the good news in word and deed, in addition to the mission of the Twelve (Luke 10:1–20). John's Gospel refers only incidentally to the Twelve, since the general and inclusive category of "disciple" carries more weight in his narrative, implicitly widening the circle of those present on various occasions, including at the Last Supper.

In addition to the close relationship he has with the apostles and other male followers, Jesus has a circle of female disciples with whom he has a deep connection of mutual love and service. These Galilean women, as we have seen, are often named and usually headed by Mary Magdalene. Not only are they devoted to Jesus in his itinerant ministry, following him from Galilee to Judea and Jerusalem and ministering to him through their financial aid, but they also remain with him in his suffering. As a consequence, they are the first to witness his empty tomb and his risen presence. Here they contrast markedly with the apostles, who vanish at the first sign of opposition. The women, in effect, replace the Twelve, acting as companions to Jesus and bearing witness to his resurrection. In this sense they have every bit as strong a claim on ministry as the Twelve. Indeed, the resurrection appearances have as much claim to bestowing quasi-ordination status on the disciples as the Last Supper.

Women and the Divine Image

Theologically speaking, one of the key issues confronting women in their ministry is whether they are capable of being icons of Christ—that is, representatives of Christ who are able to embody in some way his living presence. Is a woman's iconic status confined to narrow boundaries that do not similarly confine a man? This section examines some of the arguments employed, showing that the tradition itself, as well as Scripture, attests theologically to women's capacity, as well as men's, to reflect the person and work of Christ in all the different aspects of Christian ministry.

The Greek word for "icon," *eikōn*, is translated into English as "image." Icons in the Eastern churches are pictorial images representing sacred events or persons from either the Scriptures or the religious tradition. They are not decorations on the plain truth but visual symbols with cognitive content, closely interwoven with theology, worship, and spirituality. Icons in this tradition open a pathway between human beings and God, without losing a sense of the divine mystery, a mystery that even revelation does not dissolve.[6] They mediate a personal relationship between the viewer and the divine realm. In this the Son is the true original *eikōn*, the image of God, in whose image human beings are created and redeemed.[7] In a metaphorical sense, Scripture also functions as a core icon of the Word of God, who is Jesus Christ.

That women are made in the image of God is theologically transparent from the creation accounts, where man and woman are both created in the "image and likeness" of God (Gen. 1:26–27). Later Christian tradition, for all its accompanying negativity about women, confirms the divine image in females as well as males, a point made by Augustine in his discussion of the communion of the church, where he goes on to quote Galatians 3:28: "Who is it, then, that would exclude women from this fellowship, since they are with us co-heirs of grace? . . . They are . . . renewed to the image of God."[8] In theological terms women share with men the same transfigured identity as "children of God," a concept that is synonymous with that of the divine image (John 1:12). Christian women and men in relationship together enter into that communion of Persons within the being of God.

In another sense, none of us are capable of becoming an icon of Christ or representing him faithfully in any task or role we undertake in our own strength. As Angela West has pointed out, "Our equality with men is founded on our equal capacity for error and sin" and our need of grace.[9] To be an icon of Christ is to depend on "the image and likeness," which is marred by human failure and disobedience, as the story of Adam and Eve relates (Gen. 2–3). The restoration of that image is the work of Christ through his incarnation, ministry, atoning death, and resurrection. The restored image in him is presented not only to the Father but also to human beings so that they enter into their true created identity and destiny. It is grace alone, in

6. See Ouspensky, "Meaning and Language of Icons," 23–49.
7. For more on this, see Lee, *Flesh and Glory*, 48–50.
8. Augustine, *On the Trinity* 12.12 (Matthews, 91). See Soskice, "Trinity and Feminism," 141.
9. West, "Justification by Gender," 37. See also West, *Deadly Innocence*, 87–200.

creation and redemption, that enables us to become icons of Christ, male and female.

Despite this key component of biblical theology—asserting the mutuality of women in community with men—one of the key arguments based on tradition is that men, possessing a historical likeness to Jesus, can represent him in ways unavailable to women. This factor works with other arguments in effectively prohibiting women from ordained ministry in some ecclesial cultures, particularly in regard to presbyteral or pastoral ministry. In this area, women are seen as incapable of serving as icons of Christ in the formal worship and teaching of the church.

An important voice in this debate is that of the Orthodox scholar Elisabeth Behr-Sigel (1907–2005), who spent the last decades of her long life arguing theologically for women's ordination and their participation in the church's teaching and sacramental ministry.[10] Although she came from the Greek Orthodox Church, her theological perceptions embrace implicitly many other Christian traditions. Behr-Sigel sees the image of Christ as much in women as in men. The challenge is posed especially for those traditions that see the presider in a eucharistic gathering as implicitly or explicitly acting *in persona Christi* (in the person of Christ). But it is equally pertinent for other traditions that might be uncomfortable with such a representative view of the Eucharist but who believe that in other contexts, such as preaching and teaching, the voice of Christ (*vox Christi*) communicates itself through the male minister or pastor. In both situations, the leader takes on an iconic function in relation to Christ, whether explicit or not, a function that prohibits women precisely on the grounds of their historical (i.e., gender) unlikeness to Christ.

The danger here is that the radically cosmic nature of Jesus's humanity is called into question by this kind of bifurcation between male and female, where maleness connects to Christ's humanity more than femaleness. The patristic maxim "What has not been assumed has not been redeemed" emphasizes that all human beings are gathered into Christ, who, by taking on their humanity and uniting it to his divinity, redeems them all.[11] To affirm that women's humanity is taken up in Christ as much as men's means that there is no difference in their fundamental status and identity in Christ. It is Jesus's *humanity* that is the issue, not his maleness, as is plain from the Nicene Creed's affirmation that he "became truly human" (*enanthropizein*).

10. Behr-Sigel, *Ministry of Women*, 165–80.
11. This need not imply a blunt version of universal salvation, as human beings are left with the choice to accept or reject what has been done in and for them in Christ.

One theological explanation for the gender distinction in salvation is the view that males by definition are more capable of representing Christ, whereas females are perhaps more readily able to represent the Spirit, with whom Mary of Nazareth is particularly associated. The implications of such a scenario reach into the nature of the Trinity as the union of three divine Persons and as transcending every human category and every created entity, including that of gender. As Behr-Sigel points out, to introduce something very like sexual distinctions into the Trinity risks core belief in the transcendence and mystery of God, who is beyond our understanding and even beyond our access, except through the grace of divine self-revelation.[12]

An earlier generation of feminism wrestled with the issue of Jesus's maleness: "How can a male Savior save women?" was the catchcry. For some, the question itself became so alienating that they left the church and Christian faith.[13] If women needed to be saved from male domination and patriarchal structures, they argued, then surely the last thing they needed was a male to rescue them; their source and means of salvation should, by definition, be female. Ironically, this perspective gives the same theological weight to Jesus's maleness as the view that only men can represent the church in the pulpit and at the altar. In both cases, women are excluded by the fact that Jesus was male.[14]

Those who remained within the orbit of Christian faith needed to find an authentic way to answer the question of Jesus's maleness and its significance for women. Behr-Sigel helped to point the way. It is Jesus's humanity that is of cosmic and universal significance, not his maleness or his Jewishness. At the same time, these aspects of his particularity are of vital importance for the genuine nature of his humanity. To be fully human Jesus needs to be located within the limitations of space and time, with all that it entails: gender, race, culture, class, and other divisions.

These features of Jesus's humanity are not thereby rendered superfluous or arbitrary. The quality of his maleness—so unlike the image of maleness in many cultures—means that it can challenge men as well as include women. His divine nature, as it is developed in the New Testament and in the later creeds and formulations, ensures that Jesus's humanity has a cosmic and representative function: extending the limits of that humanity to all human beings, however diverse their particularities. Why we so frequently confine the iconic function we are given in Christ to males—and often enough to white males—is something of an enigma, as well as a serious distortion of the authentic theological tradition.

12. Behr-Sigel, *Ministry of Women*, 45–48.
13. See Christ, "Feminist Theology," 79–96.
14. For more on this, see Lee, "Feminist Theology."

Women and the Virgin Mary

At the same time, and paradoxically, the humanity of Jesus in the biblical witness depends on a woman who is a virgin and so requires no male assistance in conceiving. Mary cooperates with the life-giving and overshadowing Spirit to assent to the incarnation, conceiving Jesus and giving birth to him (Matt. 1:18–25; Luke 1:26–38).[15] In modern biology we know that a woman's ovaries provide the egg that unites with the sperm to conceive a child and that in utero everything that the fetus requires for healthy growth as a human being is given through the mother's body, even to the deprivation of her own. This is to say nothing of the actual process of giving birth, with its labor pains, the exhausting effort of pushing the baby down the birth canal, and all the associated dangers for both mother and child. In general experience, the woman is no passive receptacle for a man's seed but an active participant in the difficult but creative work of generating a child.

An important theological point is at issue in all this biology. No sexual union takes place between Mary and the Holy Spirit in the conception of Jesus, according to Matthew and Luke. It cannot be reduced to a simplistic formula in which the Spirit supplies the male seed while Mary produces the egg that enters her womb. Though that may seem to explain the two natures of Christ in Christian orthodoxy—that the Spirit impregnates Mary—there is no basis in the Gospels for this conclusion: "Nowhere in scripture is the Spirit's action that 'comes upon' and 'overshadows' a person analogous to sexual intercourse. Rather, these verbs indicate the presence of God who empowers and protects."[16] Jesus's humanity depends on a more profound union between the Spirit and Mary, which is as much spiritual as physiological; it depends as much on her yes to God, her faith (Luke 1:38), as on the cycles of her ovulation.

Andrew Lincoln, in a thoughtful and well-argued study, maintains that the virginal conception is a minor tradition within the New Testament and that the notion of Jesus's normal parentage from a human father and mother is more common.[17] Questioning whether the concept is present at all in Matthew's birth narratives,[18] Lincoln also argues that, while it is evident in Luke's annunciation story, elsewhere the Lukan writings testify to Jesus as born

15. On the issue of the virginal conception and historicity, see Keener, *Gospel of Matthew*, 83–86.

16. E. Johnson, *Truly Our Sister*, 251.

17. Lincoln, *Born of a Virgin?*

18. Against Lincoln on his exegesis at this point (*Born of a Virgin?*, 68–98), the angel's message to Joseph seeks precisely to reassure him that Mary has not been unfaithful and that the child has come not from a human father but from the Holy Spirit (Matt. 1:20).

naturally of human parents, Joseph and Mary;[19] the same is true, he asserts, for the Gospel of John and for Paul. Lincoln is not attempting here to deny the incarnation but to recover New Testament traditions that recognize that Jesus's humanity, alongside his divinity, is genuine and consistent with our own.[20] This is particularly important given that ancient biology saw the male seed as the architect of the child's essence, the maternal role being that of an incubator that provides for the flesh and its nourishment.[21]

It may be that other New Testament writers are not aware of the tradition of the virginal conception (e.g., John 6:42), but it is hard to argue that it is absent from the Gospel of Matthew or that Luke is seeking to balance two contradictory traditions. Other factors, after all, are at play. In Matthew, Joseph agrees to marry Mary only when he is assured that her pregnancy is not the result of anything but the work of the Holy Spirit (*ek pneumatos . . . hagiou*, Matt. 1:20). The references in Acts to Jesus as the descendant of David need not be interpreted in a strictly biological way but may have a symbolic force, especially if Joseph's adoption of Jesus is taken seriously.[22] As Lincoln points out, there is a problem where the later tradition, in associating the sinlessness of Jesus with the absence of a male conception, sees the sexual act as itself transmitting original sin.[23] Later belief in Mary's perpetual virginity, which cannot of itself be demonstrated in the New Testament (Matt. 1:25), takes the virginal conception into new territory, where the danger is that sex can be regarded not as the divine gift that it is in Scripture but as inherently sinful and problematic.

If we understand the virginal conception not as a guarantee of purity and not as something that can be proved historically beyond doubt but as an article of faith, then it has a compelling theological place within the Christian tradition. It acts as a sign of the mystery of the incarnation, pointing to the divine identity of Jesus and the dynamic working of the Spirit.[24] Yet something deeper and more astonishing is at play here. Mary's humanity is sufficient *in*

---

19. Lincoln, *Born of a Virgin?*, 115–24.

20. Lincoln, *Born of a Virgin?*, 275–90.

21. Lincoln quotes Tertullian, who vividly depicts ancient understandings of biology and endeavors to resolve them with his own view of the virginal conception while at the same time denying that Mary's virginity continued during and after Jesus's birth (*Born of a Virgin?*, 195–98).

22. E.g., Acts 13:22–23; 15:16–17; 20:29–36. See also Rom. 1:3 and 2 Tim. 2:8. Note that Gal. 4:4 refers to Jesus as "born of a woman" (*genomenon ek gynaikos*), which is too general to refer to the virginal conception; see Bruce, *Epistle to the Galatians*, 195–96.

23. Lincoln, *Born of a Virgin?*, 193–213.

24. For a succinct and sensitive overview of the four basic historical theories (that Joseph was the father, that an unknown man seduced Mary, that she was raped by a Roman soldier, and that her pregnancy was miraculous), see E. Johnson, *Truly Our Sister*, 227–33.

itself to guarantee that the divine *logos* (Word) becomes genuinely and fully human, a humanity that is itself sustained by grace. The continued emphasis of the tradition on Mary's virginity at the point of Jesus's conception—with or without belief in her perpetual virginity—underscores the point that female humanity alone, with the initiating and creative work of God but without male aid, has generated the humanity of the second Person of the Trinity. In one way, in the terms of modern biology, it makes more rather than less sense, given that the mother, too, is the architect of the child's life. In this sense, the emphasis of the virginal conception is not so much on the virginity of Mary but rather on her willing cooperation with God as a woman in generating and giving birth to Jesus.

It is painfully ironic that Mary's role in orthodox Christian theology as the "God-bearer" (*Theotokos*),[25] the one who conceives and carries the Son of God in her womb—who nurtures him through her placenta and who feeds him with her breast when he is born—could lead to a diminished perspective on women's relationship to Christ. Mary is the only human being named positively in the Nicene Creed apart from Jesus himself. Jesus is bound in a unique and compelling way to his mother from his conception to his death and resurrection. By being the sole guarantor of his humanity, Mary raises women's status as nothing else could; his human nature drawn from her body and from her extraordinary faith confirms the dignity of all women's humanity and their potential, not only for *theosis* (deification, sanctification) but also for playing an iconic role in the church's life. Christian belief in the virginal conception confirms that women are as closely bound to Christ as men are. Their historical unlikeness in one sense is compensated by their oneness to Christ in another sense—their gender confirmed in Jesus's female-generated humanity. Jesus as male is connected to females by his unique conception and birth. He possesses a physiological and spiritual solidarity with women through his mother that other men do not and cannot possess.

There is also an equally vibrant link between women and the Holy Spirit. In the New Testament the Spirit has a far-reaching connection with women, inspiring their prophetic ministry alongside that of men. The daughters who will prophesy at Pentecost along with the sons (Acts 2:17; Joel 2:28) are prefigured by Mary of Nazareth, whose pregnancy and prophecy are both the result of the Spirit's work and who is present at Pentecost with the Galilean women (Acts 1:14). Traditions of the Pentecost icon in Eastern Orthodoxy sometimes display Mary as present and central in the teacher's seat, the tongues of fire on

---

25. On the Council of Ephesus in 431 CE, the debates between Nestorius and Cyril of Alexandria, and the title *Theotokos* in the earlier period, see Price, "Virgin as Theotokos," 67–77.

her head.[26] The daughters who will prophesy at Pentecost are also prefigured by Elizabeth and Anna, who prophesy in the birth stories (Luke 1:35, 41, 45–56; 2:36–38). This dimension of women's ministry is then followed up beyond Pentecost by the reference to the four daughters of Philip the evangelist, who are famous as prophets in the years that follow (Acts 21:8–9).

Gender and the Trinity

If a sharp, eschatological division exists between men and women, the connection of the incarnation to those who do not share Jesus's gender, and other specific features of his human existence, is weakened. Gender is not an absolute value in theological terms (cf. Mark 12:25),[27] but it has significance because it is bodily and the body is theologically significant since it is created by God and destined for transfiguration through resurrection. The body matters because, as Sarah Coakley puts it, "It is about differentiated, embodied relationship—first and foremost to God, but also to others."[28] She goes on to say that gender, as "embodied difference," is "not to be eradicated . . . but to be transformed."[29] With the future coming of Christ, the hope, for women as much as for men, is that "we will be like him, for we will see him as he is" (1 John 3:2). If Christ represents—and in so doing redeems—females as well as males, gentiles as well as Jews, slaves as well as free people, then the concomitant is also the case. Any human being, by virtue of the humanity that she or he shares by virtue of being made in the divine image and remade in Christ through the incarnation (Heb. 2:14–18), is capable of representing Christ, a representation dependent not on gender but on vocation—whether at the altar or in the pulpit, whether in day-to-day acts of service or in martyrdom.

The nature of baptism and its christological significance establish this theological principle. Grounded in faith, baptism (as we have already seen in our study of Paul),[30] is precisely what enables us, through faith, to enter into the redeeming work of Christ—and not only his work but also his person, as we come to share his identity as Son of God. In this way we become daughters and sons of God by entering his status, his identity, his oneness with the Father. This aspect, as we have already seen, is a particular emphasis of the Gospel of John, where the message Mary Magdalene is to take

---

26. See, e.g., "Pentecost Icon as an Icon of the Church."
27. Behr-Sigel, *Ministry of Women*, 40–41.
28. Coakley, *God, Sexuality, and the Self*, 53.
29. Coakley, *God, Sexuality, and the Self*, 55.
30. See above, chap. 6, "Baptism into Christ (Gal. 3:26–29)."

back to Jesus's brothers and sisters includes the words "I am ascending to my Father and your Father, to my God and your God" (John 20:17).[31] Here there is a careful distinction between Jesus's relationship with the Father, which has primacy, and the disciples' relationship with the Father, which is the consequence. We become children of God by entering into Jesus's own identity as Son (John 1:12–14).[32] This is effected by the work of the Holy Spirit, who, in Coakley's words, "causes me to see God no longer as patriarchal threat but as infinite tenderness," but who also "painfully darkens my prior certainties . . . and so invites me ever more deeply into the life of redemption in Christ."[33] If women by definition cannot represent the one who in the incarnation has come in order to redeem them and to draw them through the divine Spirit into the fullness of his filiation, then their eschatological salvation cannot be assured.

We have already touched on the question of the Father-Son imagery for God and Jesus in the New Testament. The use of "Father" language for God in the tradition is meant to be consonant with New Testament usage, though it often falls far short. It is helpful, therefore, to remind ourselves of how the language works in the New Testament. God functions as Father in relation first and foremost to Jesus as Son; in the New Testament God's revealed identity is as the "God and Father of our Lord Jesus Christ" (Eph. 1:3). As is widely attested, this usage finds its origin in Jesus's own relationship with God, with the use of the Aramaic *abba* (Mark 14:36; Rom. 8:15; Gal. 4:6) and the more frequent use in the New Testament of the Greek emphatic phrase "*my* Father" (*ho patēr mou*).[34] Reflecting on this usage, the early church elaborated a trinitarian theology that asserted the equality of essence between the three divine Persons, without subordination of any kind: "The patriarchal ordering implied by the kinship titles was subverted early on by Christian insistence that the Son is one with the Father, equal to the Father, co-eternal with the Father and Spirit."[35]

The language of Father, Son, and Holy Spirit is a core symbol of the New Testament and the tradition, portraying "the interruptive desire of the trinitarian God for fallen creation."[36] The symbolism badly needs to be

---

31. As we noted above, this is a case where *adelphoi* should be translated inclusively (chap. 3, "Women's Presence").

32. See above, chap. 4, "Mary Magdalene."

33. Coakley, *God, Sexuality, and the Self*, 56.

34. See Matt. 7:21; 10:32–33; 11:27; 12:50; 16:17; 18:10, 19; 20:23; 25:34; 26:39, 42, 53; Luke 10:22; 22:29; 24:49; John 5:17; 6:32, 40; 8:19, 49, 54; 10:18, 29; 14:7, 20, 23; 15:1, 8, 15, 23; 20:17; Rev. 2:28; 3:5, 21.

35. Soskice, "Trinity and Feminism," 142.

36. Coakley, *God, Sexuality, and the Self*, 59.

reclaimed over against its patriarchal and domineering distortions:[37] "The *true* meaning of 'Father' is to be found in the Trinity, not dredged up from the scummy realm of human patriarchal fatherhood."[38] Like any other metaphor, the threefold designation of God as Father-Son-Spirit contains an "is" and an "is not" dimension; that is, the symbol is both like and unlike the reality that it conveys. The "is" depicts the familial intimacy that the Trinity indwells and into which God invites us, a depiction that goes back to Jesus himself, whereas the "is not" requires us to understand that God is in no sense male.[39] To make such an assumption about God is idolatrous, an idolatry of maleness on which patriarchal religion thrives. This latter dimension—the "is not"—has often been overlooked, leading understandably to the rejection of the trinitarian formula by those who do not wish to identify with paternalistic religion.[40]

It does not follow from this that the symbolism is exclusive. On the contrary, it needs to be extended, precisely to emphasize the "is not" dimension, that God is not male. Efforts to replace the classical trinitarian formula often make the mistake of falling into abstraction or tritheism, both of which are distortions of the intimacy and unity within God.[41] We need, therefore, to make two moves: (1) to reclaim the strengths of the core symbolism itself and at the same time (2) to explore other figures of speech—though their presence is much less overt in Scripture and tradition—such as motherhood imagery, since "all three Persons can be styled in the imagery of the human masculine and the human feminine."[42] The theology of Julian of Norwich, set within the patriarchal medieval church, is a prime example of how it can be done with theological perspicacity and sensitivity, and with awareness of the self-revealing God in engagement with culture.[43] What is vital here is the knowledge that God "is beyond all positive and negative attributes we may hope to lard upon God."[44]

37. See Soskice, "Can a Feminist," 81–94.
38. Coakley, *God, Sexuality, and the Self*, 324.
39. On how metaphor works, see Lee, *Flesh and Glory*, 16–20.
40. In worship and liturgy God is often referred to as "almighty," so that the phrase "Almighty God" or "Almighty Father" seems to render God more distant and autocratic. Yet the Greek *pantocratōr*, which is a characteristic title for God in the book of Revelation, really means the "all-ruling" or "all-holding" one, signifying the way in which God holds all things in being with loving sovereignty over creation (Rev. 1:8; 4:8; 11:17; 15:3; 16:7, 14; 19:6, 15; 21:22).
41. Soskice, "Trinity and Feminism," 141–42.
42. Soskice, "Trinity and Feminism," 146.
43. Coakley is wary of using female pronouns only for the Spirit, while male pronouns are used for the Father and the Son (*God, Sexuality, and the Self*, 326).
44. Coakley, *God, Sexuality, and the Self*, 324.

Conclusion

Women's sense of calling in the contemporary church is not primarily a product of Western feminism—though it has played its part—but largely a re-calling of the church to its evangelical roots, not only in the New Testament but also in the early centuries of the church's life.[45] It is grounded in a theological understanding of Jesus Christ and his significance for the life of the church and for Christian identity. Baptism is the primary symbol that draws women and men into a relationship with Christ that transcends all human barriers, whether of race, class, or gender, and unites them in a communion of persons without discrimination. Through baptism all Christians have the capacity to communicate Christ to others and to share his life in multiple forms of ministry. As there is no restriction on the basis of race, so there can be no restriction by way of gender. This is the church's story, and it is grounded not primarily in its ethics of inclusion and justice but more significantly in its christological understanding of what it means to be "in Christ Jesus."

What theology confirms is that the tradition itself, at its heart, makes room for the representative role of women as coequal icons of Christ with men. This is nowhere more apparent than in the martyrdom stories, something of which we have already seen in the previous chapter, where gender equality spontaneously emerges and strict gender roles become irrelevant. Paradoxically, martyrdom was one area in which Christian women could demonstrate not only remarkable love and courage but also their capacity to stand in the place of Christ, a powerful witness for their fellow sufferers, for their executioners, and for the Christian community as a whole.[46] The female martyrs alongside the male martyrs were (and are) effective icons of Christ and of his cosmic, redemptive suffering.

There is a powerful example of this theological point from the history of the church. In the persecution under Marcus Aurelius, a slave woman, Blandina, was subjected to dreadful tortures and was later hung on a stake in the arena for refusing to relinquish her Christian faith. She was not alone in being martyred but, being a slave, could be subject to any form of torture and any method of execution. Hanging on the stake, she became a Christlike figure for the spectators and an inspiration to her fellow martyrs: "She seemed to be hanging in the shape of a cross, and by her continuous prayer gave great zeal to the combatants . . . [who] saw in the form of their sister him who was

45. On the Christian origins of feminism in the nineteenth century, see Porter, "Christian Origins of Feminism," 208–24.
46. See Lashier, "In the Company of the Fathers."

crucified for them."[47] As Elizabeth Goodine points out, there is an overturning here of power, "a re-distribution of power that changes the perception of this slave-woman from one who is victim to one who is victor; from one who is tortured to one who causes torturers to stand in amazement."[48] In theological terms, if women can act as icons of Christ and represent him vividly in their martyrdom, they can also represent him at the altar and in the pulpit, at the font and by the graveside. Women's ministry as pastors and priests confirms all women in their capacity to represent Christ in the form of discipleship to which each is called, lay and ordained alike.

47. Eusebius, *Ecclesiastical History* 5.1.41 (Lake, 427).
48. Goodine, *Standing at Lyon*, 98.

Conclusion

THOSE WHO DISCOUNT WOMEN as leaders in the church come from a particular theological perspective on gender where maleness is given idolatrous value within a doctrinal construct that sharply delineates maleness from femaleness. Most of those opposing women's ordination these days refrain from the language of superiority and inferiority, or of greater and lesser status. Instead they focus on different roles, with the proviso that women's dignity and contribution to the life of the church are important. Even the idea of the equality of the sexes manages—at least theoretically—to be confirmed in this so-called complementarian perspective.

The issue of the difference between the sexes is not fundamentally the question. Gender difference is not in itself a sufficient reason to disqualify women from ordination or other forms of leadership. Paul argues strongly for gentile inclusion in the church without gentiles having first to become Jews. The universal nature of the church—its catholicity—derives precisely from a conviction that originates in Jesus himself: "I tell you that many will come from East and West and recline at table with Abraham, Isaac, and Jacob in the kingdom of heaven" (Matt. 8:11).

The weighting of maleness over femaleness in leadership takes two rather different forms. On the one hand, the biblical argument from marriage affirms male headship of the home that is seen to extend, by definition, to the "family" of the church. On the other hand, arguments associated with tradition claim that male representation is a key element of the Eucharist and that ordained ministry has always been male throughout the history of the church. Whatever the argument, the result is the same: a theological priority given implicitly to maleness over femaleness. There is indeed "male and female" in the church, despite the mutual and all-encompassing nature of the gospel.

The New Testament itself in various ways, and in its own contexts, envisages a community without authoritarian structures or prohibitive divisions: one in which slavery is accorded no spiritual and therefore no social significance, thereby undermining its very existence, and one in which women are accepted in full mutuality of discipleship and ministry. The women of Jesus's and Paul's ministries are testimony to this broader vision, where faith becomes the test of one's true status and identity and where all disciples are gathered into Christ—bearing his name—and are equally bound to him. This makes faith in Jesus a source not only of identity but also of freedom—containing within it a revolutionary principle that draws into the present the transforming, future reign of God.

Order of Creation

Some who oppose women's ministry speak of an order of creation that determines very different roles for men and for women, where female subordination and obedience is integral to God's vision for the world. But if that is the order of creation, intended by God from the beginning, we might well ask why it is not pertinent to the whole of human life. Why would God ordain such a structure unless there was something inherent within the nature of man and woman that fitted them for very different roles? It should mean that headship or leadership is a quality given to men in creation, while supporting and serving is more natural to women. That was certainly the traditional view of the gender division for many generations, where women belonged in the private sphere and men in the public, where men led and women followed, where men made decisions and women obeyed. It was true in the home, in the church, and in the wider society at every level. It made sense within its own narrow, paternalistic framework.

In the contemporary world, such a neat division of labor based on "nature" is no longer commonly accepted. Women, to a much greater extent than in the past, lead as well as serve. They work as teachers, academics, scientists, politicians, lawyers, and in medicine, technology, engineering, the police, the armed forces, sports, entertainment, and management, as well as in many other places. Whatever the differences between the sexes, these no longer constrain women's lives in the world outside the home as they once did.

If there is a patriarchal ordering of creation, then this contemporary phenomenon goes directly against it. If women cannot lead in the church or home by divine decree, they cannot lead anywhere; their very nature tells them so. Yet those who hold this view do not argue—at least not openly—that women should be excluded from leadership roles in society. They seem happy to support their children of all ages being taught by women, to accept being represented in government by women, being given orders by female police officers, being instructed by female doctors and lawyers, benefiting from the leading work of female scientists, and being defended by women in the armed forces.

There is a serious inconsistency here, one that is hard to press because of the harsh consequences for women's lives. If women can excel in all the areas traditionally given over to men, and if they are able to show leadership in this remarkable variety of ways in the external world—which is, if anything, increasing—then they should be given the opportunity to test their gifts in leadership within church and home. Either they can lead or they cannot. And if so, it should be the same across all areas of human activity, and the natural gifts of leadership should not be sequestered to the home and the church.

This is not to say that women have achieved the level of recognition in secular society that they desire and deserve. They are still vastly outnumbered in senior leadership positions, despite the many demonstrations of their competence. Governments are still largely run by men, despite the large number of women whose interests they represent; organizations prefer men at their head; and boards are dominated by men. This is true not only for women but also for men from other-than-European backgrounds, who are also, and often, excluded from senior positions and from representation on boards and committees.

In short, the current context points to women's increasing position in social leadership and to a flowering of the insights they bring for the healthy exercise of authority. Women are as gifted as men in the exercise of authority, though it may be carried out in different ways. To deny them such authority within the home and church despite their capacity to wield it everywhere else is little short of abuse. It is not, of course, physical abuse, as revealed in the alarming statistics of domestic and family violence. And it may not necessarily be emotional abuse, but it is a form of spiritual abuse. The church is subjecting gifted women to a real and painful form of exclusion that, in theological terms, denies the nature and reality of their faith and baptism.

For women sitting in the pews to see only male leadership in preaching, teaching, presiding at the sacraments, and leading is to communicate a message to all women present that their gifts are not as needful and valued as those of men. Even in contexts where these or similar words are never said, the imagery has the same effect on the women who are present, consciously or unconsciously. Male authority acknowledged and public, while female authority is forbidden, gives all women present a sense of being less substantial than men. It is as if they are less visible not only to the community but also to God. That sense of hidden substance lies at the root of women's lack of confidence in their own gifts. Affirming these gifts in those who possess them is important for women, but even more important is the encouraging of a sense of substance that is as real for them as for men.

None of this is to place women on a pedestal, as if their gifts and graces surpass those of men. Idealizing women is as dangerous as demeaning or dismissing them. Women are as capable of sin as men and can misuse authority and leadership as well as men. Where women and men are genuinely equal, however, is precisely in their common need of grace and their access to the gifts given them by the Spirit for the upbuilding of the church. Women's identities are grounded as much in Christ as men's, creation and baptism equally giving them a sense of substance that depends, from beginning to end, on divine grace. We cannot deprive women of this substance and these gifts, despite their fallibility—which God can also use for the divine glory.

Why are women's gifts for ministry, including that of preaching, teaching, and celebrating the sacraments, denied in parts of the church today—including the gifts of religious women and married women? We have argued throughout the book that there is no biblical basis for such an exclusion and that neither can the experience of the early church be used to justify it. Those who do so continue to speak about the order of creation and claim a commitment to women's equality, but these are empty words in the contemporary world and fail to grasp the essential principles of the gospel. Women are not equal if their gifts can be exercised anywhere but in the church, if they hold authority anywhere but church and home.

Such words are empty rhetoric arising from a deeper and not easily eradicable spiritual form of misogyny that lurks behind concerns for biblical authority and proper order. Those who support women's full access to authority and ministry and who do not concede male headship in the home are equally concerned with biblical authority and the proper ordering of the church's life. Their interpretation takes them in the opposite direction, leading them to see equality as something more than words or rhetoric—as the practical authorizing of women for the gifts that God has so clearly bestowed on them for the good of the church and the extension of the gospel. Anything less means a spirituality that is both misogynistic and abusive.

The church always faces the danger of falling back into the old age and letting go the freedoms and grace of the new age, despite the guidance and presence of the Holy Spirit. An equivalent danger lies in not living out the full implications of the gospel in a context where such realization becomes possible. Those who oppose women's participation in ministry in the church are like the Christians of Paul's Letter to the Galatians, wishing to pull back from the liberating promises of the gospel and lapsing back into the old age. But it is not the truth of the liberating and life-giving gospel. Our task today is to be transformed by the New Testament's theological vision and to live it out—more fully than the early communities were able to do—so that we ourselves become a sign to the world of what it means to be called to be the body of Christ by embracing the mutuality and unity of all within it. This mutuality encourages believers to minister in accordance not with prejudice and ranking based on gender but with the gifts of the Spirit with which they have been plentifully endowed.

The issue here is not only about Jesus but also about the Spirit and the church. Where the church is deprived of its Spirit-given gifts, its ministry suffers and women continue to be marginalized. In his own day, Paul had to fight his detractors, who wanted to maintain the classification between Jew and gentile with the reimposition of Jewish cultural norms on gentiles, an imposition that he passionately resisted. He opposed it not on political or ideological grounds but theologically, on the basis of the universal significance of Christ and the meaning of faith and baptism, where believers enter into Christ's death and so share his resurrection. In a similar way, we need to resist on theological grounds those detractors who want to uphold traditional structures of role and status in male-female relationships. Following the New Testament vision, we need to confirm that where the detractors have failed is a theological problem above all else: the failure to grasp the cosmic nature of Christ, the freedom of the Spirit, and the significance of faith, along with the transformed identity it confers in the eschatological life of the church.

Summary

This study of women in the New Testament has sought to catch a glimpse of women's ministry within a variety of literary forms, different voices, and diverse theologies. The New Testament text does not have as its main concern female discipleship and leadership but rather the proclamation of the gospel of Jesus Christ and the creation of the community of faith around that central proclamation. Yet we have asked our questions all the same, questions that have arisen from our struggles and our dilemmas, addressing them in hope to this archaic text in which we believe we hear the echoing voice of the Spirit—the modern world seeking remedies from the ancient. The answers have been sometimes direct and more often indirect, but overwhelmingly constructive, providing encouragement for women's compassionate and authoritative ministry in the church today, whether in lay or ordained forms of service.

Beginning with the Gospels and their related writings, we explored together the presence of women as disciples, finding first in Matthew and Mark women's openness to Jesus's ministry and their astonishingly courageous presence at his passion, when his closest male disciples have fled. In Luke-Acts we pondered the plethora of women in the first volume and the paucity of explicit presence in the second. Taking Luke the Evangelist on his own terms, we were able to see something of the inclusive nature of his reading of the good news, a theme going back to Jesus himself; even in Acts there were unexpected women who rose from their patriarchal context to give blessing to the female reader.

The Johannine Gospel gave us the most explicit panoply of women disciples who were able, through struggle and misunderstanding, to understand and bear witness to the gospel of divine glory revealed in Jesus's ministry, death, and resurrection. The Johannine women are outstanding exemplars of faith, courage, and resilience. Particular attention was paid to the extraordinary figure of Mary Magdalene as the apostle of the resurrection and the primary witness to God's triumph over death in Jesus.

The controversial figure of Paul, in his own writings, is always something of a bumpy ride, with the need to retain a sense of the profundity of his theology alongside accusations of misogyny. New readings of old texts cut a way through the variegated nature of his letters, whether or not he himself literally wrote them all. In the end, we saw how his apocalyptic vision attracted women as well as men into leadership in the mission of the church: female deacons, apostles, prophets, evangelists, all laboring alongside him with the same love and the same vision. There were difficult texts for us to read, especially the household codes, but these were set within their sociohistorical context, as we compared them to our own very different structures and practices today. These texts called for careful reinterpretation and attentive reading to ensure that we were not importing contradictions into Pauline teaching that did not exist. Paul's vision, as it turns out, cohered with that of the Gospels in their presentation of women as faithful disciples, supporting the mission of Jesus and following him on his travels, leaving behind their homes and families.

From the remaining New Testament texts, we saw that there was no real opposition to women's authority as leaders and teachers, particularly if these texts were interpreted within their own contexts. The General Epistles do not give much evidence of ministry structures, but they do support the inclusive vision we found in the Gospels and Paul. We also examined the androcentric language to find its genuinely inclusive impetus. The book of Revelation was more difficult to grasp, but it, too, gave a message of salvation that included female and male, despite some of the more difficult and bewildering symbols.

Finally, we glanced briefly at the story of the early church, challenging the myth of male-only leadership from the first days onward and seeing something of the hidden history of women as deacons, presbyters, and even bishops in the early days. This story led to a reconsideration of the theological issues undergirding that history, drawn from an understanding of New Testament theology and its message of hope and reconciliation, confirming women's capacity to represent Christ in various contexts as much as men. The early church in its diversity and enthusiasm embraced the ministry of women, and both material art and texts reveal their presence as fully recognized sisters in the community of Christ and as leaders within those early gatherings. Yes, their ministry was eroded with the increasing formalization of Christianity as the main religion in the Mediterranean world. But it was there in the first centuries and only petered out because of forces that worked to subject them to the mores of popular culture.

Women in the New Testament are witnesses to Jesus's birth, ministry, death, and resurrection, and they proclaim the good news of salvation and God's triumph over death in Christ with joy and faith. Mary Magdalene in her encounter with the Risen Lord proclaims not only his resurrection but also the inestimable privilege of preaching and teaching Christ, a privilege accorded to women who have followed her: "I have seen the Lord!" Along with Mary the God-bearer, who bears in her own body the life of God incarnate; Mary the "Fortress" and proclaimer of the Risen Christ; Prisca the theologian; Junia the apostle; Phoebe the deacon; Lydia; Tabitha; Mary and Martha of Bethany; Joanna; Susanna; Salome; and Mary the wife/mother of Clopas, we are called to testify to the life-giving presence of God among us in Jesus Christ through the enlivening power and presence of the Spirit.

Bibliography

Aasgaard, Reidar. *"My Beloved Brothers and Sisters!" Christian Siblingship in Paul.* Journal for the Study of the New Testament: Supplement Series 265. London: T&T Clark, 2004.

"The Acts of Paul and Thecla." In *The Apocryphal New Testament: A Collection of Apocryphal Christian Literature in an English Translation*, edited by J. K. Elliott, 364–72. Oxford: Oxford University Press, 1993.

Akala, Adesola Joan. *The Son-Father Relationship and Christological Symbolism in the Gospel of John.* Library of New Testament Studies. London: Bloomsbury T&T Clark, 2014.

Alter, Robert. *The Art of Biblical Narrative.* New York: Basic Books, 1981.

Anderson, Paul N. *The Riddles of the Fourth Gospel: An Introduction to John.* Minneapolis: Fortress, 2011.

"Apostle of the Apostles." Decree from the Congregation for Divine Worship, June 3, 2016. http://www.vatican.va/roman_curia/congregations/ccdds/documents/articolo–roche–maddalena_en.pdf.

Attridge, Harold W. *A Commentary on the Epistle to the Hebrews.* Hermeneia. Philadelphia: Fortress, 1989.

Augustine. *On the Trinity.* Books 8–15. Edited by Gareth B. Matthews. Cambridge Texts in the History of Philosophy. Cambridge: Cambridge University Press, 2002.

Aune, David. *Revelation.* 3 vols. Word Biblical Commentary 52A–C. Dallas: Word, 1997–98.

Aymer, Margaret. "Acts of the Apostles." In Newsom, Ringe, and Lapsley, *Women's Bible Commentary*, 536–46.

Bailey, Kenneth E. *Paul through Mediterranean Eyes: Cultural Studies in 1 Corinthians.* Downers Grove, IL: IVP Academic, 2011.

Balch, David L. *Let Wives Be Submissive: The Domestic Code in 1 Peter.* Chico, CA: Scholars Press, 1981.

Barnes, Nathan J. *Reading 1 Corinthians with Philosophically Educated Women.* Eugene, OR: Pickwick, 2014.

Barrett, C. K. *The Acts of the Apostles.* 2 vols. International Critical Commentary. London: T&T Clark, 1998.

———. *The Gospel according to St John: An Introduction with Commentary and Notes on the Greek Text.* 2nd ed. London: SPCK, 1978.

———. *The Pastoral Epistles.* Oxford: Clarendon, 1963.

Bauckham, Richard. *The Climax of Prophecy: Studies in the Book of Revelation.* Edinburgh: T&T Clark, 1993.

———. *Gospel of Glory: Major Themes in Johannine Theology.* Grand Rapids: Baker Academic, 2015.

———. *Gospel Women: Studies of the Named Women in the Gospels.* Grand Rapids: Eerdmans, 2002.

———. *The Testimony of the Beloved Disciple: Narrative, History, and Theology in the Gospel of John.* Grand Rapids: Baker Academic, 2007.

Beale, G. K. *The Book of Revelation: A Commentary on the Greek Text.* New International Greek Testament Commentary. Grand Rapids: Eerdmans, 1999.

Behr-Sigel, Elisabeth. *The Ministry of Women in the Church.* Translated by S. Bigham. Redondo Beach, CA: Oakwood, 1991.

Beirne, Margaret. *Women and Men in the Fourth Gospel: A Genuine Discipleship of Equals.* Journal for the Study of the New Testament: Supplement Series. London: Sheffield Academic, 2003.

Beker, J. Christiaan. "The Authority of Scripture: Normative or Incidental?" *Theology Today* 49 (1992): 376–82.

———. *Paul the Apostle: The Triumph of God in Life and Thought.* Philadelphia: Fortress, 1980.

Belleville, Linda L. "Exegetical Fallacies in Interpreting 1 Timothy 2:11–15." *Priscilla Papers* 17 (2003): 3–11.

———. *Women Leaders and the Church: Three Crucial Questions.* Grand Rapids: Baker Books, 2000.

Betsworth, Sharon. *The Reign of God Is Such as These: A Socio-literary Analysis of Daughters in the Gospel of Mark.* Library of New Testament Studies. London: T&T Clark, 2010.

Bilezikian, Gilbert. "Beyond Sex Roles: Priscilla as the Author of Hebrews." *Priscilla Papers* 31 (2017): 37–38.

Billings, Bradly S. "The End of Mark's Gospel and the Markan Community: A Fresh Look in an Old Place." *Colloquium* 46 (2014): 42–54.

Bird, Jennifer G. *Abuse, Power and Fearful Obedience: Reconsidering 1 Peter's Commands to Wives.* Library of New Testament Studies. London: T&T Clark, 2011.

Bird, Michael F. *The Gospel of the Lord: How the Early Church Wrote the Story of Jesus*. Grand Rapids: Eerdmans, 2014.

Blomberg, Craig L. "Today's New International Version: The Untold Story of a Good Translation." CBE International, January 31, 2004. https://www.cbeinternational.org/resources/article/other/todays-new-international-version.

Boring, M. Eugene. "The Gospel of Matthew: Introduction, Commentary, and Reflections." In *The New Interpreter's Bible*, edited by L. Keck, 8:87–505. Nashville: Abingdon, 1994.

———. *Mark: A Commentary*. New Testament Library. Louisville: Westminster John Knox, 2006.

———. *Revelation*. Interpretation: A Bible Commentary for Teaching and Preaching. Louisville: John Knox, 1989.

Bovon, François. *Luke 1: A Commentary on the Gospel of Luke 1:1–9:50*. Hermeneia. Minneapolis: Fortress, 2002.

———. *Luke 2: A Commentary on the Gospel of Luke 9:51–19:27*. Hermeneia. Minneapolis: Fortress, 2013.

Bovon, François, and Christopher R. Matthews. *The Acts of Philip: A New Translation*. Waco: Baylor University Press, 2012.

Brant, Jo-Ann A. *John*. Paideia: Commentaries on the New Testament. Grand Rapids: Baker Academic, 2011.

Breed, Gert. "*Diakonia*: In Conversation with John N. Collins." *Ecclesiology* 13 (2017): 349–68.

Breu, Clarissa, ed. *Biblical Exegesis without Authorial Intention? Interdisciplinary Approaches to Authorship and Meaning*. Biblical Interpretation Series 172. Leiden: Brill, 2019.

Briggs, Sheila. "Galatians." In Schüssler Fiorenza, *Feminist Commentary*, 218–36.

Brooten, Bernadette. *Women Leaders in the Ancient Synagogue: Inscriptional Evidence and Background Issues*. Chico, CA: Scholars Press, 1982.

Broussard, Karlo. "Did Jesus Make the Apostles Priests at the Last Supper?" Catholic Answers, February 1, 2017. https://www.catholic.com/magazine/online-edition/did-jesus-make-the-apostles-priests-at-the-last-supper.

Brown, Jeannine K. *The Disciples in Narrative Perspective: The Portrayal and Function of the Matthean Disciples*. Society of Biblical Literature Academia Biblica 9. Atlanta: Society of Biblical Literature, 2002.

Brown, Raymond E. *The Community of the Beloved Disciple: The Life, Loves, and Hates of an Individual Church in New Testament Times*. New York: Paulist Press, 1979.

———. *The Gospel according to John*. 2 vols. Anchor Bible 29–29A. New York: Doubleday, 1966.

Bruce, F. F. *The Book of the Acts*. New International Commentary on the Greek Testament. Rev. ed. Grand Rapids: Eerdmans, 1988.

―――. *The Epistles to the Colossians, to Philemon, and to the Ephesians*. The New International Commentary on the New Testament. Grand Rapids: Eerdmans, 1984.

―――. *The Epistle to the Galatians*. New International Greek Testament Commentary. Grand Rapids: Eerdmans, 1982.

Bultmann, Rudolf. *The Gospel of John*. Translated by G. R. Beasley-Murray. Oxford: Basil Blackwell, 1971.

Burer, M. H., and D. Wallace. "Was Junia Really an Apostle? A Re-examination of Rom 16.7." *New Testament Studies* 47 (2001): 76–91.

Burk, Denny. "Mark Driscoll on Women in Ministry." July 2007. https://www.denny burk.com/mark-driscoll-on-women-in-ministry-2/.

Burridge, Richard. *John: The People's Bible Commentary*. A Bible Commentary for Every Day. Glasgow: The Bible Reading Fellowship, 1998.

―――. *What Are the Gospels? A Comparison with Graeco-Roman Biography*. 2nd ed. The Bible Resource Series. Grand Rapids: Eerdmans, 2004.

Byers, Andrew J. *Ecclesiology and Theosis in the Gospel of John*. Society for New Testament Studies Monograph Series 166. Cambridge: Cambridge University Press, 2017.

Byrne, Brendan. *The Hospitality of God: A Reading of Luke's Gospel*. Rev. ed. Collegeville, MN: Liturgical Press, 2015.

―――. *Life Abounding: A Reading of John's Gospel*. Collegeville, MN: Liturgical Press, 2014.

―――. *Lifting the Burden: Reading Matthew's Gospel in the Church Today*. Collegeville, MN: Liturgical Press, 2004.

―――. *Paul and the Christian Woman*. Homebush, Australia: St. Paul Publications, 1988.

―――. "A Pauline Complement to *Laudato Si'*." *Theological Studies* 77 (2016): 308–27.

―――. *Romans*. Sacra Pagina 6. Collegeville, MN: Liturgical Press, 1996.

Byrne, Lavinia. *Women before God: Our Own Spirituality*. London: SPCK, 1988.

Byron, Gay L. "James." In Newsom, Ringe, and Lapsley, *Women's Bible Commentary*, 613–15.

Camery-Hoggatt, Jerry. "Images of Mary Magdalene in Christian Tradition." *Priscilla Papers* 18, no. 4 (2004): 19–24.

Carter, Warren. *Matthew: Storyteller, Interpreter, Evangelist*. Peabody, MA: Hendrickson, 2004.

Cartlidge, David R. "Thekla: The Apostle Who Defied Women's Destiny." *Bible Review* 20 (2004): 1–14.

Chennattu, Rekha M. *Johannine Discipleship as a Covenant Relationship*. Peabody, MA: Hendrickson, 2006.

Christ, Carol P. "Feminist Theology as Post-traditional Theology." In *The Cambridge Companion to Feminist Theology*, edited by S. F. Parsons, 79–96. Cambridge Companions. Cambridge: Cambridge University Press, 2002.

Chryssavgis, John. *The Way of the Fathers: Exploring the Patristic Mind.* Analecta Vlatadon 62. Thessaloniki: Patriarchal Institute for Patristic Studies, 1998.

Clason, M. A. "Feminism, Generic 'He' and the TNIV Bible Translation Debate." *Critical Discourse Studies* 3 (2006): 23–35.

Clements, E. Anne. *Mothers on the Margin? The Significance of Women in Matthew's Genealogy.* Eugene, OR: Pickwick, 2014.

Coakley, Sarah. *God, Sexuality, and the Self: An Essay "On the Trinity."* Cambridge: Cambridge University Press, 2013.

Cohick, Lynn. "The 'Woman at the Well': Was the Samaritan Woman Really an Adulteress?" In *Vindicating the Vixens: Revisiting Sexualized, Vilified, and Marginalized Women of the Bible*, edited by Sandra Glahn, 249–53. Grand Rapids: Kregel Academic, 2017.

———. *Women in the World of the Earliest Christians: Illuminating Ancient Ways of Life.* Grand Rapids: Baker Academic, 2009.

Cohick, Lynn H., and Amy Brown Hughes. "Aelia Pulcheria, 'Protectress of the Empire,' and Empress Eudocia, a Theological Poet." In Cohick and Hughes, *Christian Women in the Patristic World*, 219–52.

———. *Christian Women in the Patristic World: Their Influence, Authority, and Legacy in the Second through Fifth Centuries.* Grand Rapids: Baker Academic, 2017.

———. "Egeria's *Itinerary* and Christian Pilgrimage." In Cohick and Hughes, *Christian Women in the Patristic World*, 127–55.

———. "Perpetua and Felicitas: Mothers and Martyrs." In Cohick and Hughes, *Christian Women in the Patristic World*, 27–64.

———. "Thecla: Christian Female Protomartyr and Virgin of the Church." In Cohick and Hughes, *Christian Women in the Patristic World*, 1–26.

Collins, Adela Yarbro. *Mark: A Commentary.* Hermeneia. Minneapolis: Augsburg Fortress, 2007.

Collins, John N. *Diakonia: Re-interpreting the Ancient Sources.* Oxford: Oxford University Press, 1990.

Collins, Raymond F. *1 & 2 Timothy and Titus: A Commentary.* New Testament Library. Louisville: Westminster John Knox, 2002.

———. *First Corinthians.* Sacra Pagina 7. Collegeville, MN: Liturgical Press, 1999.

———. *Letters That Paul Did Not Write: The Epistle to the Hebrews and the Pauline Pseudepigrapha.* Good News Studies 28. Wilmington, DE: Michael Glazier, 1988.

Collinson, Sylvia Wilkey. "Women Disciples." In Kroeger and Evans, *IVP Women's Bible Commentary*, 571–73.

Coloe, Mary L. "Anointing the Temple of God: John 12:1–8." In *Transcending Boundaries: Contemporary Readings of the New Testament; Essays in Honor of Francis J. Moloney*, edited by R. M. Chennattu and M. L. Coloe, 105–18. Biblioteca di Scienze Religiose 187. Roma: Libreria Editrice Vaticana, 2005.

———. *God Dwells with Us: Temple Symbolism in the Fourth Gospel*. Collegeville, MN: Liturgical Press, 2001.

Conway, Colleen M. "Gender and the Fourth Gospel." In *The Oxford Handbook of Johannine Studies*, edited by J. M. Lieu and M. de Boer, 220–36. Oxford: Oxford University Press, 2018.

———. *Men and Women in the Fourth Gospel: Gender and Johannine Characterization*. Society of Biblical Literature Dissertation Series. Atlanta: Society of Biblical Literature, 1999.

Corley, Kathleen E. "1 Peter." In Schüssler Fiorenza, *Feminist Commentary*, 349–51.

———. *Private Women, Public Meals: Social Conflict in the Synoptic Tradition*. Grand Rapids: Baker Academic, 1993.

———. "Slaves, Servants and Prostitutes: Gender and Social Class in Mark." In Levine and Blickenstaff, *A Feminist Companion to Mark*, 191–221.

———. "Women's Inheritance Rights in Antiquity and Paul's Metaphor of Adoption." In Levine and Blickenstaff, *A Feminist Companion to Paul*, 98–121.

Cotter, Wendy. "Mark's Hero of the Twelfth-Year Miracles: The Healing of the Woman with the Hemorrhage and the Raising of Jairus' Daughter (Mark 5.21–43)." In Levine and Blickenstaff, *A Feminist Companion to Mark*, 54–78.

———. "Women's Authority Roles in Paul's Churches: Countercultural or Conventional?" *Novum Testamentum* 36 (1994): 350–72.

Cousar, Charles B. *Reading Galatians, Philippians, and 1 Thessalonians*. Reading the New Testament. Macon, GA: Smyth & Helwys, 2001.

Crossan, John Dominic. "The Search for the Historical Paul: Which Letters Did He Really Write?" Huffington Post, July 5, 2011. https://www.huffpost.com/entry/apostle-paul-letters_b_890387.

Culpepper, R. Alan. *John the Son of Zebedee: The Life of a Legend*. Columbia: University of South Carolina Press, 1994.

D'Angelo, Mary Rose. "Hebrews." In Newsom, Ringe, and Lapsley, *Women's Bible Commentary*, 608–12.

———. "'I Have Seen the Lord': Visionary, Early Christian Prophecy, and the Context of John 20:14–18." In *Mariam, the Magdalen, and the Mother*, edited by Deirdre Good, 95–122. Bloomington: Indiana University Press, 2005.

———. "Women in Luke-Acts." *Journal of Biblical Literature* 109 (1990): 441–61.

David. "Going Up? Icons of the Ascension." David's blog, October 16, 2016. Icons and Their Interpretation: Information for the Objective Student of Russian, Greek and Balkan Icons. https://russianicons.wordpress.com/tag/ascension-icon.

Davies, W. D., and Dale C. Allison. *A Critical and Exegetical Commentary on the Gospel according to Saint Matthew*. 3 vols. International Critical Commentary. Edinburgh: T&T Clark, 1988–97.

Davis, Garth, director. *Mary Magdalene*. London: Film4, 2018.

deSilva, David A. *Perseverance in Gratitude: A Socio-rhetorical Commentary on the Epistle "to the Hebrews."* Grand Rapids: Eerdmans, 2000.

Dewey, Joanna. "Women in the Gospel of Mark." *Word & World* 26 (2006): 22–29.

Dodd, C. H. "A Hidden Parable in the Fourth Gospel." In *More New Testament Studies*, 30–40. Manchester: Manchester University Press, 1968.

Donaldson, T. L. *Jesus on the Mountain: A Study in Matthean Theology.* Sheffield: JSOT Press, 1985.

Dunn, James D. G. *Romans.* 2 vols. Word Biblical Commentary 38A–B. Dallas: Word, 1988.

Edmondson, Jonathan. "Slavery and the Roman Family." In *The Ancient Mediterranean World*, edited by K. Bradley and P. Cartledge, 337–61. Vol. 1 of *The Cambridge World History of Slavery*. Cambridge: Cambridge University Press, 2011.

Ehrman, Bart D. *Forged: Writing in the Name of God—Why the Bible's Authors Are Not Who We Think They Are.* New York: HarperCollins, 2011.

Ehrman, Bart D., and Zlatko Pleše, eds. and trans. *The Apocryphal Gospels: Texts and Translations.* Oxford: Oxford University Press, 2011.

Ellingworth, Paul. *The Epistle to the Hebrews.* New International Greek Testament Commentary. Grand Rapids: Eerdmans, 1993.

Elowsky, Joel C., ed. *John 1–10.* Ancient Christian Commentary on Scripture: New Testament 4a. Downers Grove, IL: IVP Academic, 2006.

———, ed. *John 11–21.* Ancient Christian Commentary on Scripture: New Testament 4b. Downers Grove, IL: IVP Academic, 2007.

Epiphanius of Salamis. *The Panarion of Epiphanius of Salamis, Books II and III; De Fide.* Translated by F. Williams. Nag Hammadi and Manichaean Studies 79. 2nd ed. Leiden: Brill, 2013.

Epp, Eldon J. *Junia: The First Woman Apostle.* Minneapolis: Fortress, 2005.

Ernst, Allie M. *Martha from the Margins: The Authority of Martha in Early Christian Tradition.* Leiden: Brill, 2009.

Eusebius. *Ecclesiastical History.* Translated by Kirsopp Lake. 2 vols. Loeb Classical Library. London: Heinemann, 1926.

Evans, Rachel Held. "For the Sake of the Gospel, Let the Women Speak." Perineal Blog, June 7, 2012. https://rachelheldevans.com/blog/mutuality-let-women-speak.

Fee, Gordon D. "The Cultural Context of Ephesians 5:18–6:9." *Priscilla Papers* 16 (2002): 3–8.

———. *1 and 2 Timothy, Titus.* New International Biblical Commentary. Peabody, MA: Hendrickson, 1988.

———. *The First Epistle to the Corinthians.* 2nd ed. New International Commentary on the New Testament. Grand Rapids: Eerdmans, 2014.

Fehribach, Adeline. *The Women in the Life of the Bridegroom: A Feminist Historical-Literary Analysis of the Female Characters in the Fourth Gospel.* Collegeville, MN: Liturgical Press, 1998.

Fernandes, Joynel. "Analyzing Art: The Iconography of the Ascension through the Ages." Aleteia, May 15, 2018. https://aleteia.org/2018/05/15/analyzing-art-the-icono graphy-of-the-ascension-through-the-ages/.

Fitzmyer, Joseph A. *The Acts of the Apostles: A New Translation with Introduction and Commentary*. Anchor Bible 31. New York: Doubleday, 1997.

———. *First Corinthians: A New Translation with Introduction and Commentary*. Anchor Yale Bible 32. New Haven: Yale University Press, 2008.

———. *The Gospel according to Luke: Introduction, Translation, and Notes*. 2 vols. Anchor Bible. New York: Doubleday, 1979.

Ford, J. Massyngbearde. *Redeemer, Friend and Mother: Salvation in Antiquity and in the Gospel of John*. Minneapolis: Fortress, 1997.

Foster, Timothy D. "1 Timothy 2:8–15 and Gender Wars at Ephesus." *Priscilla Papers* 30 (2016): 3–10.

France, R. T. *The Gospel of Mark: A Commentary on the Greek Text*. New International Greek Testament Commentary. Grand Rapids: Eerdmans, 2002.

———. *The Gospel of Matthew*. New International Commentary on the New Testament. Grand Rapids: Eerdmans, 2007.

———. *Women in the Church's Ministry: A Test Case for Biblical Hermeneutics*. Milton Keynes, UK: Paternoster, 1995.

Frank, David B. "Do We Translate the Original Author's Intended Meaning?" *Theology* 2 (2016): 653–67. https://doi.org/10.1515/opth-2016-0051.

Frey, Jörg. *The Glory of the Crucified One: Christology and Theology in the Gospel of John*. Translated by W. Coppins and C. Heilig. Waco: Baylor University Press, 2018.

Friedrichsen, Timothy A. "The Commissioning of Women Disciples: Matthew 28:9–10." In *Transcending Boundaries: Contemporary Readings of the New Testament; Essays in Honor of Francis J. Moloney*, edited by Rekha M. Chennattu and Mary L. Coloe, 270–78. Roma: Libreria Editrice Vaticana, 2005.

Garrow, Alan. "Streeter's 'Other' Synoptic Solution: The Matthew Conflator Hypothesis." *New Testament Studies* 62 (2016): 207–26.

Gaventa, Beverly Roberts. *The Acts of the Apostles*. Abingdon New Testament Commentaries. Nashville: Abingdon, 2003.

———. "Is Galatians Just a 'Guy Thing'? A Theological Reflection." *Interpretation* 54 (2000): 267–78.

———. "Listening to Phoebe Read Romans." Lecture given at the Annual Susan Draper White Lectures in Women's Studies, United Theological Seminary of the Twin Cities, St. Paul, March 12, 2012. YouTube video, 47:51. https://www.youtube .com/watch?v=89TeH0HbelI.

———. "Listening to Romans with Junia and Her Sisters." Lecture given at the Annual Susan Draper White Lectures in Women's Studies, United Theological Seminary

of the Twin Cities, St. Paul, March 13, 2012. YouTube video, 47:21. https://www
.youtube.com/watch?v=VD-zGxapNcw&t=337s.

———. *Mary: Glimpses of the Mother of Jesus*. Studies on Personalities of the New
Testament. Columbia: University of South Carolina Press, 1995.

———. *Our Mother Saint Paul*. Louisville: Westminster John Knox, 2007.

———. *When in Romans: An Invitation to Linger with the Gospel according to Paul*.
Grand Rapids: Baker Academic, 2016.

Giles, Kevin. *What the Bible Actually Teaches on Women*. Eugene, OR: Cascade
Books, 2018.

Goodacre, Mark. *The Case against Q: Studies in Markan Priority and the Synoptic
Problem*. Harrisburg, PA: Trinity Press International, 2002.

Gooder, Paula. *Phoebe: A Story (with Notes); Pauline Christianity in Narrative Form*.
London: Hodder & Stoughton, 2018.

Goodine, Elizabeth A. *Standing at Lyon: An Examination of the Martyrdom of Blandina of Lyon*. Gorgias Studies in Early Christianity and Patristics 25. Piscataway,
NJ: Gorgias, 2014.

Gorman, Heather M. "What Has Aeneas to Do with Paul? Gender, Head Coverings,
and Ancient Appeals to Origin Stories." *Priscilla Papers* 30 (2016): 11–17.

Gorman, Michael J. *Reading Paul*. Milton Keynes, UK: Paternoster, 2008.

"The Gospel according to Mary." In Ehrman and Pleše, *Apocryphal Gospels*, 592–99.

Gospel of Bartholomew. Translated by M. R. James. Oxford: Clarendon, 1924. Added
to the Gnostic Society Library, 1995. Corrected 2011. http://gnosis.org/library
/gosbart.htm.

Gospel of Peter. Translated by R. E. Brown. Early Christian Writings. Accessed May
17, 2020. http://www.earlychristianwritings.com/text/gospelpeter-brown.html.

"The Gospel of Philip." Translated by W. W. Isenberg. In *The Nag Hammadi Library
in English: The Definitive Translation of the Gnostic Scriptures*, edited by James M.
Robinson, 139–60. 2nd ed. Leiden: Brill, 1988.

Gospel of Thomas. In *Synopsis Quattuor Evangeliorum*, edited by Kurt Aland, 517–
30. 3rd ed. Stuttgart: Deutsche Bibelgesellschaft, 1985.

Gray, Patrick, and Amy Peeler. *Hebrews: An Introduction and Study Guide*. T&T
Clark Study Guides to the New Testament. London: Bloomsbury T&T Clark,
2020. Kindle.

Green, Joel B. "Acts." In *The New Interpreter's Bible: One Volume Commentary*,
edited by Beverly Roberts Gaventa and David L. Petersen, 735–67. Nashville:
Abingdon, 2010.

———. *The Gospel of Luke*. New International Commentary on the New Testament.
Grand Rapids: Eerdmans, 1997.

Green, Mary E. *Eyes to See: The Redemptive Purpose of Icons*. New York: Morehouse, 2014.

———. "Mary Magdalene the Myrrh Bearer." In *Eyes to See: The Redemptive Purpose of Icons*. New York: Morehouse, 2014.

Gregory of Nyssa. *The Life of St. Macrina*. Translated by W. K. Lowther Clarke. London: SPCK, 1916.

———. *The Soul and the Resurrection*. Translated by Catherine P. Roth. Crestwood, NY: St. Vladimir's Seminary Press, 1993.

Grudem, Wayne A. *Evangelical Feminism and Biblical Truth: An Analysis of More Than One Hundred Disputed Questions*. Wheaton: Crossway, 2012.

Guyette, Fred. "The Genre of the Call Narrative: Beyond Habel's Model." *Jewish Bible Quarterly* 43 (2015): 54–58.

Haddad, Mimi. "What Language Shall We Use? A Look at Inclusive Language for People, Feminine Images for God, and Gender-Accurate Bible Translations." *Priscilla Papers* 17 (2003): 3–7.

Hagner, Donald A. *Matthew*. 2 vols. Word Biblical Commentary 33A–B. Nashville: Nelson, 2000.

Harrison, P. N. *The Problem of the Pastoral Epistles*. Oxford: Oxford University Press, 1921.

Haskins, Susan. *Mary Magdalene: Myth and Metaphor*. New York: Riverhead Books, 1993.

Hauerwas, Stanley. *Matthew*. Brazos Theological Commentary on the Bible. Grand Rapids: Brazos, 2006.

Hays, Richard B. *First Corinthians*. Interpretation: A Bible Commentary for Teaching and Preaching. Louisville: Westminster John Knox, 2011.

———. "Paul on the Relation between Men and Women." In Levine and Blickenstaff, *A Feminist Companion to Paul*, 137–47.

Heffernan, Thomas J. *The Passion of Perpetua and Felicity*. Oxford: Oxford University Press, 2012.

Heine, Susanne. *Women and Early Christianity: Are the Feminist Scholars Right?* Translated by J. Bowden. London: SCM, 1987.

Heinen, Sandra. "Exegesis without Authorial Intention? On the Role of the 'Author Construct' in Text Interpretation." In Brue, *Biblical Exegesis without Authorial Intention?*, 7–23.

Held, H. J. "Matthew as Interpreter of the Miracle Stories." In *Tradition and Interpretation in Matthew*, edited by G. Bornkamm, G. Barth, and H. J. Held, 165–211. Translated by P. Scott. New Testament Library. 2nd ed. London: SCM, 1982.

Henderson, Suzanne Watts. *Christology and Discipleship in the Gospel of Mark*. Society of New Testament Studies Monograph Series. Cambridge: Cambridge University Press, 2006.

Hewitt, E. C., and S. R. Hiatt. *Women Priests: Yes or No?* New York: Seabury, 1973.

Holladay, Carl R. *Acts: A Commentary*. New Testament Library. Louisville: Westminster John Knox, 2016.

Hooker, Morna D. "Authority on Her Head: An Examination of 1 Cor 11:10." *New Testament Studies* 10 (1963): 410–16.

———. *The Gospel according to St Mark*. Black's New Testament Commentary. London: Black, 1991.

Hoppin, Ruth. *Priscilla's Letter: Finding the Author of the Epistle to the Hebrews*. Fort Bragg, CA: Lost Coast, 1997.

Hoskyns, E. C., and F. N. Davey. *The Fourth Gospel*. 2 vols. London: Faber & Faber, 1939.

Hutson, Christopher R. *First and Second Timothy and Titus*. Paideia: Commentaries on the New Testament. Grand Rapids: Baker Academic, 2019.

Hylen, Susan. *A Modest Apostle: Thecla and the History of Women in the Early Church*. Oxford: Oxford University Press, 2015.

Irenaeus. *Against Heresies*. Translated by Alexander Roberts and William Rambaut. In vol. 1 of *The Ante-Nicene Fathers*, edited by Alexander Roberts, James Donaldson, and A. Cleveland Coxe. 10 vols. Buffalo: Christian Literature, 1885. Revised and edited by Kevin Knight. New Advent, 2017. http://www.newadvent.org/fathers/0103.htm.

Iverson, K. R. *Gentiles in the Gospel of Mark: "Even the Dogs under the Table Eat the Children's Crumbs."* Library of New Testament Studies. London: T&T Clark, 2007.

Jennings, Willie James. *Acts*. Belief: A Theological Commentary on the Bible. Louisville: Westminster John Knox, 2017.

John Chrysostom. *Homily 31 on Rom. xvi.5*. In *Saint Chrysostom: Homilies on the Acts of the Apostles and the Epistle to the Romans*, edited by Philip Schaff, 553–59. Vol. 11 of *Nicene and Post-Nicene Fathers*. Series 1, edited by Philip Schaff. Edinburgh: T&T Clark, 1889.

———. *Six Books on the Priesthood*. Translated by Graham Neville. London: SPCK, 1964.

John Paul II. *Ordinatio Sacerdotalis: Apostolic Letter of John Paul II to the Bishops of the Catholic Church on Reserving Priestly Ordination to Men Alone*. Vatican: Holy See, 1994. http://www.vatican.va/content/john-paul-ii/en/apost_letters/1994 /documents/hf_jp-ii_apl_19940522_ordinatio-sacerdotalis.html.

Johnson, Elizabeth. *Truly Our Sister: A Theology of Mary in the Communion of Saints*. New York: Continuum, 2003.

Johnson, Luke Timothy. *Brother of Jesus, Friend of God: Studies in the Letter of James*. Grand Rapids: Eerdmans, 2004.

———. *The First and Second Letters to Timothy: A New Translation with Introduction and Commentary*. Anchor Bible. New York: Doubleday, 2001.

———. *The Gospel of Luke*. Sacra Pagina 3. Collegeville, MN: Liturgical Press, 1991.

Jones, Victoria Emily. "The Unnamed Emmaus Disciple: Mary, Wife of Cleopas?" *Art & Theology* (blog), April 28, 2017. https://artandtheology.org/2017/04/28/the -unnamed-emmaus-disciple-mary-wife-of-cleopas/.

Josephus. *Jewish Antiquities*. Translated by L. H. Feldman. 6 vols. Loeb Classical Library. London: Heinemann, 1965.

Just, Arthur A. *Luke 1:1–9:50*. Concordia Commentary: A Theological Exposition of Sacred Scriptures. St. Louis: Concordia, 1996.

———. *Luke 9:51–24:53*. Concordia Commentary: A Theological Exposition of Sacred Scriptures. St. Louis: Concordia, 1997.

Karris, Robert J. "Women and Discipleship in Luke." *Catholic Biblical Quarterly* 56 (1994): 1–20.

Kateusz, Ally. *Mary and Early Christian Women: Hidden Leadership*. Cham, Switzerland: Palgrave Macmillan, 2019. Kindle.

Keener, Craig S. *Acts: An Exegetical Commentary*. 4 vols. Grand Rapids: Baker Academic, 2012–15.

———. *The Gospel of John: A Commentary*. 2 vols. Peabody, MA: Hendrickson, 2004.

———. *The Gospel of Matthew: A Socio-rhetorical Commentary*. 2nd ed. Grand Rapids: Eerdmans, 2009.

———. *Paul, Women, and Wives: Marriage and Women's Ministry in the Letters of Paul*. 2nd ed. Grand Rapids: Baker Academic, 2004.

Kennedy, James M. "Jeremiah." In *The New Interpreter's Bible: One Volume Commentary*, edited by Beverly Roberts Gaventa and David L. Petersen, 425–50. Nashville: Abingdon, 2010.

King, Fergus J. *Opening the Scroll: An Introductory Commentary on the Revelation of John*. Cologne: Lambert Academic Publishing, 2014.

———. "'Pointing the Bone': Sorcery Syndrome and Uncanny Death in Acts 5:1–11." *Irish Biblical Studies* 30 (2012): 12–34.

Kingsbury, Jack Dean. *Matthew: Structure, Christology, Kingdom*. Philadelphia: Fortress, 1975.

Kittredge, Cynthia Briggs. "1 Peter." In Newsom, Ringe, and Lapsley, *Women's Bible Commentary*, 616–19.

———. "Hebrews." In Schüssler Fiorenza, *Feminist Commentary*, 430–34.

Klauck, Hans-Josef. *Der erste Johannesbrief*. Neukirchen-Vluyn: Neukirchener Verlag, 1991.

Kloppenburg, John S. *Q, the Earliest Gospel: An Introduction to the Original Stories and Sayings of Jesus*. Louisville: Westminster John Knox, 2008.

Koester, Craig R. *Revelation: A New Translation with Introduction and Commentary*. Anchor Bible. New Haven: Yale University Press, 2015.

Kopas, Jane. "Jesus and Women: Luke's Gospel." *Theology Today* 42 (1986): 192–202.

Köstenberger, Andreas J., and Margaret E. Köstenberger. *God's Design for Man and Woman: A Biblical-Theological Survey*. Wheaton: Crossway, 2014.

Kovacs, Judith L. "'Now Shall the Ruler of This World Be Driven Out': Jesus' Death as Cosmic Battle in John 12:20–36." *Journal of Biblical Literature* 114 (1995): 227–47.

Krause, Deborah. *1 Timothy*. London: T&T Clark, 2004.

Kroeger, Catherine C., and Mary J. Evans, eds. *The IVP Women's Bible Commentary*. Downers Grove, IL: InterVarsity, 2002.

Lashier, Jackson. "In the Company of the Fathers: The Female Martyrs." Seedbed, April 25, 2014. https://www.seedbed.com/company-fathers-female-martyrs/.

Lee, Dorothy A. "Christological Identity and Authority in the Gospel of Mark." *Phronema* 33 (2018): 1–20.

———. "Clean and Unclean: Multiple Readings of Mark 7:24–30/31." In *Terror in the Bible: Rhetoric, Gender, and Violence*, edited by M. Melanchthon and R. Whittaker. Atlanta: SBL Press, 2021.

———. *Creation, Matter and the Image of God: Essays on John*. Scholars Collection. Adelaide, SA: ATF, 2020.

———. "The Faith of the Canaanite Woman, Mt. 15.21–28: Narrative, Theology, Ministry." *Journal of Anglican Studies* 13 (2015): 12–29.

———. "Feminist Theology." In *Jesus in History, Thought, and Culture: An Encyclopedia*, edited by L. Holden, 1:281–88. Santa Barbara, CA: ABC Clio, 2003.

———. "Fictive Kinship and Its Symbolism in the Literary Structures of 1 John." In *Anatomies of the Gospels and Beyond: Essays in Honour of R. Alan Culpepper*, edited by M. C. Parsons, E. S. Malbon, and P. N. Anderson, 388–404. Leiden: Brill, 2018. A slightly revised version appears in Lee, *Creation, Matter and the Image of God*, 253–71.

———. *Flesh and Glory: Symbolism, Gender and Theology in the Gospel of John*. New York: Crossroad, 2002.

———. *A Friendly Guide to Matthew's Gospel*. Mulgrave, Australia: Garratt, 2013.

———. "The Gospel of John and the Five Senses." *Journal of Biblical Literature* 129 (2010): 115–27. A slightly revised version appears as "The Five Senses" in Lee, *Creation, Matter and the Image of God*, 19–33.

———. *The Gospels Speak: Addressing Life's Questions*. New York: Paulist Press, 2017.

———. "Martha and Mary: Levels of Characterization in Luke and John." In *Characters and Characterization in the Gospel of John*, edited by Christopher W. Skinner, 197–220. Library of New Testament Studies. London: Bloomsbury T&T Clark, 2013. A slightly revised version appears as "Martha and Mary" in Lee, *Creation, Matter and the Image of God*, 111–35.

———. "Partnership in Easter Faith: The Role of Mary Magdalene and Thomas in John 20." *Journal for the Study of the New Testament* 58 (1995): 37–49. A slightly revised version appears in Lee, *Creation, Matter and the Image of God*, 77–89.

———. "Presence or Absence: The Question of Women Disciples at the Last Supper." *Pacifica* 6 (1993): 1–20. A slightly revised version appears in Lee, *Creation, Matter and the Image of God*, 155–76.

———. "The Significance of Moses in the Gospel of John." *Australian Biblical Review* 63 (2015): 52–66. A slightly revised version appears as "The Significance of Moses" in Lee, *Creation, Matter and the Image of God*, 137–54.

———. *The Symbolic Narratives of the Fourth Gospel: The Interplay of Form and Meaning*. Journal for the Study of the New Testament Supplement Series. Sheffield: JSOT Press, 1994.

———. *Transfiguration*. New Century Theology. London: Continuum, 2004.

———. "Witness in the Fourth Gospel: John the Baptist and the Beloved Disciple as Counterparts." *Australian Biblical Review* 61 (2013): 1–17. A slightly revised version appears in Lee, *Creation, Matter and the Image of God*, 91–110.

———. "Women as 'Sinners': Three Narratives of Salvation in Luke and John." *Australian Biblical Review* 44 (1996): 1–15.

Leonard, Richard. *Beloved Daughters: 100 Years of Papal Teaching on Women*. Melbourne: David Lovell, 1995.

Léon-Dufour, Xavier. *Lecture de l'Évangile selon Jean*. 4 vols. Parole de Dieu. Paris: Éditions du Seuil, 1996.

Levine, Amy-Jill. "Discharging Responsibility: Matthean Jesus, Biblical Law, and Hemorrhaging Woman." In *A Feminist Companion to Matthew*, edited by A.-J. Levine and M. Blickenstaff, 70–87. Feminist Commentary on the New Testament. Sheffield: Sheffield Academic, 2001.

Levine, A.-J., and M. Blickenstaff, eds. *A Feminist Companion to Mark*. Feminist Companion to the New Testament. Sheffield: Sheffield Academic, 2001.

———. *A Feminist Companion to Paul*. London: T&T Clark, 2004.

Lieu, Judith M. "The Mother of the Son in the Fourth Gospel." *Journal of Biblical Literature* 117 (1998): 61–77.

Lightfoot, R. H. *The Gospel Message of St Mark*. Oxford: Oxford University Press, 1950.

Lincoln, Andrew T. *Born of a Virgin? Reconceiving Jesus in the Bible, Tradition and Theology*. London: SPCK, 2013.

———. *The Gospel according to Saint John*. Black's New Testament Commentary. London: Continuum, 2005.

The Li Tim-Oi Foundation. 2010–2019. https://www.ltof.org.uk.

Loader, William. *The New Testament on Sexuality*. Grand Rapids: Eerdmans, 2012.

Lu, Shi-Min. "Woman's Role in New Testament Household Codes: Transforming First Century Roman Culture." *Priscilla Papers* 30 (2016): 9–15.

Luz, Ulrich. *Matthew 21–28: A Commentary*. Hermeneia. Minneapolis: Fortress, 2005.

Maccini, Robert Gordon. *Her Testimony Is True: Women as Witnesses according to John*. Journal for the Study of the New Testament Supplement Series. Sheffield: Sheffield Academic, 1996.

Macy, Gary. *The Hidden History of Women's Ordination: Female Clergy in the Medieval West*. Oxford: Oxford University Press, 2008.

Madigan, Kevin, and Carolyn Osiek, eds. and trans. *Ordained Women in the Early Church: A Documentary History*. Baltimore: Johns Hopkins University Press, 2005.

Maguire, Marjorie Reiley. "Bible, Liturgy Concur: Women Were There." *National Catholic Reporter*, June 5, 1998. Republished by the Wijngaards Institute for Catholic Research. http://www.womenpriests.org/scriptur/maguire.asp.

Malbon, Elizabeth Struthers. *In the Company of Jesus: Characters in Mark's Gospel*. Louisville: Westminster John Knox, 2002.

———. "The Poor Widow in Mark and Her Poor Rich Readers." In Levine and Blickenstaff, *A Feminist Companion to Mark*, 111–27.

Malherbe, Abraham J. *The Letters to the Thessalonians: A New Translation with Introduction and Commentary*. Anchor Bible. New York: Doubleday, 2000.

Malina, Bruce J., and John J. Pilch. *Social Science Commentary on the Book of Acts*. Minneapolis: Fortress, 2008.

Marcus, Joel. *Mark 1–8: A New Translation with Introduction and Commentary*. Anchor Bible. New Haven: Yale University Press, 2000.

———. *Mark 8–16: A New Translation with Introduction and Commentary*. Anchor Bible. New Haven: Yale University Press, 2009.

Marlowe, Michael. "Confusion of Semantics with Linguistic Pragmatics in the Defense of the TNIV." Bible Research, May 2005. http://www.bible-researcher.com/blomberg.html.

Marshall, I. Howard. *The Epistle to the Philippians*. Epworth Commentary Series. London: Epworth, 1991.

———. *The Gospel of Luke: A Commentary on the Greek Text*. New International Greek Testament Commentary. Grand Rapids: Eerdmans, 1978.

Matthews, Christopher R. "Acts of the Apostles." In *The Oxford Encyclopedia of the Books of the Bible*, edited by Michael D. Coogan, 12. Oxford: Oxford University Press, 2011.

Maximus the Confessor. *The Life of the Virgin*. Edited and translated by Stephen J. Shoemaker. New Haven: Yale University Press, 2012.

McCarty, V. K. "A Glimpse into the Wisdom of the Desert Mothers: Bibliography & Prayer for Modern-Day Practitioners." General Theological Seminary, April 2018. Academia.edu. https://www.academia.edu/7457293/A_Glimpse_into_the_Wisdom_of_the_Desert_Mothers_Bibliography_and_Prayer_for_Modern–day Practitioners day_Practitioners_by_VK_McCarty.

McGowan, Anne, and Paul F. Bradshaw. *The Pilgrimage of Egeria: A New Translation of the "Itinerarium Egeriae" with Introduction and Commentary*. Collegeville, MN: Liturgical Press, 2018.

McKnight, Scot. *The Letter of James*. New International Commentary on the New Testament. Grand Rapids: Eerdmans, 2011.

Metzger, Bruce M. *A Textual Commentary on the Greek New Testament*. 2nd ed. Stuttgart: United Bible Societies, 1994.

Miller, James D. *The Pauline Letters as Composite Documents*. Society of New Testament Studies Monograph Series 93. Cambridge: Cambridge University Press, 1997.

Milton, Michael A. "Can Women Be Pastors? The Ordination of Women to Pastoral Ministry." BibleStudyTools.com, October 23, 2019. https://www.biblestudytools.com/bible-study/topical-studies/can-women-be-pastors.html.

Mitchell, Joan L. *Beyond Fear and Silence: A Feminist-Literary Reading of Mark*. New York: Continuum, 2001.

Moloney, Francis J. *The Gospel of John*. Sacra Pagina. Collegeville, MN: Liturgical Press, 1998.

———. *The Gospel of Mark: A Commentary*. Peabody, MA: Hendrickson, 2002.

———. *Johannine Studies 1975–2017*. Wissenschaftliche Untersuchungen zum Neuen Testament. Tübingen: Mohr Siebeck, 2017.

———. *The Living Voice of the Gospel: The Gospels Today*. Mulgrave, Australia: Garratt, 2006.

———. *The Resurrection of the Messiah: A Narrative Commentary on the Resurrection Accounts in the Four Gospels*. New York: Paulist Press, 2013.

———. "Woman and Mother in the Fourth Gospel." In *Johannine Studies 1975–2017*, 270–79. Wissenschaftliche Untersuchungen zum Neuen Testament. Tübingen: Mohr Siebeck, 2017.

Moltmann-Wendel, Elisabeth. *The Women around Jesus: Reflections on Authentic Personhood*. London: SCM, 1982.

Montague, George T. *First Corinthians*. Catholic Commentary on Sacred Scripture. Grand Rapids: Baker Academic, 2011.

Moo, Douglas. "What Does It Mean Not to Teach or Have Authority over Men?" In *Recovering Biblical Manhood and Womanhood: A Response to Evangelical Feminism*, edited by John Piper and Wayne A. Grudem, 176–92. Wheaton: Crossway, 1991.

Mostert, Christiaan. "Catholicity of the Church and the Universality of Theology." *Pacifica* 16 (2003): 123–36.

Moxnes, Halvor. "Patron-Client Relations and the New Community in Luke-Acts." In *The Social World of Luke-Acts: Models for Interpretation*, edited by J. H. Neyrey, 242–50. Peabody, MA: Hendrickson, 1991.

Murphy-O'Connor, Jerome. *Paul: A Critical Life*. Oxford: Oxford University Press, 1996.

Newsom, Carol A., Sharon H. Ringe, and Jacqueline E. Lapsley, eds. *Women's Bible Commentary*. 3rd ed. Louisville: Westminster John Knox, 2012.

Nolland, John. *Luke 1–9:20*. Word Biblical Commentary 35A. Dallas: Word, 1989.

———. *Luke 18:35–24:53*. Word Biblical Commentary 35C. Dallas: Word: 1993.

O'Connor, Kathleen M. "Jeremiah." In Newsom, Ringe, and Lapsley, *Women's Bible Commentary*, 267–77.

O'Day, Gail R. "John." In Newsom, Ringe, and Lapsley, *Women's Bible Commentary*, 517–30.

———. "John 7:53–8:11: A Study in Misreading." *Journal of Biblical Literature* 111 (1992): 631–40.

Oden, Thomas C. *First and Second Timothy and Titus*. Interpretation: A Bible Commentary for Teaching and Preaching. Louisville: John Knox, 1989.

Okure, Teresa. *The Johannine Approach to Mission: A Contextual Study of John 4:1–42*. Wissenschaftliche Untersuchungen zum Neuen Testament. Tübingen: Mohr, 1988.

Olsson, B. *A Commentary on the Letters of John: An Intra-Jewish Approach*. Eugene: Pickwick, 2013.

Osiek, Carolyn and David L. Balch, *Families in the New Testament World: Households and House Churches*. Louisville: Westminster John Knox, 1997.

Ouspensky, L. "The Meaning and Language of Icons." In *The Meaning of Icons*, edited by L. Ouspensky and V. Lossky, 23–49. New York: St. Vladimir's Seminary Press, 1989.

Pagels, Elaine. *The Gnostic Gospels*. New York: Vintage Books, 1979.

Painter, John. *1, 2, and 3 John*. Sacra Pagina. Collegeville, MN: Liturgical Press, 2002.

———. *Just James: The Brother of Jesus in History and Tradition*. London: Bloomsbury, 2005.

Parkhouse, Sarah. "Matter and the Soul: The Bipartite Eschatology of the Gospel of Mary." In *Connecting Gospels: Beyond the Canonical/Non-Canonical Divide*, edited by F. Watson and S. Parkhouse, 216–32. Oxford: Oxford University Press, 2018.

Parsons, Mikeal C. *Acts*. Paideia: Commentaries on the New Testament. Grand Rapids: Baker Academic, 2008.

Payne, Philip B. *Man and Woman, One in Christ: An Exegetical and Theological Study of Paul's Letters*. Grand Rapids: Zondervan, 2009.

———. "Wild Hair and Gender Equality in 1 Corinthians 11:2–26." *Priscilla Papers* 20 (2006): 10–11.

Peeler, Amy L. B. "Junia/Joanna: Herald of the Good News." In *Vindicating the Vixens: Revisiting Sexualized, Vilified, and Marginalized Women of the Bible*, edited by Sandra Glahn, 273–85. Grand Rapids: Kregel Academic, 2017.

———. *You Are My Son: The Family of God in the Epistle to the Hebrews*. Library of New Testament Studies. London: Bloomsbury, 2014.

Pelikan, Jaroslav. *Christianity and Classical Culture: The Metamorphosis of Natural Theology in the Christian Encounter with Hellenism*. Gifford Lectures. New Haven: Yale University Press, 1993.

"Pentecost Icon as an Icon of the Church." A Reader's Guide to Orthodox Icons. June 14, 2011. https://iconreader.files.wordpress.com/2011/06/17c-assumption -cathedral-kem-rus.jpg.

Peppiatt, Lucy. *Rediscovering Scripture's Vision for Women: Fresh Perspectives on Disputed Texts*. Downers Grove, IL: IVP Academic, 2019.

Perkins, Pheme. *First Corinthians*. Paideia: Commentaries on the New Testament. Grand Rapids: Baker Academic, 2012.

Pippin, Tina. "Revelation/Apocalypse." In Newsom, Ringe, and Lapsley, *Women's Bible Commentary*, 628–29.

"Pistis Sophia." In *The Coptic Gnostic Library: With English Translation, Introduction and Notes*, edited by Carl Schmidt. Translated by Violet MacDermot. The Institute for Antiquity and Christianity. Leiden: Brill 1978.

Pliny. *Letters II*. Translated by W. Melmoth. Loeb Classical Library. London: Heinemann, 1927.

Porter, Muriel. "The Christian Origins of Feminism." In *Freedom and Entrapment: Women Thinking Theology*, edited by M. Confoy, D. A. Lee, and J. Nowotny, 208–24. Melbourne: Dove, 1995.

———. *Women in Purple: Women Bishops in Australia*. Melbourne: Garratt, 2008.

———. *Women in the Church: The Great Ordination Debate*. Melbourne: Penguin, 1989.

Price, Richard. "The Virgin as Theotokos at Ephesus (AD 431) and Earlier." In *The Oxford Handbook of Mary*, edited by Chris Maunder, 67–77. Oxford: Oxford University Press, 2019.

"The Proto-Gospel of James." In Ehrman and Pleše, *Apocryphal Gospels*, 31–71.

Reid, Barbara. *Choosing the Better Part? Women in the Gospel of Luke*. Collegeville, MN: Liturgical Press, 1996.

Reinhartz, Adele. "The Jews of the Fourth Gospel." In *The Oxford Handbook of Johannine Studies*, edited by J. M. Lieu and M. de Boer, 121–37. Oxford: Oxford University Press, 2018.

Rhoads, D. "Jesus and the Syrophoenician Woman in Mark: A Narrative-Critical Study." *Journal of the American Academy of Religion* 62 (1994): 343–75.

Ricci, Carla. *Mary Magdalene and Many Others: Women Who Followed Jesus*. Translated by P. Burns. Tunbridge Wells, UK: Burns & Oates, 1994.

Ricoeur, Paul. *Interpretation Theory: Discourse and the Surplus of Meaning*. Fort Worth: Texas Christian University Press, 1976.

Ringe, Sharon H. "A Gentile Woman's Story, Revisited: Rereading Mark 7:24–31." In Levine and Blickenstaff, *A Feminist Companion to Mark*, 79–100.

Ristine, Jennifer. *Mary Magdalene: Insights from Ancient Magdala; Unveiling the Mystery with Perspectives from Archaeology, Scriptures, and Historical Traditions.* Rome: Libreria Editrice Vaticana, 2018.

Rohrbaugh, Richard L. "The Pre-industrial City in Luke-Acts: Urban Social Relations." In *The Social World of Luke-Acts: Models for Interpretation*, edited by J. H. Neyrey, 125–49. Peabody, MA: Hendrickson, 1991.

Rosner, Brian S. *Paul and the Law: Keeping the Commandments of God.* New Studies in Biblical Theology. Downers Grove, IL: InterVarsity, 2013.

Runesson, A. *Exegesis in the Making: Postcolonialism and New Testament Studies.* Leiden: Brill, 2011.

Sawyer, Deborah F. *Women and Religion in the First Christian Centuries.* London: Routledge, 1996.

Sayers, Dorothy L. "The Human-Not-Quite-Human." In *Unpopular Opinions*, 121–22. London: Victor Gollancz, 1946.

Schaberg, Jane D., and Sharon H. Ringe. "The Gospel of Luke." In Newsom, Ringe, and Lapsley, *Women's Bible Commentary*, 493–511.

Schneiders, Sandra M. "Women in the Fourth Gospel and the Role of Women in the Contemporary Church." *Biblical Theology Bulletin* 12 (1982): 35–45.

———. *Written That You May Believe: Encountering Jesus in the Fourth Gospel.* New York: Crossroad, 1999.

Schnelle, Udo. *Das Evangelium nach Johannes.* Leipzig: Evangelische Verlagsanstalt, 1998.

———. "Johannine Theology: Introduction to the Christian Faith." In *Theology of the New Testament*, translated by M. E. Boring, 659–750. Grand Rapids: Baker Academic, 2009.

———. "Revelation: Seeing and Understanding." In *Theology of the New Testament*, translated by M. E. Boring, 751–72. Grand Rapids: Baker Academic, 2009.

Schrader, Elizabeth. "Was Martha Added to the Fourth Gospel in the Second Century?" *Harvard Theological Review* 110 (2017): 360–92.

Schüssler Fiorenza, Elisabeth, ed. *A Feminist Commentary.* Vol. 2 of *Searching the Scriptures.* New York: Crossroad, 1994.

———. *In Memory of Her: A Feminist Theological Reconstruction of Christian Origins.* London: SCM, 1983.

———. *Revelation: Vision of a Just World.* Proclamation Commentaries. Minneapolis: Fortress, 1991.

Schweizer, Eduard. *The Good News according to Matthew.* Translated by D. E. Green. Louisville: John Knox, 1975.

Seim, Turid Karlsen. *The Double Message: Patterns of Gender in Luke and Acts.* Nashville: Abingdon, 1994.

———. "The Gospel of Luke." In Schüssler Fiorenza, *Feminist Commentary*, 728–62.

Senior, Donald P. *1 Peter, Jude and 2 Peter*. Sacra Pagina. Collegeville, MN: Liturgical Press, 2003.

Shoemaker, Stephen J. *Mary in Early Christian Faith and Devotion*. New Haven: Yale University Press, 2016.

Sim, David C. *The Gospel of Matthew and Christian-Judaism: The History and Social Setting of the Matthean Community*. Studies of the New Testament and Its World. Edinburgh: T&T Clark, 1998.

Sloyan, G. S. *Walking in the Truth: Perseverers and Deserters; The First, Second, and Third Letters of John*. Valley Forge, PA: Trinity Press International, 1995.

Smith, D. Moody. *Johannine Christianity: Essays on Its Setting, Sources, and Theology*. Edinburgh: T&T Clark, 1984.

Smith, Yancy W. "Women's Ordination in Hippolytus' Commentary *On the Song of Songs* and the Question of Provenance." In *Finding a Woman's Place: Essays in Honor of Carolyn Osiek*, edited by D. L. Balch and J. T. Lamoreaux, 311–35. Princeton Theological Monograph Series. Eugene, OR: Wipf & Stock, 2011.

Soskice, Janet Martin. "Can a Feminist Call God 'Father'?" In *Speaking the Christian God: The Holy Trinity and the Challenge of Feminism*, edited by A. J. Kimel, 81–94. Grand Rapids: Eerdmans, 1992.

———. "Trinity and Feminism." In *The Cambridge Companion to Feminist Theology*, edited by S. F. Parsons, 135–50. Cambridge Companions. Cambridge: Cambridge University Press, 2002.

Sowers, Brian P. *In Her Own Words: The Life and Poetry of Aelia Eudocia*. Hellenic Studies Series. Washington, DC: Center for Hellenic Studies, 2019.

Stagg, Evelyn, and Frank Stagg. *Women in the World of Jesus*. Philadelphia: Westminster, 1978.

Stephens, F. Scott. *The Gospel of Luke and Acts of the Apostles*. Interpreting Biblical Texts. Nashville: Abingdon, 2008.

Strauss, Mark L. "Current Issues in the Gender-Language Debate: A Response to Vern Poythress and Wayne Grudem." In *The Challenges of Bible Translation: Communicating God's Word to the World*, edited by G. G. Scorgie, M. L. Strauss, and S. M. Voth, 115–41. Grand Rapids: Zondervan, 2003.

Suetonius. "The Deified Claudius." In *The Lives of the Caesars*, translated by J. C. Rolfe, 1–84. 2 vols. Loeb Classical Library. Cambridge, MA: Harvard University Press, 1970.

Sunberg, Carla D. *The Cappadocian Mothers: Deification Exemplified in the Writings of Basil, Gregory, and Gregory*. Eugene, OR: Pickwick, 2017.

Swan, Laura. *The Forgotten Desert Mothers: Sayings, Lives, and Stories of Early Christian Women*. Mahwah, NJ: Paulist Press, 2001.

Swidler, Leonard. *Biblical Affirmations of Women*. Philadelphia: Westminster, 1979.

Tamez, Elsa. "Hagar and Sarah: A Case Study in Freedom." *Word & World* 20 (2000): 265–71.

———. "James." In Schüssler Fiorenza, *Feminist Commentary*, 383–91.

Taylor, Joan E. "Missing Magdala and the Name of Mary 'Magdalene.'" *Palestine Exploration Quarterly* 146 (2014): 205–23.

Tertullian. *De Baptismo*. In *Homily on Baptism*, edited and translated by Ernest Evans. London: SPCK, 1964.

Tetlow, E. M. *Women and Ministry in the New Testament*. New York: Paulist Press, 1980.

Thiselton, Antony C. *The First Epistle to the Corinthians*. New International Greek Testament Commentary. Grand Rapids: Eerdmans, 2000.

———. *The Two Horizons: New Testament Hermeneutics and Philosophical Description*. Grand Rapids: Eerdmans, 1980.

Thompson, Marianne Meye. *John: A Commentary*. New Testament Library. Louisville: Westminster John Knox, 2015.

Thompson, Mark D. *A Clear and Present Word: The Clarity of Scripture*. New Studies in Biblical Theology. Downers Grove, IL: IVP Academic, 2006.

Thurston, Bonnie Bowman. "Mark." In Kroeger and Evans, *IVP Women's Bible Commentary*, 547–61.

———. "Widows." In Kroeger and Evans, *IVP Women's Bible Commentary*, 745.

Tilley, Maureen A. "The Passion of Perpetua and Felicity." In Schüssler Fiorenza, *Feminist Commentary*, 828–58.

Torjesen, Karen Jo. *When Women Were Priests: Women's Leadership in the Early Church and the Scandal of Their Subordination in the Rise of Christianity*. New York: HarperSanFrancisco, 1993.

Traverso, V. M. "Art and the Gospels: Who Was St. Salome?" Aleteia, July 20, 2018. https://aleteia.org/2018/07/20/art-and-the-gospels-who-was-saint-salome/.

Troost-Cramer, Kathleen. *Jesus as Means and Locus of Worship in the Fourth Gospel: Sacrifice and Worship Space in John*. Eugene, OR: Pickwick, 2017.

Vandrei, Martha. "Claudia Rufina." In *Making and Remaking Saints in Nineteenth-Century Britain*, edited by G. Atkins, 60–76. Manchester: Manchester University Press, 2016.

Vanhoozer, Kevin J. *Is There a Meaning in This Text? The Bible, the Reader and the Morality of Literary Knowledge*. Leicester, UK: Apollos, 1998.

Vinson, Richard B. *Luke*. Smyth & Helwys Bible Commentary. Macon, GA: Smyth & Helwys, 2008.

Wainwright, Elaine Mary. *Towards a Feminist Critical Reading of the Gospel according to Matthew*. Beihefte zur Zeitschrift für die neutestamentliche Wissenschaft. Berlin: de Gruyter, 1991.

Wall, Robert W., and Robert W. Steele. *1 & 2 Timothy and Titus*. Two Horizons New Testament Commentary. Grand Rapids: Eerdmans, 2012.

Wasserman, Tommy. "Bringing Sisters Back Together: Another Look at Luke 10:41–42." *Journal of Biblical Literature* 137 (2018): 439–61.

Wesley, Margaret. *Son of Mary: The Family of Jesus and the Community of Faith in the Fourth Gospel*. Australian College of Theology Monograph Series. Eugene, OR: Wipf & Stock, 2015.

West, Angela. *Deadly Innocence: Feminism and the Mythology of Sin*. London: Cassell, 1995.

———. "Justification by Gender: Daphne Hampson's *After Christianity*." In *Challenging Women's Orthodoxies in the Context of Faith*, edited by S. F. Parsons, 35–71. Heythrop Studies in Contemporary Theology, Religion and Philosophy. Aldershot: Ashgate, 2000.

Westfall, Cynthia Long. *Paul and Gender: Reclaiming the Apostle's Vision for Men and Women in Christ*. Grand Rapids: Baker Academic, 2016.

Wijngaards, John. *The Ordination of Women in the Catholic Church: Unmasking a Cuckoo's Egg Tradition*. London: Darton, Longman and Todd, 2001.

———. *Women in Holy Orders? The Women Deacons of the Early Church*. Norwich: Canterbury, 2002.

Williams, Rowan. *Resurrection: Interpreting the Easter Gospel*. 2nd ed. London: Darton, Longman & Todd, 2002.

Willimon, William H. *Acts*. International Biblical Commentary for Teaching and Preaching. Atlanta: John Knox, 1988.

Wilson, Brittany E. "Mary Magdalene and Her Interpreters." In Newsom, Ringe, and Lapsley, *Women's Bible Commentary*, 512–16.

Wire, Antoinette Clark. *The Corinthian Women Prophets: A Reconstruction through Paul's Rhetoric*. Minneapolis: Fortress, 1990.

Witherington, Ben, III. *John's Wisdom: A Commentary on the Fourth Gospel*. Louisville: Westminster John Knox, 1995.

———. *Letters and Homilies for Hellenized Christians: A Socio-rhetorical Commentary on 1–2 Peter*. Downers Grove, IL: IVP Academic, 2007.

———. *Letters and Homilies for Jewish Christians. A Socio-rhetorical Commentary on Hebrews, James and Jude*. Downers Grove, IL: IVP Academic, 2007.

"Women as Clergy." Parts 1 and 2. Religious Tolerance. Accessed May 18, 2020. http://www.religioustolerance.org/femclrg13.htm.

Wright, N. T. *Paul and the Faithfulness of God*. 2 bks. Christian Origins and the Question of God 4. Minneapolis: Fortress, 2013.

Young, Norman H. "The Figure of the *Paidagōgos* in Art and Literature." *Biblical Archaeologist* 53 (1990): 80–86.

Zimmermann, Ruben. "Eschatology and Time in the Gospel of John." In *The Oxford Handbook of Johannine Studies*, edited by J. M. Lieu and M. de Boer, 292–310. Oxford: Oxford University Press, 2018.

———. *Puzzling the Parables of Jesus: Methods and Interpretation*. Minneapolis: Fortress, 2015.

Zumstein, Jean. *L'Évangile selon Saint Jean*. 2 vols. Commentaire du Nouveau Testament 4, Deuxième Série. Geneva: Labor et Fides, 2007.

Author Index

Scripture and Ancient Writings Index